THE
NORTH
AMERICAN
DEMOCRATIC
PEACE

THE NORTH AMERICAN DEMOCRATIC PEACE

Absence of War and Security Institution-Building in Canada-US Relations, 1867-1958

Stéphane Roussel

Published for the School of Policy Studies and the
Centre for International Relations, Queen's University
by McGill-Queen's University Press
Montreal & Kingston • London • Ithaca

National Library of Canada Cataloguing in Publication

Roussel, Stéphane, 1964-
    The North American democratic peace : absence of war and security institution-building in Canada-US relations, 1867-1958 / Stéphane Roussel.

Includes bibliographical references and index.
ISBN 0-88911-939-2 (bound).—ISBN 0-88911-937-6 (pbk.)

    1. Canada—Foreign relations—United States. 2. United States—Foreign relations—Canada. 3. Canada—Foreign relations—1867-. 4. United States—Foreign relations—1865-. 5. North America—Defenses—History. 6. Peace. I. Queen's University (Kingston, Ont.). School of Policy Studies II. Queen's University (Kingston, Ont.). Centre for International Relations III. Title.

FC249.R69 2004   327.71073'09'034   C2004-902038-2

À Fernand, parti trop tôt pour en voir le début,

À Denise, partie trop tôt pour en voir la fin.

Contents

Foreword

Depending upon how one measures these things, the Canadian-American relationship constitutes either the world's longest-standing "security community," or its second-oldest such entity, ranking just behind the Swedish-Norwegian couple. Security communities are interstate groupings characterized by dependable expectations of peaceful change, meaning that members neither use nor threaten to use force as a means of conflict resolution within the group. And whether number one or two in longevity, the Canadian-American security community is remarkable, in that it has been nearly two centuries since the two countries last fought against each other, and a century since either made a credible threat of force against the other.

It is the explication of this "long peace" in North America that Stéphane Roussel has made his task in this monograph. He has succeeded marvellously. On offer here is a remarkably original account of the continental security community, in which the author skillfully employs insights gleaned from a body of theory that most typically finds application elsewhere than in North America: democratic peace theory. Roussel sets out to show that the seeming puzzle of North America's asymmetrical balance of power — namely how to account for Canada's doing as well as it has done given America's overwhelming might — is no puzzle at all. Rather than being dependent upon an extracontinental "balancer," as some claim, or simply being an anomaly that proves the general rule about life in the international anarchy being nasty, brutish, and short, the long North American peace has really rested upon a normative foundation. It is the two countries' liberal-democratic domestic orders that accounts for the North American security community, says Roussel.

Not only do these respective domestic orders predispose the continent toward peace, but they also serve to enhance the quality of security and defence cooperation between the neighbours, making the North American "democratic alliance" one of the world's premier collective defence structures. For anyone interested in how that alliance took shape, and how it is likely to evolve given the uncertainties of the current war on terror, Roussel's book makes timely and invaluable reading. Queen's School of Policy Studies is proud to have facilitated its publication in English translation.

David G. Haglund
Sir Edward Peacock Professor of Political Studies
Queen's University, Kingston

Preface and Acknowledgements

Canadian-American relations are intriguing, for two reasons. First is that it has been nearly two hundred years since the countries last engaged in warfare against each other, and this has to be recognized as a very rare (and happy) outcome when set against the normal historical experience of small countries who have found themselves living next door to great powers. Second, and even more remarkable, is that the two states have been able to develop cooperative relations that just do not reflect the skewed differential in power in North America. Alone, neither phenomenon gets the attention it deserves; together, the two aspects cry out for systematic inquiry. And it is precisely this that I undertake in this book, which makes the argument that in large measure, the irenic and cooperative quality of Canadian-American relations is owing to the fact that both countries are liberal democracies whose political leaders acknowledge each other's liberal-democratic credentials. Their relations, thus, are a manifestation of both the "democratic peace" and "cooperation between democracies."

Although this study examines the history of Canadian-American security relations, it is not a work of history. In it, I have not sought to uncover any new historical evidence; instead, I have endeavoured to propose a new interpretation for well-known events. I have sought to do this primarily by resorting to a body of theory that typically does not inform the scholarly analysis of Canadian foreign policy. I have borrowed heavily from international relations theory, and in particular from the approach known as social constructivism, which has done so much to advance our understanding of democratic peace theory.

The book is organized as follows. Part One sets out the theoretical issues that appertain to Canadian-American relations. The chapters in this portion of the book variously explore the great North American puzzle, namely of why vast differentials in capability should not have resulted in considerable harm befalling the smaller power, Canada. My own way of solving the puzzle, as the reader will discover, takes the form of a liberal-constructivist explication.

The book's Part Two consists in a series of three cases, which constitute the empirical tests of that explication. These cover, respectively, the periods from 1867 to 1914, from 1914 to 1945, and from 1945 to 1958; these periods witnessed the evolution and progressive deepening of Canadian-American security cooperation, from conflict resolution to the articulation of the common defence. My concluding chapter asks whether, in light of the epochal events on and subsequent to 11 September 2001, the cooperative pattern might be subject to further evolution.

***

It is hardly an accident that this book should accord such importance — some hold, *too much* importance — to theory; it started out, after all, as a dissertation in the department of political science at the Université de Montréal (U de M). In this regard, I owe a debt to many more people than I can thank here, who contributed directly or indirectly, willingly or not, to my intellectual development. To all who, during my years in graduate school, offered counsel and encouragement, shared their insights, steered me to some unknown source, or simply spurred me on to completion by their skeptical bantering as to whether one ever could (or did) finish a thesis — to all these people I extend my gratitude.

Included in this group are some people I wish especially to acknowledge, starting with Michel Fortmann, my supervisor. For supporting me in more endeavours than I can remember, allowing free rein to my intellectual curiosity when others might have tried to throw a lasso over me, and for always treating me as a friend and a colleague, I thank Michel warmly. My thanks go as well to another U de M professor, André-J. Bélanger, who painstakingly read, weighed, and queried every word in that dissertation: countless discussions at a Montréal restaurant that has unfortunately since closed for good, as well as the in and out boxes of his e-mail system, bear witness to the hours he dedicated to my project. To me, those exchanges will always be worth much more than any number of diplomas; to him, goes my gratitude for his generosity. And to Thomas Risse I acknowledge my debt for his having written a book that did so much to inspire my own work, as well as for his having so kindly and patiently shared his thoughts with me during a long conversation that took place between Toronto and Montreal back in March 1997.

Of course, it is every dissertationist's dream to see the manuscript that so painstakingly began life as a thesis metamorphose into something else — a volume bearing its own cover, and even finding its way into book stores. This transformation could never have occurred if I did not have a backer in my corner. That part was played by David G. Haglund, of Queen's University, who encouraged me every step of the way; in every sense, he is the book's godfather, and without his involvement, I doubt it would ever have materialized.

My thanks go to two other Queen's professors, whose institutional support for this project is greatly appreciated. Douglas Bland, holder of the Chair of Defence Management Studies, and Charles C. Pentland, director of the Centre for International Relations. I want especially to acknowledge the translator, Susan M. Murphy, for the manner in which she was able to take a manuscript that must have seemed as dry as it was obscure and endow it, through her diligence and professionalism, with a new-found elegance. Also, my thanks go to Valerie Jarus, Mark Howes, Gerald Lefevbre, Marie-Eve Desrosiers, and Nicolas-Dominic Audet.

I would be remiss if I did not take the opportunity here to acknowledge those sources of financial support that sustained the project in its very earliest stages: the Université de Montréal Département de science politique, for a scholarship held between 1991 and 1994; the Military and Strategic Studies Program (today, Security and Defence Forum) of the Canadian Department of National Defence, for a fellowship held between 1991 and 1994; and the Social Sciences and Humanities Research Council of Canada, for a grant held in 1994 and 1995.

Finally, words of thanks to both Chantal and Thomas, the first for having been there for me on 26 April in 1998 and 1999, and the second for having answered the call on 10 January 2001. What a pleasure it is to write this, knowing that they are so close.

St-Sauveur, Québec
28 March 2004

CHAPTER ONE

A North American "Liberal Order"?

THE ANOMALY OF CANADIAN-AMERICAN RELATIONS

In one of Richard Rohmer's novels there is a dramatic recounting of an unfolding crisis in Canadian-American relations, triggered by a dispute over natural gas reserves in the High Arctic — a crisis replete with ultimata, threats of annexation, and the menace of war.[1] The book appeared at a time in the early 1970s when hydrocarbon and energy crises were headline issues in international relations, as well as in Canadian-American relations. But even then, few in either country could bring themselves to think of Rohmer's work as representing anything other than the fantasizings of a novelist. Interestingly, one of the rare groups that, logically, should have been prepared to accord credibility to such a scenario as Rohmer's was a particular camp of international relations theorists, the "structural" (sometimes confusingly called "neo"-) realists.

After all, if we accept, as these theorists instruct us, that the international system is first and foremost characterized by anarchy, we should also concede that there are precious few checks upon the strong when it comes to their dealings with the weak. In this context, the "distribution of power" is the critical factor accounting for the quality of interstate relations: those who have power are able, and more than likely, to lord it over those who lack it.

Thus it should hardly be astonishing to find that the structural realists characterize relations between the great and the "secondary" powers as being, from the latters' perspective, fraught with peril. All things being equal, these lesser powers constantly find themselves at risk of aggression in a myriad of forms: invasion, incursion, total or partial occupation of their territory, sanctions, and so on. Even "cooperative" relationships are not spared from this sombre assessment, being themselves subject to divers pressures, threats, coercive gestures, interventions disguised as assistance, and other moves intended to get the weaker country to do what the stronger wishes it to. This is especially so in the realm of security and defence, sometimes labelled the arena of "high politics," a sphere that concerns the very survival of the state.

And though small states might find succour in allying themselves with larger neighbours, they can and do regard such security pacts as being themselves far from unqualified blessings, given their worry about being subordinate to, if not absorbed by, their great power protector. From their point of view, asymmetrical alliances can lead to a loss of decisionmaking autonomy and possibly even political independence. It is not such a large step to move from the status of ally to that of "satellite" and, eventually, of "province."[2] Accordingly, one can discern a "double security dilemma" for secondary powers: what they might gain at the start in security, they forfeit ultimately in sovereignty.

The twentieth century provided numerous examples of secondary powers having to pay a high political price for the cooperative relations they established with powerful neighbours.[3] From the century's first decade on, "cooperative" relations between the US and its Latin American neighbours were frequently marked by the unilateral nature of decisionmaking in Washington — notwithstanding the later dispensations of the Rio Treaty or the Organization of American States (OAS) — and punctuated by the adoption of coercive measures. Quite apart from the extreme cases of military intervention in Guatemala (1954), the Dominican Republic (1965), Grenada (1983), and Panama (1989), there were dozens of demonstrations of American force in the region. Nor was there any absence of occasions in which Latin American countries had to bear the brunt of subversive maneuvers (Chile in 1973) or economic embargo.[4]

In Central and Eastern Europe (CEE), the "allies" of the Soviet Union enjoyed precious little freedom of maneuver in the decades between the close of the Second World War and the end of the Cold War; during those years, CEE states lived in a tightly constrained security galaxy, one in which any deviation on their part could be expected to be met by severe reprisals, at times even outright invasion. Each in its own way, the Monroe doctrine for Latin America and the Brezhnev doctrine for the CEE epitomized systemic asymmetries at the regional level.

On the other side of the ledger, America's dealings with the industrialized states — the Western European countries, Japan, Australia, and Canada — failed to display those typical attributes of asymmetrical relationships. Not only were coercive gestures and unilateral decisions rare (the dispute over the 2003 war with Iraq being a dramatic departure from the pattern), but the cooperative linkages themselves have tended to be fashioned on the basis of such norms as consultation, transparency, collegiality, sharing of responsibilities, and respect for sovereignty. And while the US stands clearly as the leader of the Western community, its partners still manage to retain a certain margin of flexibility when it comes to defence policies. Thus we can qualify these cooperative relations as more "egalitarian" (without their necessarily being "equal") than a strict reading of power categories would lead us to expect.[5] Structural realists can and do try to ascribe this state of affairs to the distribution of power within the overall strategic context: Western Europe and Japan, after all, are far away from the US, and the power differentials separating it from them are hardly as pronounced as those that characterize US relations with the Latin Americans. As for Australia, it is not only even farther away, it does not reside in a part of the world held to be central to American strategic interests — at least as those interests were traditionally assessed prior to the events of 11 September 2001 and the ensuing campaign against terrorism.

Illustratively, none of the above distinctions apply to the Canadian case. Notwithstanding its proximity to the US, the importance of its territory for America's own physical security (more so now than at any time during the past three decades), and the vast differential in power between it and its southern neighbour, Canada enjoys a bilateral security relationship with the US that is qualitatively comparable to Washington's relations with London, Berlin, Canberra, or Tokyo. Moreover, while Canada might have developed very close defence ties with the US, it has not really suffered adversely as a result, save perhaps for a couple of years during the Second World War, from 1942 to 1944, when the presence of American troops on Canadian soil raised deep concerns about sovereignty. Ever since that war, Canadian-American defence collaboration has proceeded apace, at both the bilateral (viz., the myriad of accords bearing upon continental defence reached in the decades since 1940)[6] and the multilateral level, the latter represented through the bonds forged within the North Atlantic Treaty Organization (NATO) context as well the common interests articulated among the allies.[7]

Though Canadians evince an habitual preference for multilateral over bilateral ties in defence, the latter have been every bit as marked by transparency and collegiality as the former. As we will discover in the following chapter, two leading scholars of interdependence have demonstrated that in bilateral conflicts with Canada, the US has been able to prevail only about half the time, even in respect of delicate matters appertaining to security. Nor is that all: Ottawa has at times succeeded in staking out positions quite at variance with those of Washington, and claims occasionally to have had some influence upon the development of *American* foreign and security policy.

For some analysts, Canadian-American relations represent an historical curiosity, if not a unique phenomenon.[8] How else are structural realists expected to interpret this bilateral relationship if not as an "anomaly," given that its egalitarian quality, especially in the sensitive area of security, seems to make a mockery of their Hobbesian logic? To be sure, one must be careful not to overstate the matter, for even within a setting of "mutual respect" the US does conserve an undoubted predominance, no more so than when it comes to assessing threats to the North American continent and developing appropriate responses thereto. That said, some questions really do need to be tackled. How are we to account for the quality of Canadian-American relations in the realm of security and defence? What is it that permits the attenuation if not elimination of the power disproportionality between the two partners? In brief, is it possible to identify one or more of these "equalizing factors"?

SOME HYPOTHESES CONCERNING THE "EQUALIZING FACTORS"

Specialists in Canadian-American relations have not lacked for explanatory frameworks in their quest to account for the anomaly that so fascinates them. Two leading competing approaches stand out. *Realists*, who take guidance from the balance of power, have to be regarded as the dominant theoretical camp. Their chief rivals have been the *transnationalists*, who lay stress upon "complex interdependence," and in so doing are themselves inspired by *institutional rationalism*.

By a large margin, it is the balance-of-power perspective that has pride of place in this theoretical competition, though it is typically only invoked implicitly.[9] Implicit or not, the logic thereof is simple: a state that finds itself on the wrong end of an unequal relationship seeks to re-equilibrate things by finding among third parties a "counterweight." From this it follows that the more success it encounters in this search for counterpoise, the less the secondary power has to worry about the pernicious effects attending its relationship with the great power.

A corollary of the hypothesis is that problems are likely to mount when dealings between the secondary and the great power take place on the bilateral level. The remedy for these is to try to keep matters "multilateralized," ideally by bringing in as many other small or middle powers as one can find. This remedy, in turn, bears all the markings of balancing behaviour, with the expectation being that rounding up enough similarly sized powers constitutes an effective means of diluting the power of the great, not only "containing" it but also gaining for the small state some influence over the large one's policymaking — and this, without having to put up with the drawbacks of a strictly bilateral relationship. What better, according to such reasoning, than *multilateral* institutions as a means of satisfying both the security and sovereignty objectives of the secondary power?[10]

Applied to the Canadian-American example, the counterweight hypothesis seems, at first blush, to do more than justice to the historical record. After all, between 1776 and the interwar years, was it not Canada's security guarantee from the United Kingdom that served to keep at bay annexationist pressures welling up in its increasingly powerful neighbour to the south, which made no secret of its having a "continental" — even "manifest" — destiny? Beginning in 1947, did not Ottawa hope to find within the Atlantic community European allies who could serve as counterweights to American influence? The balance-of-power hypothesis, however superficially convincing and elegant it might be, in the end comes up short, because it simply does not rest upon a very solid empirical foundation. Notwithstanding the countless times the counterweight metaphor has been summoned to explain Canadian policy behaviour, there has never been any sustained, systematic, attempt to demonstrate that it actually constituted the foundation of Canadian decisionmaking.

As for the principal alternative theory, complex interdependence, it has to be conceded that it has failed to gain much of a foothold, primarily but not exclusively because of its ahistorical character, a point to which I shall return in the next chapter. Specifically, transnationalists have never been able convincingly to account for the emergence of transgovernmental linkages of sufficient density to serve as equalizing factors. Likewise, while institutionalists might give a satisfactory explanation for the staying power of institutions *once established*, they are less able to provide a compelling account for the emergence of such institutions in the first place. If the distribution of power and the interests of actors are the only variables worth heeding when it comes to the creation of institutions, then it really must remain a puzzle why such asymmetrical entities in inspiration can evolve along more egalitarian lines.

Perhaps there is a more satisfactory theoretical approach that can enable us to resolve the dilemmas both of realism and transnationalism? In the next section, I argue that there is such an alternative, an approach that elevates values and norms to the status of explanatory variables. It goes under the label, "constructivism."

THE CONSTRUCTIVIST ALTERNATIVE: COOPERATION AMONG DEMOCRACIES

"Constructivism" connotes a very sweeping current of ideas, the most important of which take the form of a sociological premise that social facts do not possess a purely objective status, but are rather the consequences of social interchange. These facts, in a word, represent "constructed" reality. To be sure, material features such as power and wealth contribute to shaping the definition of an actor's "interests," but it is a definition that is largely dependent upon the interpretation actors give to material reality. To use a classical example, naval maneuvers organized under the aegis of the United States will be interpreted in a radically different manner by Ottawa (which will take them to represent a legitimate exercise in enhancing the common defence) than they will by Havana (which takes them to be an intimidating gesture); this is because of the quality of the relations the two capitals have had with Washington. In other words, it is this social environment that generates explanatory impact in this particular case. And not just this particular case: what constructivism does is to throw into question assumptions about the relatively fixed and invariant nature of *all* state interests as these latter have so often been deductively identified.

The constructivist approach offers a way to solve the puzzle of the anomalous Canadian-American security relationship, and does so by invoking the explanatory prowess of "democratic peace theory." This latter postulates that democracies do not go to war against other democracies. The values, norms, and political processes typically associated with "liberal democracy" seem to have determinative impact upon the management of conflict, because they speak directly to the issue of whether or not to resort to force in dispute settlement.[11] The convergence of these liberal-democratic values fosters a "sense of community," or collective identity, that leads members of the community to regard fellow members in a way fundamentally different from the manner in which they assess states lying outside the group: they simply do not take seriously that the former represent potential aggressors. In so doing, what Kant has called the "republican federation" succeeds in eradicating the Hobbesian state of nature.

Thomas Risse-Kappen has pushed the logic of the argument farthest.[12] If democratic norms can have such an influence over conflictive relations, why cannot they also come into play in cooperative ones? To answer this requires, for the constructivists, that we dissolve those analytical barriers, so dear to realist and institutionalist alike, held to demarcate the international from the domestic level. For the constructivists, it is precisely these unit-level qualities that explain the dynamics of international relations. To the extent that we see the entrenchment of liberal values and norms within the domestic political arena, then to that extent we shall see these values and norms accounting for international outcomes among members of the group. Thus the same mechanisms that reduce the returns to power at home can and do reduce the returns to power abroad, within the democratic community of states. Therefore, the anomaly is resolved: power differentials become less significant, and the way is open for secondary powers to gain influence in the decisionmaking of great powers.

Apart from offering a novel solution to the puzzle of egalitarian relations between unequal partners, constructivism generally, and democratic peace theory more specifically, allows us to reinterpret some of the hypotheses of the transnationalists. Such a synthesis can account for the origins of transnationalism, which are seen to reside in the congruency of political values and processes. Seen in this light, transnational institutional linkages between democracies take shape in precisely the same manner as did domestic ones within them. Constructivism remedies as well a second, related, deficiency of the institutional rationalism that inspires transnationalism, by insisting that both the form and the content of international institutional practices are dependent upon the values, norms, and cultures of *interacting* societies. They are not simply the "objective" product of interest and of power differentials, but they depend as well upon a subjective construe that itself emerges from social intercourse within an institutional setting.

The focus of Risse-Kappen's study was the transatlantic security relationship between the US and the European allies during the Cold War. His findings are impressive. Through six case studies, he has demonstrated that notwithstanding discrepancies in power, the European allies were able to exercise a significant degree of influence over American policy. *A priori*, Risse-Kappen's hypothesis should also be applicable to the Canadian-American security relationship. That said, there are some ambiguities in Risse-Kappen's framework, of an empirical as well as theoretical nature.

The first stems from the fact that though Canada might be grouped with the "European" allies in Risse-Kappen's case studies, it never is given any sustained analytical attention. Rather it is the United Kingdom and France who have the starring roles in this story, and one is left with the impression that what applies to them must also apply to Canada. Rather than simply accept that this is so, we need to do some careful thinking if we are to conclude that the Risse-Kappen thesis does possess applicability for Canadian-American security relations.

From the point of view of that thesis, my argument in these pages possesses a certain interest, for the Canada-US relationship could be said to constitute the "hard case" (or the least probable case) for testing the validity of Risse-Kappen's account. This is because the disparity in power between the US and Canada is much greater than that between the US and the major European allies, and was so even for the 1945-55 decade, when Canada was at the peak of its relative power and Western Europe was still recovering from the war. Moreover, Canada cannot avail itself of the kind of physical separation that Europe has from America. If the distribution of power really does play such a minimal role compared with the impact of values and institutions (as predicted by the "cooperation among democracies" version), then Canada's experience should resemble that of the European allies. If this turns out to be so, then the Canadian example might prove useful even to those researchers who normally think *only* of the US and Europe when they focus their gaze upon transatlantic security relations.

The second, more theoretical, ambiguity of the Risse-Kappen account inheres in its multilateral framework (viz., the Atlantic alliance). Can it be said that what works in this context might also apply to a different structure of relations, say the bilateral one? Risse-Kappen himself answers in the negative, since the very multilateral character of institutions he holds to be necessary and not just convenient for the process of interallied decisionmaking.[13] In this respect he adheres to the conventional wisdom of which structural realists, neoliberals, and constructivists alike partake. However, there is nothing in his own theory that requires him to do this. To the contrary, if one is going to endow norms and institutions with influence independent of power relations, there is no place in the analysis for a variable such as the number of participants (implying as it must a balancing game enabled by multilateralism): whether there are two participants or sixteen should have no impact upon the actors' attitudes toward the norms and institutions.

Since there exists no systematic study of *bilateral* cooperative relations between *liberal* states, it is impossible to resort to the literature to resolve the matter. Indeed, trying to show how irrelevant the number of participants is, which is the burden of my argument in the chapters that follow, not only goes against the grain of the above-mentioned conventional wisdom in international relations, but it also flies in the face of the entrenched lore of Canadian foreign policy. In the process, it obliges us to take a new, and critical, look at the widespread skepticism evinced by Canadians when they contemplate the asymmetries of their bilateral relationship with the US. It also leads us to reflect upon the presumed virtues of multilateralism as a safeguard against those power imbalances.

My perspective on these issues is influenced not only by Risse-Kappen's views on "cooperation among democracies"; it is also pays tribute to the John Owen's explication of the "democratic peace."[14] The crux of the argument I make in this book is this:

- Decisionmakers who regard each other as expressing the preferences of societies founded upon liberal-democratic norms and values will tend to apply those same domestic norms and values in their reciprocal (interstate) relations, and will do so whether they are dealing with a conflictive or a cooperative context.

This claim depends upon the application, at the international level, of the same elements that regulate the internal politics of the societies under examination. The independent variable consists not only in the nature of these societies' political system — namely, liberal democracy — but also in the *perceptions* held by decisionmaking elites in respect of the political system of the state with which they are dealing, which must also be regarded as liberal democratic.

The dependent variable, i.e., the internationalization of liberal values and norms, is operationalized here by two conditions that bear upon the quality and content of the interactions under examination. The first is the actors' understanding of the *intentions* of their counterparts. The second is the *form and content of the practices and institutions* that structure the cooperation between participating states. It is the benefit of the doubt that democracies accord each other, as well as the liberal-democratic character of their institutional cooperative links, that explain the egalitarian dynamic of their relations, even when power assets may be very asymmetrically apportioned among them. This applies both in a context of conflict and cooperation.

Applied to the specific case of the Canadian-American relationship, my argument can be refined thusly:

- The more that decisionmaking elites in Canada and the US recognize the basic liberal-democratic nature of the other's political system, the greater will be their tendency to impute benign intentions to the other, and to strive to forge bilateral institutions that embody the norms of equality, reciprocity, and consultation.

My primary objective in these pages will not only be to determine why there has been no war between the two countries for nearly two centuries, but also to account for how they have been able to manage their bilateral conflicts and at the same time arrange for the common defence of North America, without the latter resulting in the subordination of the weaker partner to the will of the stronger one. In other words, my objective is to find evidence for the existence of a North American *liberal order*.

Notes

[1] Richard Rohmer, *Exxoneration* (Toronto: McClelland and Stewart, 1974).

[2] Robert L. Rothstein, *Alliances and Small Powers* (New York: Columbia University Press, 1968), p. 61; Allen Sens, "La coopération selon le néoréalisme: la cooptation des petits États d'Europe centrale et de l'Est," *Études internationales* 26 (December 1995): 770; Jean-Claude Allain, "Principes et gestion des alliances à l'époque contemporaine," *Documents et enquêtes*, no. 18 (1992), pp. 7-8.

[3]In comparing Canadian-American relations with other bilateral cases, William T. R. Fox has noted: "Among the other pairs of neighbouring states of grossly unequal power — the Soviet Union and Finland, Germany and Austria, Germany and Denmark, Britain and Ireland, the United States and Mexico, India and Pakistan — Finland, Austria, Denmark, Pakistan and Mexico have all been invaded by their great neighbors in the twentieth century. The Irish had to fight a bitter war to bring an independent Irish state into being." *A Continent Apart: The United States and Canada in World Politics* (Toronto: University of Toronto Press, 1985), p. 74.

[4]See David R. Mares, "Looking for Godot? Can Multilateralism Work in Latin America this Time?" in *Multilateralism and Regional Security*, ed. Michel Fortmann, S. Neil MacFarlane, and Stéphane Roussel (Cornwallis, NS: Canadian Peacekeeping Press, 1997), pp. 81-103.

[5]In this regard, see the six criteria of power postulated by Kenneth N. Waltz, *Theory of International Politics* (Reading, MA: Addison-Wesley, 1979), p. 131.

[6]These vary in number from 300 to 800, according to how one measures these things; in fact, if we are to believe a recent Canadian ambassador to Washington, no one really knows the exact number of these bilateral accords. Lecture delivered by Ambassador Raymond Chrétien, l'Université du Québec à Montréal, 22 April 1997. But a committee of the Canadian Senate has put a number, 330, to these accords, including some 80 treaties. See Government of Canada, Senate, Standing Committee on National Security and Defence, *Defence of North America: A Canadian Responsibility* (Ottawa, September 2002), p. 28.

[7]To avoid making things unnecessarily complicated at this stage, let it suffice simply to recall the existence of the Canada-US Regional Planning Group (CUSRPG), charged with developing plans for North American defence within an overall alliance context. It should be noted that Canada-US defence cooperation also takes place within such other institutional fora as the UN and the OAS.

[8]Among those who have best expressed this "anomalous" or "unique" condition are Robert O. Keohane and Joseph Nye, *Power and Interdependence: World Politics in Transition* (Boston: Little, Brown, 1977), chap. 7: Kalevi J. Holsti, "Canada and the United States," in *Conflict in World Politics*, ed. Steven L. Spiegel and Kenneth N. Waltz (Cambridge, MA: Winthrop, 1971), pp. 375-96; David Baldwin, "The Myths of the Special Relationship," in *An Independent Foreign Policy for Canada?*, ed. Stephen Clarkson (Toronto: McClelland and Stewart, 1968), pp. 5-6; Donald Barry, "The Politics of 'Exceptionalism': Canada and the United States as a Distinctive International Relationship," *Dalhousie Review* 60 (Spring 1980): 114-37; John Kirton, "Canada and the United States: A More Distant Relationship," *Current History* 79 (November 1980): 117; and John Mueller, *Retreat from Doomsday: The Obsolescence of Major War* (New York: Basic Books, 1989), pp. 240-50.

[9]In fact, the term itself is rarely employed, even though the logic is. More commonly, one encounters the term "counterweight," which on reflection is simply another way of saying "balance." For one of the explicit usages of balance of

power in the North American context, see Kenneth Bourne, *Britain and the Balance of Power in North America* (London: Longmans and Green, 1967).

[10]Rothstein, *Alliances and Small Powers*, pp. 124-27; Allen Sens, "The Security of Small States in Post-Cold War Europe," in *From Euphoria to Hysteria: Western European Security After the Cold War*, ed. David G. Haglund (Boulder: Westview, 1993), pp. 235-36.

[11]To simplify things, when I use "democracy" I am implying the existence of a "liberal state," and when I employ the adjective "democratic" I mean to imply "liberal democracy." I say this because it can rightly be argued that democracies are not necessarily liberal (for instance, ancient Greece); those democracies, by contrast, about which I write in this book are invariably liberal democracies. See Bruce Russett, *Grasping the Democratic Peace: Principles for a Post-Cold War World* (Princeton: Princeton University Press, 1993), pp. 43-71; and John M. Owen, *Liberal Peace, Liberal War: American Politics and International Security* (Ithaca: Cornell University Press, 1997), pp. 15-16.

[12]Thomas Risse-Kappen, *Cooperation Among Democracies: The European Influence on U.S. Foreign Policy* (Princeton: Princeton University Press, 1995).

[13]Risse-Kappen, in response to a question put by the author during a seminar at the Université de Montréal, 26 March 1997. Risse-Kappen's caution on this score brings to mind similar reservations about bilateralism made by John Ruggie, to which I will return in chapter 4.

[14]John M. Owen, "How Liberalism Produces Democratic Peace," *International Security* 19 (Autumn 1994): 87-125; and Owen, *Liberal Peace, Liberal War*.

PART ONE

THEORIZING BILATERAL DEFENCE AND SECURITY

CHAPTER TWO

Asymmetry and Its Discontents

GENERAL FEATURES OF THE BILATERAL RELATIONSHIP

W e should hardly be surprised to learn that theorists of international relations are only rarely moved to test their assumptions against the backdrop — if not backwater — of Canadian-American relations. What is a bit astonishing is to discover that analysts of Canadian foreign policy are only slightly more likely to frame their assumptions within the context of established IR theories, or at least to do so explicitly. Nevertheless, if we look for it, we can find some "virtual" connection between the foreign policy analysts and the IR theorists, and it will be the burden of this chapter to demonstrate more directly that connection. I will do this both by providing an overview of those bodies of IR theory I deem most germane to the study of the Canadian-American relationship, and by referring to empirical works that I believe depend upon logical postulates derived from one or the other of the theoretical schools. I begin by examining some of the most useful writings on the bilateral relationship, with a view to teasing out from these the dominant ideas, recurrent themes, and above all, general tone of the debate surrounding the field of Canadian-American relations.

Everywhere Canadians venture in the analysis of the Canadian-American relationship they come face to face with the reality of asymmetry, and this holds for the scientific community as much as for anyone else. But as much as this structural condition has preoccupied Canadian students of the relationship, it has not been accorded anything like comparable importance by their American counterparts.

This respective difference shows up as well in the attention governments pay to asymmetry. Simply put, Canada defines itself in relation to the United

States, and has always done so. The forging of Canadian federation (officially, "Confederation") in 1867 has been presented as a direct response to the challenge posed by the US, at a time when it appeared as if the British were preparing to withdraw from their North American garrisons.[1] Since the turn of the twentieth century, commercial ties between the two countries had expanded dramatically: in 1900, exports to the American market accounted for 30 percent of Canada's overall exports; by 1994, the proportion had reached 80 percent. As John Holmes noted: "Coping with the fact of the USA is and always has been an essential ingredient of being Canadian. It has formed us just as being an island formed Britain."[2] Quite naturally, the relationship with the US has developed into *the* central preoccupation of Canadian foreign policy, to such a degree that the latter can be reduced to a constant quest for equilibrium between continentalism and internationalism[3] — or, as one book puts it, "between the United States and the world."[4] Not surprisingly, there is an abundance of writing on Canadian-American relations, almost all of it by Canadians.[5]

In contrast, American political scientists are not much drawn to the study of the bilateral relationship. As Thompson and Randall remind us, few among them have built their careers in this area of scholarship, with some of the most notable exceptions being Seymour Martin Lipset, Alfred Hero, Annette Baker Fox, Charles Doran, Joseph Jockel, and Chris Sands.[6] In general works on American history, Canada largely disappeared after the ending of the nineteenth century, with the resolution of many of the conflicts between the two countries.[7] In studies that concentrate on US foreign policy, Canada's presence is often limited to its having been one of the founding members of NATO, in respect of which it is regarded as being a loyal if at times irritating ally.[8]

Notwithstanding its limited quantity, American intellectual activity in this area is sufficiently qualitatively developed to enable us to draw some comparisons with perceptions conveyed in the literature written by Canadians. Authors on either side of the border might agree on a number of points, but there are times when their assessments of the bilateral relationship diverge substantially.

Both Americans and Canadians agree that the relationship can be characterized as a *friendly* one. The "long peace" that took root in the first half of the nineteenth century continues to this day. In the early part of the twentieth century this relationship, so bereft of animosity, moved not a few commentators and leaders in both countries to see in it proof positive that North Americans had discovered how to escape from the dragons of war, whose fiery breath seemed still to afflict the Europeans. The flowering of such concepts as "North Americanism" and "exceptionalism" were reaffirmations of this conviction. With the passage of time, one heard less and less of these conceits, in large part because "exceptionalism" itself grew to enjoy a wider ambit, becoming eventually applicable in Western Europe as well as in North America.

Another point of substantial agreement between Canadian and American students of the bilateral relationship is their assessment that the latter demonstrates a high degree of *interdependence*, manifested at the economic, political, and even socio-cultural levels.[9] Geographic proximity, the density of bilateral exchanges, a community of interests, and even cultural and ideological convergence are all cited as factors promoting interdependence.

A third category of agreement concerns the fundamentally *informal* nature of bilateral interstate relations.[10] A few formal institutions apart (viz., the International Joint Commission, NAFTA, or the Permanent Joint Board on Defence) policy coordination and conflict resolution are the province of informal bilateral networks exemplifying "transgovernmentalism," or even of simple protocols of agreement drawn up by relevant agencies or ministries. Thus, the majority of bilateral activities occur on an ad hoc basis, as the situation dictates. Nevertheless, this informal quality does not mean that there is an *absence of institutions*. Principles, norms, rules, and procedures certainly exist,[11] even if these have largely escaped systematic study, a point to which I return later in this chapter.

A fourth theme that recurs frequently in the works on Canadian-American relations is *asymmetry*. This quality literally leaps into full view; and if we employ Kenneth Waltz's criteria for establishing hierarchies of power — namely, population and territory, economic capacity, resource endowment, military power, political stability, and competence[12] — we find the US dominating Canada in nearly all domains, save for size of territory and political stability.[13] Beyond this widespread recognition of an unassailable fact, there is divergence between the Canadian and American scholars as to the consequences of asymmetry. This divergence often turns out to be more apparent than real, however, since the authors tend to isolate different variables in coming to their conclusions.

The study of asymmetrical relationships has given rise to a large body of literature in Canada[14] — no more so than in the spheres of economics and culture — of which the vast majority of works have concentrated upon the *negative* aspects of asymmetry. Canadian unease is rooted in the recognition that, all things being equal, Canada must find itself at the mercy of its powerful neighbour. During the nineteenth century this unease took a rather direct and traditional form of worry about either an invasion or the outright annexation of the country. But as time passed and exchanges developed, the concern became more subtle, though perhaps more pernicious: that the US weight would always be preponderant in all facets of Canadian existence. In cooperating closely with the US, Canada ran the risk of having to give up, under its neighbour's relentless pressure, layer after layer of its sovereignty, until such time as there was simply nothing left to cede. Thus the unequal relationship with the US constitutes *the* question of Canadian existence, touching as it does upon the country's survival as a sovereign political entity.[15]

Sovereignty fears have frequently been encountered in the debates over political, economic, and cultural issues. During the 1960s in particular, there were numerous expressions of grave concern about the implication of the country's economic dependence upon the US.[16] This anxiety gave rise, at the start of the 1970s, to a policy of economic nationalism at the federal level (viz. the creation of an agency charged with monitoring foreign investment, attempts at trade diversification, and a national energy policy). There was a rebirth of economic nationalism toward the end of the 1980s, touched off by the debate over a free trade agreement with the US.

These Canadian preoccupations would find their echo in the area of defence and security. From the very outset of defence cooperation during the Second World War, Canadian decisionmakers manifested concern about sovereignty. These concerns would later reappear, only this time in the writings of Canadian defence specialists, and in the early 2000s, with the so-called "security perimeter."[17] Nor was it any surprise that the literature on Canadian foreign policy should be chock-a-block with recommendations as to how to limit the American impact upon national sovereignty — recommendations running the gamut from finding a European counterweight to declaring neutrality.

American analysts tended to see things differently.[18] At a time when one Canadian after another was demanding stern measures aimed at "re-Canadianizing" the country's economy and culture, American researchers were observing that asymmetry to the contrary notwithstanding, the bilateral relationship was more egalitarian (or at least heading in that direction) than realized. Those who chose to emphasize a postulated American "domination" of Canada were few in number. More commonly encountered were arguments such as that made by Robert O. Keohane and Joseph Nye, to the effect that it was *interdependence* not *dependence* that best characterized the bilateral relationship, and that this diluted the impact of power asymmetries. Compartmentalizing the relationship into "issue areas," and tracing the growth of transgovernmental and transnational channels for decisionmaking, the two authors reached the conclusion that both countries experienced a roughly equal number of successes and failures in their bilateral dealings.[19]

Thus while the relationship might look to be "asymmetrical," it was really "egalitarian." To account for this ostensible paradox, recourse was had to a subtle distinction between "power" and "influence." Canadians worried most about encroachments that might be unintended or dictated by extraneous developments. They realized that the relationship with the US was a friendly one, and that there was absolutely no risk of invasion, subversion, or annexation. When they denounced economic or cultural domination, it was a reflection of a worry about impersonal socio-economic "forces" inherent in any liberal society, and not a manifestation of anxiety about intentions. The allegory of the elephant and the mouse, a staple of Canadian discourse, spoke directly to their misgivings about unintended harm befalling the country as a result of the asymmetries of North American existence. In this sense, what Canadians distrusted was the power of the American economy not the Americans themselves — until, that is, the advent of the George W. Bush administration in 2001. This mistrust predicated on power differentials would have an impact upon the totality of the interactions between the two states, and would lie at the base of sentiments associated with the country's "anti-Americanism."[20]

American authors, for their part, were more inclined to focus upon certain *socio-political* forces (e.g., the development of transgovernmental relations) and their effect upon state and interstate behaviour. More and more, they paid attention to motivations, calculations, and actors' intentions. Their primary interest lay in determining how external constraints might effect voluntary and conscious interaction. What they most looked for was the *influence* that relevant actors were able to exercise. In sum, relationships that might initially appear to be very asymmetrical when viewed solely from the perspective of power imbalance, could turn out to look very differently, once one factored in the influence of intergovernmental or transgovernmental forces.[21]

There exists one final element, so often evoked in the corpus of scholarship on Canadian-American relations, that warrants our attention here. Both North American countries are *democracies* whose political processes are firmly situated within the *liberal* tradition. That said, the majority of writers who draw attention to this feature do so to determine differences between the two political systems, especially insofar as institutions and political culture are concerned. These differences are located notably at the level of division of powers (between executive and legislative, or between central and regional levels of government), in socio-political cleavages (racial in the US, linguistic in Canada), and in values (individualism being less pronounced in Canada, which accords greater importance to social welfare).

Applied to the domain of foreign policy, reference to differences serves to highlight obstacles to bilateral negotiations. In this respect, Canadians and Americans alike profess to see the problem as lying with the political system of the *other* country.[22] Only rarely do authors put the stress on resemblances and convergences. Withal, there may be great merit in contemplating, *mutatis mutandis*, the two states as representing variants on the same democratic theme. Seizing upon a comparative approach so as to bring into focus the differences rather than the similarities presents its own set of difficulties, of which two stand out. The first is that it blurs the extent and impact of policy convergence between the two states.[23] The second is that it blinds us to the possibility of the two states forming part of the same "whole" (say, a "community" or a "region"), one possessing its own distinct logic rather than merely being the sum of its parts. Indeed, if Canadian-American relations are sometimes cited as illustrative of the concept of community,[24] it remains the case that there is no reference to their constituting a "democratic community" for analytical purposes. This omission is odd, given the interesting theoretical reward that awaits such a consideration of the bilateral relationship.

THEORIES OF CANADIAN FOREIGN POLICY AND OF INTERNATIONAL RELATIONS

Works on the foreign policies of the two countries can provide theoretical orientations additional to those in the preceding section. Certainly, the analysis of America's foreign policy, including its relations with allies and neighbours, derives much of its theoretical inspiration from the broader sphere of international relations (and much the same can be said in re-verse, given that America's relations with other states so often constitute the empirical record against which IR theories are tested). But when we turn to the literature on Canada, the "fit" between IR theory and foreign policy theory is not so tight. Perhaps because they grew disenchanted with theoretical models developed to account for the foreign policies of *great* powers, Canadian researchers have tried to elaborate conceptual schema that are more reflective of their own preoccupations (or at least of the pre-occupations of Canada's diplomats). Thus, theories of Canadian foreign policy can be split into three categories, each with applicability for Cana-da's special setting: internationalism (i.e., Canada as a middle power), peripheral dependence (Canada as a satellite of the US), and "complex neo-realism" (Canada as a "principal power").[25]

"Classical" internationalism derives its inspiration from scholarship on functionalism, yet the discourse and preoccupations of its adherents curi-ously owe much to a "realist" logic, because they so frequently acknowledge that need for Canada to find the means of exerting influence appropriate to its status as "middle" power. The problem of managing the relationship with the US, conceived as an inequitable one, seems to be the chief con-cern of theorists within this tradition. International institutions are explicitly regarded as the means not only of attenuating the power differentials in-herent in unbalanced relationships but also of expanding the influence of secondary powers. Functionalist-internationalist ideas have heavily influ-enced the discussion of Canadian foreign policy since 1945, and have given it a pronounced "institutionalist" orientation.[26]

From a body of work intended initially to guide policy, it was not at all difficult for internationalism to make the leap into the realm of theory, where its chief contribution resided in its being able to furnish a coherent framework within which could be situated Canada's place in the interna-tional system.[27] Central to this framework have been the concepts of middle power and "middlepowermanship." However, the theory suffered from the same shortcomings of the policy advocacy from which it sprang; while it might have spawned a number of normative propositions, it was rather anemic when it came to generating explanatory hypotheses or guiding empirical research. More to the point, its central concepts were simply too fuzzy, therefore nearly useless for the purposes of comparison or generali-zation. Recent works in this genre, sometimes labelled "second-generation" internationalist theory, have helped redress somewhat these shortcomings.[28]

Middle power is now more carefully defined, allowing us to have a better understanding of the universe of states that fit into this category, as well as to observe more clearly their attempts at coalition building intended to equilibrate their relations with the great powers.[29]

As for the theory of "peripheral dependence," it had clear affinities with the neo-Marxian theory of "dependency" that made such headway during the 1960s. *Dependencia* might have been conceived in a Latin American setting, but for Canadians who subscribed to it there was appeal to be had both to nationalism and to the inequitable quality of Canadian-American relations. They saw Canada as nothing more than an economic, political, and military satellite of the US. What most appealed to them in this body of theory was not its explanatory prowess but its ability to be massaged into a program of action. A good number of the policy ideas that were making the rounds during the late 1960s and over the next few years — including calls for Canada to declare its neutrality[30] — have to be regarded as products of the peripheral dependence mindset. The allure of this theoretical school would diminish greatly subsequent to the failure of the "Canadianization" initiatives launched during the early Trudeau years, targeted on economics (viz. the trade-diversification strategy) and defence (the reduction of Canada's contribution to NATO). Until recently, little work was being done within this theoretical clustering, but the events subsequent to 11 September 2001 have caused some critics to question anew the deepening of bilateral cooperation.[31]

Finally, the "complex neo-realist" perspective,[32] which was based partly on realist ideas stressing the power and capacity of a state to defend its interests, and partly on theories of complex interdependence (especially the dissolution of the category of power into divers issue areas of functional specificity), never did succeed in spinning off any sustained and systematic research programs.[33] Moreover, it appeared to be singularly ill-suited for studying questions related to security, given that in the defence sphere it is a quite a stretch to present Canada as a "principal" power! (We will revisit this problem later.)

So what can we conclude from this brief foray into theories of Canadian foreign policy? Notwithstanding the obvious importance Canadians attach to the relationship with the US, and regardless of the rich bounty of documentation on that relationship, the theory is impoverished, offering next to nothing in the way of guidance. First, its core concepts are little more than echoes from international relations theory, and if this is so, why not go directly to that source itself in our bid to understand the bilateral relationship? Secondly, the Canadian literature gives the impression of having been stimulated more by normative considerations linked to various political agendas than by any thirst for scientific explanation. Thus when — or if — a research program manages to arise from this body of writing, it is only because of political not scientific considerations, and any hypotheses stemming therefrom will have limited relevance to other areas of inquiry, whether for the purposes of comparison or of generalization. Not for nothing have critics of this body of theory attacked its idiosyncratic and ad hoc character. And even at its most interesting, the link between its analytical framework and international relations theory is too often either ambiguous, implicit, or reductionist. Research on Canadian foreign policy gives the appearance of having been undertaken within a "closed circuit," with little or no attempt being made to situate the product within any *problématique* inspired by international relations theory.[34]

For all these reasons, it seems better to root a research project on Canada-US relations within the soil of international relations theory, and to avoid excessive reference to established modes of analyzing Canadian foreign policy. As the reader will gather from chapter three, this is indeed what I do in this book, which is premised upon an hypothesis derived from recent IR theory. It is not that the Canadian foreign policy literature lacks all utility; it can be helpful if it serves as a gloss upon IR theory, or if spawns empirical work enabling us to determine the strengths and weaknesses of the theory. But it is to IR theory that primary recourse will be had. Which body of the latter holds out the greatest promise? Realists and structural realists, institutionalists, and constructivists can all, in their own way, yield explanations about cooperative relations between states of unequal power. Our task, therefore, becomes one of determining how satisfactorily they can answer the following three questions:

- How can we account for certain states being able to interact closely with much larger states yet still manage to preserve their independence, and possibly even to achieve a measure of influence over their larger partner?

- Which variables determine the dynamic of cooperative interaction, particularly within the security domain, among a group of actors with marked differentials in power?

- How should we distinguish between cooperative strands woven at the bilateral and at the multilateral levels?

As we saw in chapter one, international relations theories are not short on explanatory accounts of the Canadian-American relationship, many of which find their echo in the discourse on Canadian foreign policy. One small passage from a speech given in 1997 by the then minister of foreign affairs, Lloyd Axworthy, is revealing in this respect:

> Multilateralism has been at the heart of Canada's foreign policy, above all because we have sought to be in good company in our dealings with our great neighbour and because we have insisted that rules — the rule of law — mitigate the unilateral impulses of other "large players" [...][35]

In one brief passage the minister managed to pull off a tour de force (no doubt involuntarily, as theoretical preoccupations generally seem to be far removed from the concerns of policymakers), making implicit reference to two opposing theoretical tendencies. He first showed himself off in realist raiements, through his quantitative appreciation of the requirements of healthy living for Canada: "be[ing] in good company" in dealings with the US is simply another way of expressing the search for a counterweight to the power and influence of America. On this view, one establishes an egalitarian relationship by amassing power. In fact, this perspective is widespread in the literature on Canadian foreign policy.

The minister then changed tack, and put on his neoliberal face through his insistence upon rules — notably those rules that bind everyone including the great powers, whose "unilateral impulses" are thereby attenuated. Note that it is not power itself that is at play here, but rather the order thought to follow from the establishment of rules-based institutions. All are deemed equal before these institutions, the mighty as well as the puny. It is no exaggeration to say that institutionalism comes close to being the theoretical negation of the counterweight dogma.

But the above two approaches hardly exhaust the category of theories to which recourse is had in pursuit of the solution to the Canadian-American puzzle. Realism, structural realism, transnationalism, and multilateralism offer up a full menu of explanations, sometimes complementary, sometimes contradictory, and often totally independent from the others. What we need to do is separate the wheat from the chaff in the existent theories, and search for guidance in new approaches. Let us begin the winnowing process in the next chapter, in which we move from realism to multilateralism.

Notes

[1]D. M. L. Farr, "Britain, Canada, the United States and Confederation: The Politics of Nation-Building during the Turbulent Years," in *Reflections from the Past: Perspectives on Canada and the Canada-U.S. Relationship* (Plattsburgh, NY: SUNY Plattsburgh Center for the Study of Canada, 1991; orig. pub. 1967); John Herd Thompson and Stephen J. Randall, *Canada and the United States: Ambivalent Allies* (Montreal and Kingston: McGill-Queen's University Press, 1994), pp. 3-4.

[2]John W. Holmes, *Life With Uncle: The Canadian-American Relationship* (Toronto: University of Toronto Press, 1981), pp. 107-8.

[3]Lloyd Axworthy, "Entre mondialisation et multipolarité: pour une politique étrangère du Canada globale et humaine," *Études internationales* 28 (March 1997): 107-9; Allan Gotlieb, "The United States in Canadian Foreign Policy," *O. D. Skelton Memorial Lecture*, Toronto, 10 December 1991; Joseph T. Jockel, *Security to the North: Canada-U.S. Defense Relations in the 1990s* (East Lansing: Michigan State University Press, 1991), p. 17; Kim Richard Nossal, *The Politics of Canadian Foreign Policy*, 3rd ed. (Scarborough: Prentice-Hall, 1997), p. 79; David Leyton-Brown, "Managing Canada-United States Relations in the Context of Multilateral Alliances," in *America's Alliances and Canadian-American Relations*, ed. Lauren McKinsey and Kim Richard Nossal (Toronto: Summerhill Press, 1988), p. 162.

[4]Panayotis Soldatos and André P. Donneur, eds., *Le Canada entre les États-Unis et le monde* (North York, ONT: Captus Press, 1989). Also see Louis Balthazar, "Les relations canado-américaines," in *De Mackenzie King à Pierre Trudeau: Quarante ans de diplomatie canadienne (1945-1985)*, ed. Paul Painchaud (Québec: Presses de l'Université Laval, 1988), pp. 251-74.

[5]If anyone doubts this claim, let them simply glance at the bibliography in Thompson and Randall, *Canada and the United States*, pp. 351-70.

[6]Ibid., p. 2.

[7]See, for example, Richard N. Current, T. Harry Williams, and Frank Freidel, *American History: A Survey*, 5th ed. (New York: Knopf, 1979); Joseph Robert Conlin, *The American Past: A Survey of American History* (San Diego: Harcourt Brace Jovanovich, 1984); and Norman K. Risjord, *America: A History of the United States* (Englewood Cliffs, NJ: Prentice-Hall, 1985).

[8]Henry Kissinger's memoirs are eloquent in this regard, because in the first volume's 1,584 pages mention is made of Canada but seven times. *À la Maison-Blanche (1968-1973)*, 2 vols. (Paris: Fayard, 1979). Also worthy of note are the

five volumes of the monumental series of American foreign policy documents, edited by Arthur M. Schlesinger, Jr., which contain no section on Canada, and very few mentions of it. *The Dynamics of World Power: A Documentary History of United States Foreign Policy, 1945-1973*, 5 vols. (New York: Chelsea House/ McGraw-Hill, 1973).

[9]David Leyton-Brown, "The Political Dimension of Canadian-U.S. Relations," in *Unequal Partners: A Comparative Analysis of Relations Between Austria and the Federal Republic of Germany and Between Canada and the United States*, ed. Harald von Riekhoff and Hans-Peter Neuhold (Boulder: Westview, 1993), pp. 137-50; Robert O. Keohane and Joseph S. Nye, *Power and Interdependence: World Politics in Transition* (Toronto: Little Brown, 1977), pp. 167-70.

[10]Kenneth M. Curtis and John E. Carroll, *Canadian-American Relations: The Promise and the Challenge* (Lexington, Mass.: Lexington Books, 1983), p. 51; Kalevi J. Holsti, *International Politics: A Framework for Analysis* (Englewood Cliffs, NJ: Prentice-Hall, 1983), p. 445; John J. Kirton, "Canada and the United States: A More Distant Relationship," *Current History* 79 (November 1980): 117; Roger Frank Swanson, "An Analytical Assessment of the United States-Canadian Defense Issue Area," in *Canada and the United States: Transnational and Transgovernmental Relations*, ed. Annette Baker Fox, Alfred Hero, and Joseph Nye (New York: Columbia University Press, 1976), pp. 191-92.

[11]Keohane and Nye, *Power and Interdependence*, pp. 170-71.

[12]Kenneth N. Waltz, *Theory of International Politics* (Reading, MA: Addison-Wesley, 1979), p. 131.

[13]So overwhelming does this asymmetry appear to be that some authors do not even bother to attempt to qualify it; see, for instance, von Riekhoff and Neuhold, *Unequal Partners*. (Leyton-Brown's chapter in this volume constitutes a partial exception, as he dedicates two short paragraphs to a definitional foray into asymmetry.)

[14]For examples, see von Riekhoff and Neuhold, *Unequal Partners*; James Eayrs, "Canada and the United States: The Politics of Disparate Power," *Centennial Review* 10 (Autumn 1966): 415-29. More generally, on the Canadian literature, see Balthazar, "Les relations canado-américaines," pp. 261-62; Charles F. Doran, *Forgotten Partnership: US-Canada Relations Today* (Baltimore: Johns Hopkins University Press, 1984); and Maureen Appel Molot, "Where De We, Should We, or Can We Sit?" *International Journal of Canadian Studies* 1-2 (Spring-Autumn 1990), pp. 77-96.

[15]The writer who most clearly summarized the predicament, ironically, was an American, Roger Frank Swanson. See his "The United States as a National Security Threat to Canada," *Behind the Headlines* 29 (July 1970): 9-16.

[16]The groundwork had been prepared during the previous decade by reports of two royal commissions, the Massey Commission in 1951 and the Gordon Commission a half dozen years later. One of the most celebrated commentaries of the 1960s of this genre was George P. Grant, *Lament for a Nation: The Defeat of*

Canadian Nationalism (Toronto: McClelland and Stewart, 1965). On the evolution of economic nationalism, see Richard Arteau, "Libre-échange et continentalisme: récapitulations," in *La politique économique canadienne à l'épreuve du continentalisme*, ed. Christian Deblock and Richard Arteau (Montréal: GRÉTSÉ-ACFAS, 1988), pp. 169-95.

[17]John English and Norman Hillmer, "Canada's Alliance," *Revue internationale d'histoire militaire*, no. 54 (1982), pp. 31-52; Kenneth McNaught, "From Colony to Satellite," in *An Independent Foreign Policy for Canada?*, ed. Stephen Clarkson (Toronto: McClelland and Stewart, 1968), pp. 173-83; Michael Byers, "Canadian Armed Forces Under US Command," a report commissioned by the Simons Centre for Peace and Disarmament Studies, Vancouver, British Columbia, April 2002.

[18]The difference was well-observed by Peyton V. Lyon, "Introduction," in *Continental Community: Independence and Integration in North America*, ed. Andrew Axline et al. (Toronto: McClelland and Stewart, 1974), p. 2.

[19]Keohane and Nye, *Power and Interdependence*, chap. 7. Also see Idem, "Introduction: The Complex Politics of Canadian-American Interdependence," in Fox, Hero, and Nye, *Canada and the United States*, pp. 3-15.

[20]See J. L. Granatstein, *Yankee Go Home? Canadians and Anti-Americanism* (Toronto: HarperCollins, 1996).

[21]Thompson and Randall recognize this distinction, in a passage that nonetheless reflects more the Canadian than the American perspective on asymmetry: "One may speak of a relationship in which influence flows in both directions, as indeed it sometimes has; but the essential reality has been the imbalance of power." *Canada and the United States*, p. 2.

[22]For an illustrative comparison, see Charles F. Doran, "Contrasts in Governing: A Tale of Two Democracies," in *Friends So Different: Essays on Canada and the United States in the 1980s*, ed. Lansing Lamont and J. Duncan Edmonds (Ottawa: University of Ottawa Press, 1989), pp. 149-59; Allan E. Gotlieb, *I'll Be With You in a Minute, Mr. Ambassador: The Education of a Canadian Diplomat in Washington* (Toronto: University of Toronto Press, 1991); and Idem, "United States in Canadian Foreign Policy."

[23]See Keith Banting, George Hoberg, and Richard Simeon, eds., *Degrees of Freedom: Canada and the United States in a Changing World* (Montreal and Kingston: McGill-Queen's University Press, 1997).

[24]Karl W. Deutsch et al., *Political Community and the North Atlantic Area: International Organization in the Light of Historical Experience* (Princeton: Princeton University Press, 1957); Sean M. Shore, "No Fences Make Good Neighbours: The Development of the Canadian-American Security Community, 1871-1940," in *Security Communities*, ed. Emanuel Adler and Michael Barnett (Cambridge: Cambridge University Press, 1998), pp. 333-67.

[25]This tripartite division is frequently found in the writings on Canadian foreign policy. Examples include Molot, "Where Do We ... Sit?," pp. 77-96; Andrew F. Cooper, *Canadian Foreign Policy: Old Habits and New Directions* (Scarborough:

Prentice-Hall, 1997), pp. 6-25; Nossal, *Politics of Canadian Foreign Policy*, pp. 53-66; and Michael K. Hawes, *Principal Power, Middle Power, or Satellite?* (Toronto: York University Research Program in Strategic Studies, 1984).

[26]John W. Holmes, *The Shaping of the Peace: Canada and the Search for World Order, 1943-1957*, vol. 1 (Toronto: University of Toronto Press, 1979); J. L. Granatstein, *The Ottawa Men: The Civil Service Mandarins, 1935-1957* (Toronto: Oxford University Press, 1982).

[27]For a recent example, see Andrew Cohen, *While Canada Slept: How We Lost Our Place in the World* (Toronto: McClelland and Stewart, 2003).

[28]David R. Black and Heather A. Smith, "Notable Exceptions? New and Arrested Directions in Canadian Foreign Policy Literature," *Canadian Journal of Political Science* 26 (December 1993): 760-61.

[29]Bernard Wood, "Towards North-South Middle Power Coalitions," in *Middle Power Internationalism: The North-South Dimension*, ed. Cranford Pratt (Montreal and Kingston: McGill-Queen's University Press, 1990), pp. 70-107.

[30]McNaught, "From Colony to Satellite"; Philip Resnick, "Canadian Defence Policy and the American Empire," in *Close the 49th Parallel etc.: The Americanization of Canada*, ed. Ian Lumsden (Toronto: University of Toronto Press, 1970), pp. 93-115; Lewis Hertzman, John Warnock, and Thomas Hockin, *Alliances and Illusions: Canada and the NATO-NORAD Question* (Edmonton: Hurtig, 1969). Today the only ones to plump for neutrality appear to be the pacifists.

[31]See, for instance, Stephen Clarkson, *Uncle Sam and Us: Globalization, Neoconservatism and the Canadian State* (Toronto: University of Toronto Press, 2002); and Michael Byers, "Canadian Forces Under American Command," *International Journal* 58 (Winter 2002-3): 89-114.

[32]For the texts most representative of this tendency, see James Eayrs, "Defining a New Place for Canada in the Hierarchy of World Power," *International Perspectives* 4 (May-June 1975): 15-24; David B. Dewitt and John J. Kirton, *Canada as a Principal Power* (Toronto: Wiley and Sons, 1983); and Norman Hillmer and Garth Stevenson, eds., *A Foremost Nation: Canadian Foreign Policy in a Changing World* (Toronto: McClelland and Stewart, 1977).

[33]Black and Smith, "Notable Exceptions?"

[34]André P. Donneur, "L'étude de la politique étrangère: une discipline essentiellement canadienne" (unpublished mss).

[35]Axworthy, "Entre mondialisation et multipolarité," p. 112 (author's translation).

CHAPTER THREE

In Search of the "Equalizing Factors": Realism, Transnationalism, and Institutionalism

REALIST THEORIES: MODIFIED POWER AS PRINCIPAL EXPLANATORY VARIABLE

For a long time, realism has held a dominant position among the theories of international relations, even for Canadian researchers.[1] Numerous propositions are deducible from realist theories, intended in one way or another to explain how it is that secondary states can resist the influence of great powers with whom they are linked in a relationship marked by asymmetries of power.

Realism itself is a broad church, embracing such denominations as "classical realism," "neo-realism," and "offensive realism." Despite their differences, these variants share certain attributes. They regard the state to be the principal actor in the international system. They hold it to be a coherent and rational entity.[2] And they consider that the environment in which states interact is bereft of any overarching authority capable of arbitrating conflict. The anarchic character of the system is, accordingly, said in large measure to determine actors' behaviour, because the pattern of relations they establish with each other must necessarily be founded upon a balance of power. Faced with a near-permanent risk of war, rationally acting states elevate survival to the top of their list of objectives. Thus they seek to maximize their power, and they can count only upon their own resources to enhance their survivability (i.e., they must rely upon "self-help"). Is it any wonder that questions of security dominate their policy agenda, or that they should be so jealous of their sovereignty? This applies not only to political and military issues, but to economic and cultural ones as well.

Realist accounts locate the "equalizing factor" *inside* the explanatory framework of the balance of power. The distribution of power remains the dominant fact of international relations, therefore any apparent anomalies must be explained by shifts in power capabilities. If the "facts of observation" do not happen to correspond to the predictions deduced from the balance of power, this does not negate the explanatory capability of the latter; it simply means that "something" has modified the power distribution. Hypotheses seeking to explain a situation in which "egalitarian" relations are developed between actors of unequal power are obliged, then, to introduce factors that might explain this modification.

To limit the explanation to the systemic effects generated by anarchy requires a certain number of corollary assumptions. It is important to establish at the outset the boundaries of what realism can and *cannot* explain. Kenneth Waltz insists that structural realism can only "tell us a small number of big and important things."[3] The same stricture can apply to the entire family of theories associated with realism, to the extent that its logical foundation, so simple and coherent, obliges its adherents to relegate to the sidelines a congeries of phenomena deemed to be of secondary relevance. This set includes those factors that structure the individual behaviour of each actor, to wit the specific content of each state's foreign policy. Realists can and do formulate propositions about actors' motivations, the impact of international institutions on behaviour, and the difference between the behaviour of great as opposed to secondary powers. But these propositions are deductions from the general theory and therefore remain subordinate to the logic of its hypotheses. An examination of the positions shared by nearly all realists can help us see more clearly how realism's answer(s) to our question are distinctly different from those of other theoretical approaches we will survey in this chapter and the one that follows.

As a general rule, realists conceive of the motivations and preferences of states as being determined by two considerations: 1) the anarchic character the international system; and 2) the rationality of state actors able both to comprehend their "interest" and to design strategies intended to maximize it. For such writers as Waltz and Hans Morgenthau, these postulates translate into states' constant quest to enhance their power, guarantee their security, and maximize their interests.[4] Others, for instance Raymond Aron, tell us that these postulates require policymakers always to adopt an attitude of "prudence."[5] Their rationality bias leads realists to reject accounts of behaviour as being driven by such factors as the pressure of public opinion or other domestic interests, considerations of a moral or ethical nature, or values and norms. These can have little to do with rationality as they conceive of it.

Realists do not attach too much importance to treaty obligations assumed by states, for the latter behave according to the dictates of their interests. Any commitment that runs counter to those interests can and should be renounced or ignored. In the absence of any supranational authority capable of obliging states to keep their promises, the risk of "cheating" is constant. The same applies to institutions, which are perceived simply as the creatures of member-states, who are free to use, abuse, or ignore them.[6] Anarchy is regarded as the ultimate and unbreachable barrier to the establishment of lasting cooperation. It is not hard, if you follow their logic, to see why realists have such difficulty accounting for cooperation, even in the short term. And when it does occur, they interpret it as having been brought about by the exertions of great powers or because of the existence of a threat to some states' security.

Not surprisingly, realists do not devote much of their energies to the study of institutions, generally held to be epiphenomena, mere reflections of power relationships and thus incapable of having an autonomous impact on state behaviour.[7] This is especially so in cases involving security, the sphere in which states are least inclined to submit their policies to external constraints.[8] For realists, alliances constitute the only institutions worthy of interest, because they serve to crystallize power relationships.

Finally, secondary powers occupy an insignificant place in the structural realist research program, in light of the premium attached to power, and the resultant hierarchy based upon capabilities of states.[9] Such notions as the "structure of the international system," of "configurations of power relationships," or of the "balance of power" pay homage chiefly to the great powers because, by definition, the secondary powers are little more than ciphers.[10] The same observation applies to Canadian-American relations.[11] For realist theory broadly stated, the *preferences* of states may be invariant, no matter whether they be superpowers or micro-states; but the *consequences* of state action are anything but invariant, and depend critically upon the power of the actor(s).[12]

As with any theory, there are refinements and adjustments that get made by many of its adherents, so we shall encounter in the pages below many realists who see things a bit differently from the way they have been described above; some of them have even adapted the general theory in such a way as to render it useful for studying the secondary powers. In the next five sections of this chapter, I group these realists according to the core concepts they articulate, taking them in the following order: hegemonic stability theorists, alliance theorists, issue structuralists, "power of the weak" theorists, and counterweight proponents.

HEGEMONIC STABILITY THEORY

The theory of hegemonic stability is perhaps the most common of the variants of realist theory, and is sometimes even confused with structural realism through its obvious affinities with the work of Kenneth Waltz. It is often associated with two other writers, however: Charles Kindelberger and Robert Gilpin.[13] Its basic message is that international relations are structured according to the wishes of the great powers, and that the secondary powers have only a limited margin of maneuver. International institutions, conceived primarily as a microcosm or subset of the international system, simply reproduce existing relationships of force between states. The "distribution of power" thus becomes as important a variable for studying this subsystem as it is for the system itself. It explains the creation and functioning of the institution, as well as the nature of commitments undertaken thereto and the distribution of gain therein; this is particularly the case of security institutions.

Hegemonic powers set up institutions as a means of managing interstate relations and enhancing their ability to stake out and maintain a dominant position. These states are perceived as "entrepreneurs," bent on reaping the gains that come from cooperation.[14] Admittedly, organizing cooperation is not a cost-free undertaking, even for the hegemon; but it puts up with the financial and political constraints in order to legitimize and safeguard its position of dominance. Doing so requires it to demonstrate a certain degree of flexibility when confronted by demands from its "client states." International institutions help hegemonic powers lock into place their favourable status against the time when their relative power begins to decline. Essential for making the institution work is the hegemon's capacity to "extract" cooperative behaviour from its partners, whether by blandishments or inducements, or a mixture of both.

According to these realists, it is pointless to distinguish between multilateral institutions and bilateral ones. What matters is not the number of partners but the quality of their relationship, meaning that it display an inequitable distribution of power as between the hegemon and the other(s). The more inequitable the distribution is, the more able is the hegemon to get its way.

Hegemonic stability theory has attracted a great deal of critical commentary.[15] Scholars who have compared its heuristic potential with competing assessments of institutions acknowledge that it at least has the merit of highlighting the role of hegemonic power, as well as the effect produced by changes in the power assets of the hegemon.[16] But how helpful can hegemonic stability theory be in accounting for the ability of secondary powers to resist the will of the hegemon?

A priori, there appears to be no check on the hegemon's imposition of its power, save that supplied by its own desire to concede to the preferences of its smaller partners on matters of slight importance to itself, so as to assure their good will. Only the hegemon's decline will permit the secondary powers to regain their full freedom of action. Failing this, their cooperation with the hegemon occurs sometimes because they have no alternative; they are forced into doing so. At other times, they may agree quite happily to play the hegemon's "game" because they hope thereby to curry favour. But even though they might succeed in extracting some concessions at the margin, they must always bend before the hegemonic state's strategic preferences, all the more so if the cooperation takes place within the confines of an alliance. Whatever margin of maneuver they possess will essentially be a function of the *manner* in which the secondary powers cooperate. More specifically, these latter have the option of playing a bilevel cooperative game. One level consists in the amount of their contribution to the common enterprise, and the other consists in the nature of the commitments they are willing to make. In this context, analyzing the attitude of the secondary powers brings us to the theorists of collective action.

Analogous to the entrepreneur who sets up a business, the hegemonic power is called upon to contribute more than his partners to the undertaking. In alliance affairs, this disproportionality is felt principally in the levels of contribution made to the common defence. On the positive side of the ledger, it also enables the hegemon to claim for itself the lion's share of decisionmaking authority, and this certainly helps it solidify its leadership role. For their part, the secondary powers can still happily enter into such an arrangement given the security it furnishes them. That said, they will display a tendency to want to "free ride," seeking to minimize their contribution to collective defence, confirmed in the knowledge that the hegemon will more than cover the difference. Only when their large partner begins to lean on them to spend more on defence, or when that partner becomes less "large" by virtue of its decline, will the secondary powers normally bestir themselves to increase the size of their contribution.[17]

Secondary powers generally seek to limit their commitments to the bare minimum, fearful that alliance constraints will compress their room for maneuver, and anxious about the plans great powers may have for the alliance. This leads to what Glenn Snyder has referred to as the "alliance dilemma." By this he has in mind the interplay between two kinds of challenges facing alliance members, above all the smaller allies: abandonment, and entrapment. *Abandonment*, at its most extreme, consists in a state's seeing its allies decamp just when they are most needed; but it can also possess another significance, in which a secondary power finds its own interests ignored by the great power that runs the show. *Entrapment*, by contrast, refers to the risk that a state will get dragged into a war as a result of things done by an ally.

The greater a state's dependence upon its allies, the greater can become the worry about being abandoned; thus for states in this position, there is a willingness to accept a certain amount of constraint if doing so fortifies the alliance ties. They may be willing to make certain sacrifices (for instance, regarding their own sovereignty) in hopes of strengthening the alliance. By contrast, a state that is not very dependent upon allies will be more concerned with entrapment, and thus less likely to put up with constraints and sacrifices.[18]

How might what the hegemonic stability theorists have to say apply to Canadian-American security relations? In two ways, mostly. First, the theory serves to blaze a trail through some of the relationship's thickets. It leads us to see how Canada might have to make concessions in terms of sovereignty in response to US pressure, as a result of basal asymmetries in the relationship. Paul Létourneau and Michel Fortmann describe this type of bilateral interaction: "Confronted with a Pentagon that almost single-handedly defines the nature of the threat, Canada seeks basically to limit American ambitions while preserving the friendly character of the relationship."[19] A bit more colourfully, Robert Keohane and Joseph Nye advance a similar thought: "It is sometimes said ... that in the North

American relationship, the Canadians win a good share of the games, but the ball park and the rules of the game are American."[20]

The theory of hegemonic stability can also clarify some of Canada's policies, notably the chronic tendency to minimize its contribution to the Atlantic alliance, especially since the 1960s, as well as to North American defence, beginning in the 1950s, when Ottawa was happy to leave the lion's share of the costs associated with building air-defence radars to Washington. Not only does Canada display a tendency toward free riding, but it also evinces considerably more concern about being entrapped by the US in a war not of its own design than it does about being abandoned by its larger ally. The reason for the lack of concern with abandonment is not hard to discern: it stems from the Canadian conviction that America extends to its northern neighbour an involuntary and automatic security guarantee.

Apart from these not-inconsiderable matters, there is precious little else that hegemonic stability theory can provide when we turn our attention to the apparently egalitarian nature of the bilateral relationship. When theorists of this kidney direct their efforts to the explication of alliance dynamics, they regularly give the Canadian-American one a wide berth, and concentrate instead on NATO, a setting that enables them to exercise their primary concern, which is to explain burdensharing inequities within the alliance.[21] Among Canadian analysts, the only ones working from a perspective approximating that of hegemonic stability are to be found in the peripheral-dependence school, discussed in the previous chapter. And even their ranks are noticeably slimmer today than they were in the salad days of that school, the 1960s and 1970s.

BALANCE-OF-THREAT THEORY AND ALLIANCES

If it is true that realists have little overall interest in international institutions, there is one striking exception to the rule: alliances. As is the case with other institutions, alliances are regarded as natural products of the balance of power and of the fact of anarchy. Nevertheless, alliances assume a special importance because of the way in which they can and do affect the balance of power. They do this by bringing into sharp relief the "structure" of the international system, and thus serve as one of the few empirical referents for the global balance. In this context, they are often seen to constitute a stabilizing element.[22] Not surprisingly, realists attach a great deal of importance to the processes that lead both to the formation of alliances and to their dissolution. They have sought to identify those factors that predispose states to choosing certain allies at certain times, and even of switching alliances.[23]

Stephen Walt has been one of the most prolific realist theorists of alliances, and is especially known for his suggestion that it is not the balance of *power* per se that generates alliances, as most realists assume, but rather the balance of *threat*.[24] States seek to create an equilibrium not against the most powerful state but rather against the most threatening one. The need to respond to threat, coupled with a community or at least complementarity of interests and the ability of allies to resolve one's particular security dilemma — these are what determine whether a state will ally and with whom.[25] Hypotheses regarding the comportment of secondary powers in alliances will, accordingly, be a function of degree of threat posed by a third party. This is all very mechanical, for the postulated "automatic" tendency of states to balance against threat makes it unnecessary to very deeply into the qualitative relations allies have with other allies.

The existence and the proximity of the threat account chiefly for the manner in which an alliance will be put together. If the alliance is created to advance certain political aims, and the threat is a distant one, then the secondary powers will tend to form bonds with others of their own size, and eschew allying with a great power. But confront them with a clear and present danger, these same secondary powers will seek safety in the embrace of a great power.[26] Geographic proximity, affinities at the level of values and ideas, and even considerations of domestic politics can and do play some part in the choice of allies, but by and large these factors remain peripheral to the dynamic.

The most well-known hypotheses stemming from balance-of-threat theory are those covering the behaviours known as *balancing* and *bandwagoning*. The former term applies to the process by which a state seeks allies to help it equalize the correlation of forces presented by the threat. The second term refers to the phenomenon of a state rallying to the side of the threat rather than confronting it. And even if the vast majority of the cases he studies fall into the first category, Walt indicates that weak states prefer bandwagoning over balancing. "In general, the weaker the state, the more likely it is to bandwagon."[27] Implied in the notion of bandwagoning is the submission of the weaker state.

Bandwagoning involves *unequal exchange*; the vulnerable state makes asymmetrical concessions to the dominant power and accepts a subordinate role ... Bandwagoning is an accommodation to pressure (either latent or manifest).... Most important of all, bandwagoning suggests a willingness to support or tolerate illegitimate actions by the dominant ally.[28]

Thus presented, genuine cases of bandwagoning are rare, and derive from peculiar if not desperate circumstances (e.g., a weak and isolated state confronted by a very powerful adversary). However, some scholars have sought to provide a more nuanced understanding of the process, and to show that small states might be tempted to bandwagon not out of necessity but rather because doing so can prove advantageous, even profitable.[29]

Whether done via balancing or bandwagoning, joining an alliance must always come at some cost, assessed either as a reduction of one's own freedom of action or in terms of the obligation to go to someone else's defence. The costs are necessarily higher for smaller states. Thus it follows, and no one expressed it better than Machiavelli, that leaders of small states should try to avoid compacting with more powerful states unless it was absolutely essential so to do.[30] The risks are hardly trivial. Not only can the weaker ally find its room for maneuver vis-à-vis its stronger ally so constrained as virtually to constitute its becoming a satellite[31] — which in itself makes a mockery of the claim that all states unfailingly seek to preserve their sovereignty — but it must put up as well with a variety of other inconveniences.

In effect, great powers have global interests, while small powers concentrate upon their own regional situation. The former are likely, therefore, to have a number of declared or potential enemies, and thus to have to go to war frequently. The latter, in tying up with a great power, inherit the same expanded set of enemies, and find themselves having to take part in conflicts that might not otherwise engage their "vital" interests. And even when they can stay out battle, they invariably discover of alliance constraints upon their foreign policy autonomy. As a result, their choice of a great power as ally generates for the small powers a "double security dilemma."

This is an interesting notion, and one that could have some applicability in the Canadian-American context. However, the alliance theorists who introduce it tend to be rather mute when it comes to proposing some way out of the two-pronged dilemma. Mostly, they claim that the dilemma will

disappear on its own. If the exigencies of the moment seem to dictate forming a pact with a great power or else suffering a military defeat, then how
important can such secondary considerations as sovereignty be, when survival itself is at stake? Security will always trump autonomy. Thus the
double dilemma turns out to be self-nullifying: sovereignty concerns will
vary in inverse and direct proportion with the gravity of the perceived security threat. There is something unsatisfactory about their *deus ex machina.*
As we will see a bit later in this chapter, some interesting work has been
done by other analysts, who propose particular policies (including search-
ing for "counterweights") as a way out of the bind.

Another problem with the alliance theorists inheres in the "acultural"
and ahistorical nature of their enterprise.[32] In putting the accent strictly on
the mechanistic and quantitative aspects of alliance formation, the theorists fail to come to grips with *qualitative* considerations, including the
preferences of actors. And if the theory may tell us *why* states align, it fails
to instruct us on *how* they do it. Alliances are simply treated as more or
less interchangeable, all subject to the same conditioning factors. However, states having to decide whether to align really must face a series of
choices covering a wide range of questions — to take just instance, why
plump for a multilateral as opposed to a bilateral pact? Realist theories of
alliance offer few accounts of the various modes of alliance.

These criticisms to the contrary notwithstanding, we may yet discover
in realist alliance theory some important insights into the problematique
of this book, namely how to account for the "egalitarian" character of an
otherwise patently unequal relationship? At first blush, it would not seem
that alliance theory could bring much to our understanding of Canadian-
American relations; there is just too little metal in this ore body. Asking
whether Canada sought to balance against the Soviet threat might be considered a trivial question. Walt himself does not even bother to apply his
own theory to the North American experience: "The United States ... has
only two countries on its borders. Neither is especially powerful. Because
U.S. policy toward both has been benevolent in recent decades, both have
chosen to ally with the United States."[33]

On the other hand, the dual security dilemma does seem to fit the Canadian situation.[34] Endowed with an immense landmass but a small population
of limited means, Canada has never on its own been able to assure its
security. From Confederation until 1940, the defence of Canada rested with
the British Empire. The latter's weakening led Canada to turn toward the

US for security guarantees. The August 1940 Ogdensburg declaration marked the beginning of Canada-US defence cooperation, which continues to this day. The decision to ally with the US can certainly be explained in terms of threat perception, even if not directly so. The Axis until 1945, and the USSR until 1991, were invoked as reasons to ally with the US. Whether the objective reality of these two threats to Canada, the country was able to derive undisputable benefit from its linkage with America, because the latter gave it a degree of protection that was simply otherwise inconceivable.

However, as Desmond Morton has pointed out, "the postwar paradox of Canadian defence was that the Soviet Union was the ultimate threat but the United States was the immediate danger."[35] The paradox was reflected in the preoccupations of Canadian policymakers, who seemed forever to be oscillating between a desire to snuggle up with the Americans and a concern about the effects of such an affair upon the country's sovereignty. In keeping with alliance theory, the balance between the two values was tied to threat perception: the greater the apparent menace, the less was the concern about sovereignty. Once the urgency of the moment had passed, Canadian leaders would possess both the leisure and the reason for worrying about sovereignty protection. How to accomplish the latter leads us directly to an examination of the final three of the realist camps surveyed in this chapter, respectively the issue structuralists, "power of the weak" theorists, and counterweight proponents.

ISSUE STRUCTURALISM

This approach first gained popularity in the 1960s and 1970s, as a contribution to the study of foreign policy.[36] It is sometimes regarded as being a response to realism, in large measure because of its origins within the school of transnationalism. But at least one of its variants has affinities with realism: "issue structuralism," the essence of which consists in trying to see how and why "power" can be relevant in some contexts but not in others.

Traditional realists have tended to regard power as a monolithic entity that is characterized by extreme "fungibility" — i.e., a property that remains invariant regardless of the domain of application. Insofar as power is primarily defined in economic and military terms, it is easy to impute to states that are dominant in both sectors a large degree of influence over all walks of international life. What issue structuralists do is to disaggregate spheres of activity, in the process seeking to evaluate the capabilities of actors in the unique sphere being analyzed. They remain realists, because they isolate power as a central element, even if they insist upon its contingent qualities.[37]

The logic of issue structuralism allows us to glimpse some of the sources of influence possessed by secondary powers. A state regarded as a small power on the military scale might turn out to be a large(r) power when it comes to certain niches in which it has greater interests, resources, and credibility even than some other states that outrank it economically and militarily. We speak of small powers exploiting their comparative advantage in a particular field so as to magnify their international influence, in a manner redolent of what Adam Smith had in mind regarding economic exchange. This is not something unique to the small powers; far from it. But because they carry fewer global burdens than the great powers, they may be more able to focus their energies upon specific niches.[38]

The strategy of specialization depends upon the formulation of a dynamic and active policy, whether in substance or in form. In substance, this might mean a state's choosing to promote "reformist" or "moralistic" positions, which in the right circumstances can enhance its influence. Not for nothing do small powers like to specialize in such areas a arms control, the environment, and developmental assistance.[39] As for form, they like to assume a high degree of international activism and to adopt certain roles, such as mediator, catalyzer, and leader in coalition-building.[40] Issue structuralism helps us see why secondary powers can get to talk as "one equal to another" with states that are endowed with much greater economic and military clout than they possess.

One drawback of issue structuralism, however, is its rather feeble applicability to security questions. This drawback is not easily overcome, given that issue structuralism's very logic seeks to isolate military power from other policy spheres.[41] One way to try to remedy the problem is to subdivide the *military* issue-area, so as to distinguish between activities related to defence per se (i.e., protection against a physical threat) and those linked more generally to the causes of international instability. The former activities touch directly upon such sensitive topics as protecting a state's sovereignty; the latter relate to more peripheral national-security problems, such as peacekeeping, conflict resolution, and arms control. Nevertheless, even in these peripheral areas, and notwithstanding whatever comparative advantage they may have developed, small powers often find themselves marginalized by the great powers, should these latter consider that any of their major interests are at stake, as is so often the case in the security arena. Thus by seeking to develop niches in these more peripheral areas, small powers may at times find they have attained no increased influence.

There is another problem. Two can play the same game of issue structuralism, meaning that in the domain of security, for instance, great powers can utilize their overwhelming advantages to put a stop to any attempt at issue linkage by small powers. Great powers can impose their own perception of the threat, along with the means of responding thereto, upon their smaller partner.

Reliance upon issue structuralism, as noted in the previous chapter, has been a characteristic of the "complex neorealists," and has also featured in the efforts of internationalists seeking to account for the influence of middle powers. Both camps have emphasized the merits of specialization. And specialization can help to account for the quality of Canadian-American interaction in certain peripheral domains of security. These latter might embrace not only arms control and peacekeeping, but also a congeries of nonmilitary security developments (e.g., those leading to the establishment of the Conference on Security and Cooperation in Europe [CSCE] during the era of detente). But, insofar as concerns the purely military defence of North America or Europe, the differential in military capability trumps all else. We have, therefore, to look elsewhere in our quest for the equalizing factors.

THE "POWER OF THE WEAK" THESIS

Not all realists are bored by the secondary powers. Those with an interest hone it trying to puzzle out the distinction between the logic of state behaviour as it varies according to the power a state possesses. They want to know in what ways secondary powers develop "rational" responses that differ fundamentally from those of strong states, with the aforementioned double security dilemmas perhaps being the best such point of difference.

In particular, realists who follow secondary powers want to know why these latter can at times wield influence out of all proportion to their objective capabilities, as well as to defend their own interests when it comes to dealing with the great powers. The phenomenon has been given a label, the "power of the weak," and this has served animate a number of research programs on the foreign policies of the Scandinavian states and the European neutrals.[42]

To account for the puzzle, analysts have advanced four hypotheses. Some authors hold the secondary powers' ability to negotiate to be in large measure a function of the configuration of the international system. Thus, a system characterized by an equilibrium between the greatest powers — especially a bipolar system — is said to favour the interests of the smaller powers. In this context, which approaches that of a zero-sum game, great powers accord certain privileges to their smaller partners for fear that the latter might switch sides and adversely affect the global balance. Seeking to increase the number of their own allies and reducing the size of their adversary's bloc, and above all worried about suffering from a "domino effect," great powers bend over backwards to make concessions to smaller ones. The more the latter are needed by the former, the more influence they will wield.

Other authors, closer to classical than to structural realism, insists instead upon focusing on particular attributes of individual smaller powers. These attributes can run the gamut, for instance, from having a favourable geographic location to being in possession of considerable strategic resources. The more one refines (and expands) the list of desirable attributes, the easier it is to invoke the power of the weak under specified circumstances.

A third approach lays the emphasis upon a particular kind of behaviour pattern said to be characteristic of smaller powers when they develop foreign policies. This characteristic is made manifest primarily through the fostering of certain attitudes. Small powers, for instance, tend to be obsessed with their sovereignty in its various manifestations — military, economic, and cultural. They develop this attitude because they fear that great powers, especially neighbouring ones, are constantly endangering their autonomy. Not infrequently, the smaller powers' policies reveal a frequent mixture of security and sovereignty motivations, sometimes in a contradictory fashion. Additionally, small powers cultivate a set of tactics (or "survival techniques") that they put on display in their dealings with great powers. One such we have already glimpsed: bandwagoning for profit. Another is to concentrate upon their own specialities, finding and defending a niche in ways we explored above.

A fourth approach puts the analytical weight upon the degree of dependence a small power experiences vis-à-vis its alliance partner(s). For secondary powers, multilateral institutions —alliances in particular — constitute the most common solution to their security dilemmas. But they do so with the drawback we know of as the double security dilemma. How do the power-of-the-weak theorists handle this drawback?

They do this, in the first instance, by trying to minimize the negative aspects of asymmetrical alliances, inter alia by stressing the other benefits apart from security that accrue to the smaller ally. A secondary power may be able to establish a privileged relationship with its great-power ally, deriving therefrom certain "marketable" benefits. Among these is the levering effect that alliance membership can have upon the political influence of decisionmakers in the smaller state; this is especially so when the latter take the threat less seriously than do decisionmakers in the larger state. When the latter are more worried, so goes this account, the smaller states gain greater voice — but only if they have been crafty enough to have aligned themselves with the great power *before* a crisis has erupted. Should tension be high, all bets are off, for if the great power senses the menace is grave, it may be tempted to impose its will arbitrarily upon its smaller security dependencies.

The above considerations take on more precise significance when they are enmeshed with a certain way of contemplating the meaning of "interdependence." One state's dependence is a function both of the degree of threat and the place of alliances in its foreign policy. To the extent a small state feels itself both threatened and reliant upon allies, then that state is dependent. Allies so constrained, or ensnared, have little leverage, apart from the threat to withdraw from the alliance. But even that can turn out to be mere bluster if the smaller state stands to lose more than its stronger ally from its departure. All is not bleak, for the small power's degree of dependence can be attenuated by certain factors, one of which is the reduction or disappearance of the threat.

Power-of-the-weak propositions do add to our ability to understand how it is that a small state might be able to establish egalitarian links with a strong partner. However, the theory suffers from the *over*specification and utter contingency of so many of its so-called "explanatory" variables; together, these render the theory next to useless as a source of generalizations and predictions. In fact, what we usually find among these theorists are not explanations per se, but rather the identification and justification of "strategies."

Consider the case of the legion of students of Canadian-American relations whose work can more or less be squeezed into the power-of-the-weak rubric: what is it that makes their accounts tick? They might refer to diplomatic technique (e.g., "quiet diplomacy" or its polar opposite, aggressive lobbying), to the concentration upon comparative advantage, to domestic institutional constraints or strategic considerations of the US, or to any number of things. No matter the so-called "explanatory" vehicle chosen, the destination of the power-of-the-weak theorist is always the same: a happy port for the Canadian ship of state, only reached as a result of the brilliant navigational skills of the captains of Canadian diplomacy.

What is wrong with these accounts? Without taking anything away from the attributes of Canadian diplomats, we still must concede that power-of-the-weak explanations suffer from being profoundly ad hoc. The diplomats could not, no matter how sterling their efforts, have eradicated from Canadian-American relations the power disparities that realists so enjoy highlighting. And while the above accounts may shed some light on individual cases, they do little to clarify the systematic dynamics of the bilateral relationship. And the latter, over the long haul, is most noteworthy for its stable and egalitarian quality. Thus it is not the isolated cases that pose the puzzle; it is the long-term trend, and regarding this the power-of-the-weak theories have nothing much to say, especially in the realm of defence and security.

COUNTERWEIGHT LOGICS

The "counterweight" hypothesis (also known as the "union of secondary powers") is one of the most well-known of the realist variants that seek to account for alliance relations between unequal partners. It borrows liberally from such other realist variants as balance of power and alliance theory. And it depends upon a strict line being drawn between bilateral as opposed to multilateral treaties.

One of the most common themes that realists highlight when they discuss the behaviour of secondary powers is *multilateralism*; small powers always are said to prefer this over bilateralism (though realists reverse the order of priority when it comes to what great powers prefer). The theme has a seductive logic. In a strictly bilateral alliance, there is nothing to check the dominance of the great-power partner. The latter is basically accorded free reign, which puts the smaller power constantly at risk of being entrapped, and at the overall mercy of its ally.

Multilateral alliances work differently, as they enable smaller powers to form intra-alliance coalitions whose aim is to counterbalance the power of the great ally. To the extent their doing so generates new channels and levers for exerting pressure, they create an entity whose influence is much greater than the sum of the individual members. And even if multilateral alliances bring some constraints of their own to the table — e.g., by complicating the attainment of consensus — they remain by far the preferred option of the smaller powers.

Despite the association of multilateralism with an "institutionalist" rhetoric, we should always bear in mind that counterweight theorizing is very much an enterprise of realists, even if it is not exclusively so. And counterweight properties reside *not* in the normative features of the institution itself, but rather in the opportunity to multiply restraints. In other words, it is the *cumulative power* of states that stands out as the core explanatory variable.

There is much to commend counterweight theorizing. It is simple, rich, coherent, and supple in its application. That said, it suffers from an unavoidable drawback: vagueness when it comes actually to operationalizing its logic. Even though rarely expressed as such, it is a logic that draws its inspiration from balance-of-power reasoning.

It is also one of the most well-rooted approaches in the historiography of Canadian foreign policy. Retrospectively, it has been pressed into service to account for the "long peace" between Canada and the US that prevailed from 1814 through 1940. In its contemporary version (which has international institutions replacing the British empire as the counterweight to the US), it saw the light of day as a policy injunction whose most ardent champion was Escott Reid.[43] This diplomat drew a lesson from the wartime cooperation between Canada and the US, namely that it was wiser to seek a multilateral institutional framework for such cooperation, for while cooperation brought untold security benefits to Canada, it implied certain risks from the point of view of sovereignty. Reid's thinking would bear fruit toward the end of the 1940s, when Canadians teamed up with British and American officials to lay the groundwork for what would become the Atlantic alliance. For the Canadians, at least, counterweight aspirations were ever-present in their thinking.[44]

Henceforth, this thinking would characterize Canada's approach to the allies. In 1968, the Robertson Report, which presaged a fair number of ideas that would become policy with the Trudeau government's 1971 *White Paper on Defence*, recalled that the principal counterweight to the US was and remained Europe.[45] Starting in 1972-73, the government would "rediscover" NATO's merits as a means of establishing privileged relations with the European allies, the Federal Republic of Germany especially, and for facilitating the working of the counterweight.[46] By the beginning of the 1980s, the evolution of the alliance and interallied relations raised concerns regarding the ongoing utility of security institutions for managing Canadian-American relations. The relative and absolute decline in Canada's military contribution to the alliance was worrisome to certain of the country's diplomats, none more so than John G. H. Halstead, who was concerned that Canada would lose its credibility with the Europeans, and along with this any ability to employ the latter as a means of balancing the US.[47] Others, especially John W. Holmes, put the government on notice about the risks it was running should the alliance become a "two-pillar" affair (one on either side of the Atlantic).[48]

The metaphor is often, even today, resorted to by Canadian diplomats. But it does not have the same resonance with their colleagues from the Department of National Defence.

> [I]t has been a part of the Canadian conventional wisdom that it is to Canada's advantage to deal with the United States through multilateral rather than bilateral channels, so that the asymmetry of power may be buffered by the obligations and involvement of others. It was striking in the research ... that while this view may prevail among academics and diplomats, it does not appear to do so among military officers. Time and time again I was told that, in the experience of the individual, one-to-one cooperation with the United States was preferable to multilateral cooperation.[49]

The academics are probably the diplomats' best mouthpieces on this issue; there has certainly been no shortage of scholarly volunteers to spread the counterweight word. The metaphor has recurred at regular intervals in academic writings on Canadian defence and security policy. Indeed, it has been a staple of such writing for half a century.

Despite its political function, the metaphor has yielded analytical payoffs for many writers, who have sought to invest it with explanatory prowess in respect of the anomaly represented by the power differential between Canada and the US. That said, the approach has generally been tangential, for rare are the scholars who have made of it the central factor in their analyses. Usually, it is invoked in a normative context, as in this typical formulation: Canada should be an active participant in NATO because this provides it with a counterpoise to American influence. This formulation received exposure in the debates that took place in 1991 and 1992, which preceded the decision to end Canada's troop stationing in Germany.[50]

It has to be said, however, that not everyone subscribed to the metaphor's logic, with analysts of a "peripheral-dependence" kidney arguing just the reverse: that the alliance was simply a means of magnifying American influence over Canada! Lost in all the argumentation was a rather simple point, and it appertained to the explicative value of the metaphor (or its reverse, in the case of those skeptics who saw NATO enslaving Canada further). Could anyone actually demonstrate how the European allies were supposed to be working their counterweight magic (or poison, to the skeptics), thereby affecting the American influence upon Canada? For that matter, how useful was the metaphor when it came to assessing the dynamics of the bilateral relationship? In short, did the hypothesis have any grounding in reality?

Balance-of-power hypotheses, of which the counterweight logic forms a part, are certainly interesting enough approaches to the anomaly of Canadian-American relations. They even offer some methodological advantages, the most important being their simplicity and elegance. After all, only two clearly identifiable variables are at play here.

In the historical context, the counterweight hypothesis would seem to have descriptive value, at least at first glance. From 1775 to the 1930s it does seem indisputable that the British backstop of Canada's security accounted for the latter's ability to resist annexationist and other impulses from the US. In 1940 Britain's weakness made the Empire useless as a means of defending Canada, and the arrival of a full-blown German threat left Ottawa with no option but to turn to Washington for a security guarantee.[51] Nevertheless, as I will relate in Chapter Six, the war did expose Canada to some sovereignty difficulties, and these looked to have been aggravated as a result of there being no counterweight to American influence at the time. This absence was remedied with the creation of the Atlantic alliance, an enterprise to which Canadian leaders attached great importance in the late 1940s.

Conceptually, therefore, the counterweight hypothesis has plausibility, and internal balancing games occurring within North America appear to be similar to balancing dynamics on display elsewhere in the international system. The hypothesis is also consistent with Canadian foreign policy behaviour, certainly from the late 1940s on and especially in the domain of security, where Canada relied upon international institutions — so much so that it built for itself a reputation as a paragon of multilateralism.[52]

But there is something lacking in the counterweight hypothesis. First of all, it has no solid empirical foundation. No matter how often analysts have alleged that balancing behaviour helped Canada preserve its sovereignty, no one has been able to demonstrate exactly how the trick was accomplished. Mainly the connection has remained in analytical suspended animation, a kind of hocus-pocus that depends more on intuition and anecdote than upon scientific, systematic examination. Its powerful normative element offers absolutely no insight into Canadian-American bilateral relations.[53]

The second problem with the hypothesis inheres in its immanently contingent nature. By this I mean that an essential condition for the exercise of counterpoise in a multilateral institution is the commonality of interest as between the secondary powers, who are supposed to be banding together to resist the pressure coming from their great-power ally.[54] But where is the evidence that this occurred on a systematic basis? It will not do simply to consider that a European counterweight had been acquired by dint of NATO's creation; two supplementary conditions required being fulfilled. First, Canadian-American disputes should have been such as to make NATO the forum for their resolution — or at least their airing. This is far from what took place in the sphere of defence and security, as evidenced by Washington's sharp rejection of John Diefenbaker's 1958 bid to establish a link between NORAD and NATO, which I discuss below, in Chapter Seven.

Secondly, the European allies and Canada would have needed to be on the same page if they were going to counterbalance the US, and how often was this the case? Only rarely, for much of the time after 1949 Canadian and European interests were divergent, not convergent. Occasionally, there was some commonality of interest, hence the contingent nature of the counterweight hypothesis. Thomas Risse has put it best: whenever the counterweight (or "realist bargaining") hypothesis has been put to the test against a contrasting hypothesis that we will explore in the next chapter, it has come up short.[55]

It is not that the realist hypotheses possess no merit, for as we have already seen, they do enable us to comprehend elements of the Canadian-American relationship in security and defence. But they cannot fundamentally resolve the paradox of egalitarian outcomes within a context of asymmetrical capabilities. Is it possible to find a better means of resolving the paradox? There is no shortage of candidates for that non-realist alternative, In the remaining sections of this chapter I examine two such candidates, transnationalism and institutionalism, and in the following chapter, I turn my attention to an alternative that I happen to believe is the most satisfactory, constructivism.

TRANSNATIONALISM (OTHERWISE KNOWN AS INTERDEPENDENCE)

The transnationalist approach arose from the work of functionalists and integrationists who had, since the 1950s, been proposing alternatives means to realism for coming to grips with international political phenomena, including and especially cooperation.[56] Interdependence can be taken to refer to the mutual influence possessed by two actors who are dependent upon each other. The degree of interdependence will be a function of the quality and the significance of their dealings. The phenomenon is characterized by: 1) a multiplicity of channels of communication (transnational, transgovernmental, and intergovernmental); 2) the proliferation of domains of activity and the absence of an hierarchical rank-ordering between them; and 3) the abjuring of recourse to force as a means of settling disputes between the actors. The degree of interdependence will be sector specific, and may take asymmetrical form if one of the parties happens to be less vulnerable or sensitive to eventual modifications in the relationship.[57]

Interdependency offers an explanation for the anomaly of a secondary power being able to preserve its independence from, and even to exert some influence over, its great power partner. What Keohane and Nye do is to appropriate certain realist hypotheses but apply them in a context of interdependence. Thus they borrow the category of "issue structuralism," but in doing so they introduce some modifications, especially one stressing the presence of barriers across domains, i.e., the compartmentalization of "issue areas." What compartmentalization does is to protect the interests of lesser powers by hiving off realms of activity one from another, thereby reducing the ability of the greater power to attempt "linkage" between issue areas. Since recourse to force is ruled out *ex hypothesi*, great powers are unable to avail themselves of their trump card, their military might. And because economic levers are generally dispersed throughout society and not held by state elites, there is little chance that the great power will seek to blackmail its partner. On the contrary,

> [P]oor weak states are not similarly inhibited from linking unrelated issues, partly because their domestic interests are less complex. Linkage of unrelated issues is often a means of extracting concessions or side payments from rich and powerful states. And unlike powerful states whose instrument for linkage (military force) is often too costly to use, the linkage instrument used by poor, weak states is available and inexpensive.[58]

Keohane and Nye borrow further from the toolbox of realism, in adducing certain "survival techniques" said to be utilizable by secondary powers. In a way redolent of the "power-of-the-weak" approaches detailed earlier in this chapter, they recognize that "on several issues, it seems to have been the intensity and coherence of the smaller state's bargaining position that led to different patterns of success."[59] Competence, political will, and perseverance seem as important to their account as they do to the realists'.

But there are also profound differences, for interdependence theory breaks with certain postulates of realism. It eliminates the hierarchy established by the realists between security questions ("high politics") and all other areas of international relations ("low politics"), and does so as a logical consequence of the disappearance of the risk of war between two interdependent states. In addition, instead of taking the state to be the principal actor in international relations, it recognizes the important role played by such other actors as individuals, transnational groups, and international organizations.

These departures from realist postulates can help to explain the sometimes surprising influence wielded by secondary powers. The neutralization of military force and the lack of hierarchy tend to eliminate the advantages great powers rely upon to impose their will. Building autonomous transnational and transgovernmental relations enables secondary powers to create alliances with interest groups capable of influencing, *from the inside*, the policies of the great power. Finally, secondary powers can use the norms and decisionmaking procedures of international institutions to undertake political initiatives and establish linkages between areas of activity.[60]

The Keohane and Nye model is more useful than "issue structuralism" in examining certain security questions, in particular those related to military cooperation between states having renounced force as a means of resolving their differences. Keohane, in using this model to attempt to explain the apparently disproportionate influence of America's smaller allies upon its foreign policy, proposes a three-part process in which the first step has secondary powers seeking to create links with portions of the American state apparatus, such as the civil service or the military. They next seek to obtain the support of private interest groups willing to lobby the American government. Finally, they attempt to gain the sympathy of the American public opinion through press and promotional campaigns.[61]

Complex interdependence theory appears to offer a convincing explanation for the influence of secondary powers and thus to be a promising approach for this study's problematique. Yet this transnationalist approach fell out of favour within a decade, it being widely critiqued as poorly adapted to the political and intellectual realities of the early 1980s at a time when structural realists were dominating the debate.[62] Its biggest failing was said to be not "contextualizing" the phenomenon of interdependence. Exactly how and why did three characteristic elements of interdependence — multiple channels and exchanges, absence of a hierarchy in areas of activity, and renunciation of the use of force — come into being in the first place? Keohane and Nye understood the critique, but did not address it head on:

> We would like to go further and have a series of studies that would allow us to say how broadly the generalizations about complex interdependence in the Canadian-American case could be extended. What are the effects, for example, of political friendship, cultural distance, or different levels of economic development? Such ambitions are beyond the practical scope of this volume.[63]

Others have sought to do better than this. Some writers found the answer to the "how" and "why" questions in the *economic* content of interdependence: force is excluded and transnational exchanges are present where there is a high level of trade between countries. Others drew attention to the impact of liberal-democratic norms, values, and institutions.

Keohane and Nye themselves conceded the importance of this variable, but from a purely tactical standpoint: "The pressure of democratic politics usually favors the smaller states in the bargaining process, because for them, politicization from below tends to lead to tough negotiating behaviour and coherent stands by government, whereas for the United States such politicization leads to fragmentation of policy."[64]

It is, however, possible to go much farther. The convergence of democratic values can explain the abolition of the resort to force, whether on its own (viz., democratic peace theory) or in combination with trade factors (as with the so-called "democratic-capitalism" thesis).[65] Further, that states might share certain norms and democratic values could help to explain the rise of a number of significant transgovernmental relations.

Transnationalist theorists, for the most part American, were very interested in the Canadian-American relationship, considered the "ideal case" for developing their model. Keohane and Nye, in particular, were among the first to note the anomalous dynamics of the bilateral relationship from the standpoint of realist theory. Moreover, they were able to demonstrate the anomaly empirically: in forty cases of conflict arising during the years 1929-39 and 1950-60, outcomes defied realist expectations because each government was able to claim "victory" (meaning a result close to its initial preference) in half of the cases, with sixteen favouring the US, sixteen Canada, and eight resulting in a "tie."[66]

But is it possible that interdependence theory loses utility if we focus upon bilateral *security* relations? That only ten of the forty cases observed had much relation to security makes us ask this question. Of those ten cases, five resulted in a decision favourable to the United States, three for Canada, and two were draws. These results may be more nuanced than the overall results, but they still throw into doubt the realist idea that the more powerful partner must always prevail.

Another cautionary note needs to be sounded: we need to distinguish between "vulnerability" and "sensitivity" interdependence. In a nutshell, Canada could be said to possess an important bargaining chip, in that its vast territory is so critical to America's own security that Washington is often forced to bow to Canadian preferences as a means of furthering its own objectives.[67] This observation, too, must be qualified. Firstly, the vulnerability interdependence of both partners diminished with the thawing, and then the ending, of the Cold War, though one could argue that since 11 September 2001 it is again increasing, for reasons intimately related to

America's doctrine of homeland security.[68] But even during the Cold War, technological changes associated with intercontinental ballistic missiles and new generation radars diminished the importance *to the US* of Canadian territory; each country's need for the other became, as a result, less impelling than during the peak years of the bipolar confrontation in the first postwar decade.

Furthermore, we can wonder whether the effects of interdependence really were as clear and important as Keohane and Nye have presented them. Joseph Jockel, for instance, argues that Canada was never really able to use its relationship with the US either to increase its influence upon its partner, or even to establish a privileged relationship with it.[69] Not only this, but it could be — indeed *has* been — claimed that bilateral transgovernmental linkages, especially military ones, more often favoured US than Canadian interests, as evidenced *inter alia* by the air defence of the Pacific coast during the Second World War, the creation of NORAD,[70] and Canada's acquisition of nuclear warheads. Perhaps the realists had it right, all along, and that interdependence was nothing other than an "instrument of penetration"?[71]

INSTITUTIONS AS THE EQUALIZING FACTOR?

Before throwing in the towel, and conceding that the realists, appearances to the contrary notwithstanding, supply the best account of Canadian-American relations — including and especially the reason why neither state uses force against the other — let us examine yet another body of literature that tries to establish the possibility of an egalitarian relationship between states of disproportionate power, and to do so by elevating international institutions to the status of independent variable. Institutions can be taken to be those interlinked and ongoing rules and mechanisms, both formal and informal, within which state actions and perceptions get shaped.[72] Institutions can take the form of principles, rules, norms, and decisionmaking procedures, with all such institutions applying to a given area of policy constituting an "international regime." Neoliberal institutionalists and other "rationalists" have done the most to develop the interest-based theory of regimes.[73]

Regime theorists have found the area of security studies to be fertile ground for the application of their theory, due to the large number both of institutions (e.g., alliances, concerts, and global as well as regional collective-security systems) and of areas of activity (e.g., conflict management and arms control).[74] The theory might also be applied to examine bilateral relationships.

The main contribution of neoliberal institutionalism to the study of international relations stems from the manner in which it accounts for the ability of actors to begin and to sustain cooperation despite the obstacles imposed by anarchy. This account depends upon the ability of the institutions to orient and reign in the behaviour of individual states in such a way as to get them to agree to modify their individual policies and preferences. Institutions do this by facilitating the free flow of information, establishing behavioural norms, allowing for the reduction of transaction costs, and by imposing some cost on those who do not respect the norms and rules. By doing these things, institutions contribute to reducing the level of uncertainty surrounding actors' intentions and future actions. This in turn results in less mistrust, simplifies decisionmakers' strategic calculations, mitigates if not complete resolves the collective-action dilemma. States agree to conform to the norms, calculating that — in accordance with the principle of reciprocity — their partners will act in like fashion.[75]

Faith in the ability of international institutions to influence behaviour and facilitate cooperation is what most sets the neoliberals apart from the neorealists. Otherwise, both schools are inspired by international political economy and share a large number of presumptions, including state-centrism, the nature of anarchy, and the motives and rationality of state actors.[76] Since the return to vogue of critical theories inspired by sociology, the convergences between the two have been so remarked upon that it is not uncommon to encounter references to a conceptual *Anschluss*, under the label of the "neo-neo" synthesis.[77] Rationality of the state actor plays a central role in this theory, since their cooperation is seen as based on the states' shared community of interests: each participant expects to receive a benefit in return for aligning its policy with that of the others. The creation of a regime thus results from a supply and demand process between states offering and states desiring a public benefit (such as security, elimination of trade barriers, and the like).[78] That the process so often, however, shows that the convergence of interests cannot fully explain the emergence of institutions. Other variants of regime theory have therefore been developed, which add such variables as power and knowledge.[79] Power-based theories refer to the ability of hegemonic states to extract cooperation from their less powerful partners, and resemble hegemonic stability theory as well as the "English school" of international relations.[80] Knowledge-based theories, taking inspiration from communication and knowledge theories, explain regime formation by reference to the actors' community of ideas and values; accordingly, these resemble certain constructivist theories, which I discuss in chapter four.

Institutionalist theories, for all their merit, fail to address three questions of importance to my argument in this book. What determines the actors' preferences concerning the substance of the institutions? How does the unequal distribution of power between actors in a regime affect their relationship? Is the theory as applicable at the bilateral level as at the multilateral? Convergence of interests and distribution of power and knowledge are useful systemic variables to explain the context of the formation of institutions, and can be considered necessary conditions. However, the attitude of individual actors during the process of creation of institutions can only be explained through an analysis of each individual's motives. This attitude will be tied to the nature of the political institutions, the interplay of different internal groups and coalitions, and the decisionmakers' perception of interests and threats. Once created, the international institutions will tend to affect the attitudes of leaders, civil servants, pressure groups, and the public; they will seek to maintain the regime and lobby for the state to conform to their prescriptions.[81]

The analysis of individual motivations is especially problematical for state-centrist, rationalistic postulates of institutional theory. This shortcoming is manifest when one tries to explain why a regime is composed of certain norms, rules, and principles rather than of others. The concept of rationality is of limited use here because in many cases the cost-benefit calculation seems to be absent or to possess little meaning.[82] In other words, it is impossible to predict the form and substance of the institutions on the sole basis of the distribution of power and the interests of the actors. NATO and the OAS, both created under the aegis of the US with a view to preserving similar security interests, do not have a similar form or content, and the relations between the US and its various allies within the two institutions are very different. In order to understand the qualitative aspects of the formation of institutions it is essential to depart from the strictly rationalist approach and to add some historical and sociological factors.

The second drawback of institutionalist theory is its handling of the question of the effect of unequal distribution of power within an institution, discussed by its proponents only from the standpoint of the hegemonic power at the beginning of the process. Secondary states are simply overlooked, even though it is these states that, as Allen Sens argues, are generally the ones that are most committed to multilateral cooperation — the very process that institutionalists profess to explicate![83]

The relations of secondary powers with international security institutions are noteworthy in that the former prefer multilateral to bilateral institutions, and their views on the size of membership are infused with a "more-the-merrier" expectation. Small states also stress political consultation, and want the group to cooperate in nonmilitary areas as well; plus, they are solicitous of protecting certain domestic policy domains from alliance "interference." The realists and the institutionalists differ on interpreting this small-state behaviour of apparently wanting to have one's cake and eat it, too. For realists, small states are simply pipe dreaming. But institutionalists are prepared to concede that the insertion of norms of equality, consensus, and reciprocity does favour the secondary powers, by dint of its abolition of the hierarchy that relative power would otherwise instil.[84]

This logic subtends the institutionalist variant of the counterweight thesis: even a small state may succeed in imposing its views on its more powerful partners in a forum where the norms of equality or consensus apply. Institutions, by placing certain constraints on states' behaviour, prevent the relationships from being based solely on the distribution of power, thereby reducing the risk that the great powers will act unilaterally and without taking into account the interests or the sovereign rights of their smaller partner. The effect is a general levelling of the power differential, since the constraints apply to the small and the great powers alike. This thesis, intriguing as it is, begs the question: why *is* it that great powers agree to adopt such measures and, once having done so, to continue to abide by them?

It needs to be noted that institutionalists rarely bother to remark qualitative differences between multilateral and bilateral relations; Ruggie was one of the first to do so, as we shall see in the next chapter. Although the term "institution" is so often used in conjunction with the adjective "multilateral" as to make one believe the words were synonyms, there is absolutely nothing in logic that prevents us from applying institutionalism to bilateral relations as well.

Curiously, scholars of Canadian foreign policy have tended to give a wide berth to institutionalist theory.[85] Occasional reference is made to the use of norms and rules of multilateral institutions as a way for Canada to exert influence, obtain information otherwise inaccessible, and so forth. However, norms and rules do not themselves play a significant role in the analysis: the perspective is a realist one, in which what is important is not so much the content of the institutions but the fact that they provide a place for confrontation and the possibility to form coalitions so as to magnify Canadian influence. Further, historical studies far outnumber theoretical analysis of Canadian participation in multilateral institutions, despite the fact that multilateralism is central to Canadian foreign policy and that the neoliberal thesis would seem to offer a promising approach. After all, Canada is often described as a "paragon of multilateralism," a state for whom international institutions are a blessed instrument indeed, enabling it to project influence.

What applies to the *general* study of Canadian foreign policy needs qualification when we turn to Canadian-American relations. Here there has been a greater emphasis upon institutions and institutionalism. John Holmes as been foremost among those who have regarded institutions as a way to protect Canadian interests in an unbalanced continent.[86] But even he does not specify *why* it is that institutions can play this role; they just play it. He does, however, acknowledge that the two countries enjoy a special relationship predicated upon certain principles, norms, rules, and decisionmaking procedures. "Exceptionalism" and "quiet diplomacy" are among the concepts used to designate the set of informal institutions structuring this relationship. Keohane and Nye also refer to the existence of a group of informal institutions aimed at managing the interdependent relationship. They refer in essence to the same procedures and rules contained in the 1965 Merchant-Heeney Report: mechanisms of consultation, separation of issues (i.e., there is to be no explicit "linkage" of issues), recourse to discrete or "quiet" diplomacy, and the depoliticizing of conflicts, whose resolution is left to bureaucratic actors.[87]

These analyses leave themselves open to the same criticism directed at institutionalism. Although the authors explain the emergence of the institutions by the existence of a common interest — the need to manage a relationship of interdependence, and, to a lesser extent, to parry the threats posed first by Germany and then the Soviet Union — they do not typically explain why these institutions led to the formation of an "exceptional" or a typically "North American" approach to international relations.[88] The attention given to formal institutions has tended to obscure the existence of *informal* ones. Although there are several thousand bilateral accords dealing with almost all dimensions of the bilateral relationship, the overwhelming majority are simple administrative accords, devoid of political content and aimed at handling administrative rather than political aspects of the exchanges. According to a study conducted in the 1970s, only twenty or so of these can properly be considered "institutions," half of the total have fallen into disuse.[89] The best known of these institutions are the International Joint Commission, the Permanent Joint Board on Defence, NORAD, and the Canada-US Free Trade Agreement. These institutions, however, are rarely seen as equalizing factors; on the contrary, they are generally considered a political sacrifice made in behalf of technical efficacy. Some Canadians even regard them as instruments used by the cunning Americans to dominate Canada!

It is possible to regard these agreements as representing something very different: as an equalizing factor in an otherwise skewed bilateral relationship. That is the task I have set for myself in this book, which explores the rationale for using bilateral institutions not so as to reduce Canadian "dependence" upon the US but rather as to manage, along with the US, defence and security "interdependence."

In order properly to apply institutionalist theses to Canadian-American defence and security relations, it is necessary to identify the origins of Canadian-American institutions and to place their development in *political* context. This requires us to broaden the category, so that we include not only formal institutions but those customs and practices that also prescribe behaviour, and in so doing provide the framework for, and shape the expectations of, interstate actors. To do this will require us to change the nature of the analytical game from economic metatheory to sociology. For although realist, neorealist, transnationalist, and neoliberal theories all provide elements of an answer to the enigma of the American-Canadian relationship, no one of them is wholly convincing. What they do *not* do is signal the application to their bilateral relationship of the two countries' domestic liberal-democratic orders. Without this application of domestic precepts and practices to an international relationship, we shall never fully be able to comprehend the grand anomaly that is the Canadian-American relationship.

To make the application, we must have recourse to the social-constructivist alternative.

Notes

[1]Bahgat Korany, "Où en sommes-nous? Au-delà de 'l'apple pie' anglo-saxon," in *Analyse des relations internationales: approches, concepts et données*, ed. Korany (Montréal: Gaëtan Morin, 1987), pp. 297-308; Jean-François Rioux, Ernie Keenes, and Gregg Légaré, "Le néo-réalisme ou la reformulation du paradigme hégémonique en relations internationales," *Études internationales* 19 (March 1988): 57-80; Axel Dorscht, Ernie Keenes, Gregg Légaré, and Jean-François Rioux, "Canada's Foreign Policy," *International Perspectives* (May-June 1986): 3-6; Kalevi J. Holsti, *The Dividing Discipline: Hegemony and Diversity in International Theory* (Boston: Allen and Unwin, 1985), pp. 94-95, 112-14.

[2]The rationality assumption enables realist writers to avail themselves of the logic and approaches utilized by scholars associated with postulates of "economic rationality" and "collective action." In particular, works on alliances have often displayed such an orientation. For examples, see Mancur Olson and Richard Zeckhauser, "An Economic Theory of Alliances," in *Alliance in International Politics*, ed. Julian R. Friedman, Christopher Bladen, and Steven Rosen (Boston: Allyn and Bacon, 1970), pp. 175-98; John R. O'Neal, "The Theory of Collective Action and Burden Sharing in NATO," *International Organization* 44 (Summer 1990): 379-402; and A. C. Conybeare and Todd Sandler, "The Triple Entente and the Triple Alliance, 1880-1914: A Collective Goods Approach," *American Political Science Review* 84 (December 1990): 1197-1206. More generally, see Vincent Lemieux, Namatié Traoré, and Nathalie Bolduc, "Coalitions, alignements et alliances interétatiques," *Études internationales* 25 (June 1994): 247-48. For critical comparisons between hypotheses inspired by collective-action theory and other realist hypotheses, see Charles A. Kupchan, "NATO and the Persian Gulf: Examining Intra-Alliance Behavior," *International Organization* 42 (Spring 1988): 317-46; and John S. Duffield, "International Regimes and Alliance Behavior: Explaining NATO Conventional Force Levels," *International Organization* 46 (Autumn 1992): 819-55.

[3]Kenneth N. Waltz, "A Response to My Critics," in *Neorealism and Its Critics*, ed. Robert O. Keohane (New York: Columbia University Press, 1986), p. 329.

[4]Hans J. Morgenthau, *Politics Among Nations: The Struggle for Power and Peace*, 6th ed. (New York: Knopf, 1985); and Kenneth N. Waltz, *Theory of International Politics* (Reading, Mass.: Addison-Wesley, 1979).

[5]Raymond Aron, "Qu'est-ce qu'une théorie des relations internationales?," in *Théories des relations internationales*, ed. Philippe Braillard (Paris: Presses Universitaires de France, 1977), pp. 96-109.

[6]Margaret P. Karns and Karen A. Mingst, "Multilateral Institutions and International Security," in *World Security: Trends and Challenges at Century's End*, ed. Michael Klare and Daniel C. Thomas (New York: St. Martin's Press, 1991), p. 267. Also see John Mearsheimer, "The False Promise of International Institutions," *International Security* 19 (Winter 1994-95): 13-14.

[7]This applies more to the structural realists, Waltz especially, than it does to the classical realists. See Randall L. Schweller and David Priess, "A Tale of Two Realisms: Expanding the Institutions Debate," *Mershon International Studies Review* 41 (May 1997): 1-32.

[8]Mearsheimer, "False Promise."

[9]"Sure, people in Luxemburg have good ideas. But who gives a damn? Luxemburg ain't hegemonic." This comment of Stephen D. Krasner's, providing a good flavour of the realist assessment of secondary powers, is quoted in Andrew F. Cooper, Richard Higgott, and Kim Richard Nossal, *Relocating Middle Powers: Australia and Canada in a Changing World Order* (Vancouver: University of British Columbia Press, 1993), p. 15, note 3.

[10]Waltz is clear on this: "The theory, like the story, of international politics in written in terms of the great powers of an era.... Concern with international politics as a system requires concentration on the states that make the most difference. A general theory of international politics is necessarily based on the great powers." *Theory of International Politics*, pp. 72-73.

[11]See this observation from the late 1960s: "In short, study of Canadian-American relations tells us almost nothing about the big problems facing the world." David A. Baldwin, "The Myths of the Special Relationship," in *An Independent Foreign Policy for Canada?*, ed. Stephen Clarkson (Toronto: McClelland and Stewart, 1968), pp. 5-6.

[12]Allen Sens, "Cooperation under Neorealism: Bringing in the Small States (of Eastern Europe)," in *Multilateralism and Regional Security*, ed. Michel Fortmann, S. Neil MacFarlane, and Stéphane Roussel (Cornwallis, NS: Canadian Peacekeeping Press, 1997), pp. 186-87; Laura J. Neak, "Beyond the Rhetoric of Peacekeeping and Peacemaking: Middle States in International Politics" (Ph.D. dissertation, University of Kentucky, 1991), p. 7.

[13]Charles P. Kindelberger, *The World in Depression, 1929-1939* (Berkeley: University of California Press, 1973); Idem, "Dominance and Leadership in the International Economy," *International Studies Quarterly* 25 (June 1981): 242-54; Robert Gilpin, *War and Change in World Politics* (Cambridge: Cambridge University Press, 1981), p. 144; Idem, *The Political Economy of International Relations* (Princeton: Princeton University Press, 1987), pp. 72-80.

[14]Robert O. Keohane, "The Demand for International Regimes," *International Organization* 36 (Spring 1982): 141-69; Idem, *After Hegemony: Cooperation and Discord in the World Political Economy* (Princeton: Princeton University Press, 1984), pp. 7-10.

[15]See Robert O. Keohane, "The Theory of Hegemonic Stability and Changes in International Economic Regimes, 1967-1977," in *Change in the International System*, ed. Ole R. Hosti et al. (Boulder: Westview Press, 1980), pp, 131-62; and Isabelle Grunberg, "Exploring the 'Myth' of Hegemonic Stability," *International Organization* 44 (Autumn 1990): 431-77.

[16]Andrew Hurrell, "Regionalism in Theoretical Perspective," in *Regional Organization and International Order*, ed. Louise Fawcett and Hurrell (Oxford: Oxford University Press, 1995), pp. 50-53.

[17]Olson and Zeckhauser, "Economic Theory of Alliances"; Stephen Brown et al., "Public-Good Theory and Bargaining between Large and Small Countries," *International Studies Quarterly* 20 (September 1976): 393-414.

[18]Glenn H. Snyder, "The Security Dilemma in Alliance Politics," *World Politics* 36 (July 1984): 471-77.

[19]Paul Létourneau and Michel Fortmann, "La politique de défense et de sécurité du Canada," in *Défense et sécurité: Onze approches nationales*, ed. Létourneau and Harold P. Klepak (Montréal: Méridien/CQRI, 1990), p. 22.

[20]Robert O. Keohane and Joseph S. Nye, *Power and Interdependence: World Politics in Transition* (Toronto: Little, Brown, 1977), p. 179.

[21]See endnote 2, above, for examples.

[22]Charles W. Kegley, Jr., and Gregory A. Raymond, *When Trust Breaks Down: Alliance Norms and World Politics* (Columbia, SC: University of South Carolina Press, 1990), p. 2.

[23]Kalevi J. Holsti, ed., *Why Nations Realign: Foreign Policy Restructuring in the Postwar World* (London: Allen and Unwin, 1982); Ole R. Holsti, P. Terrence Hopmann, and John D. Sullivan, *Unity and Disintegration in International Alliances: A Comparative Study* (New York: Wiley and Sons, 1973).

[24]See Stephen M. Walt, *The Origins of Alliances* (Ithaca: Cornell University Press, 1987); and Idem, "Alliance Formation and the Balance of World Power," *International Security* 9 (Spring 1985): 3-43.

[25]Stephen M. Walt, "Alliances in Theory and Practice: What Lies Ahead?" *Journal of International Affairs* 43 (Summer/Autumn 1989): 4-5; Glenn H. Snyder, "Alliances, Balance, and Stability," *International Organization* 45 (Winter 1991): 121-42.

[26]Heinz Gärtner, "Small States and Security Integration," *Coexistence* 30, 3 (1993): 308; Robert Rothstein, *Alliances and Small Powers* (New York: Columbia University Press, 1968), pp. 50-52, 117, 168-78.

[27]Walt, *Origins of Alliances*, p. 29.

[28]Stephen M. Walt, "Alliance Formation in Southwest Asia: Balancing and Bandwagoning in Cold War Competition," in *Dominoes and Bandwagons: Strategic Beliefs and Great Power Competition in the Eurasian Rimland* (New York: Oxford University Press, 1991), p. 55.

[29]Randall L. Schweller, "Bandwagoning for Profit: Bringing the Revisionist State Back In," *International Security* 19 (Summer 1994): 72-107.

[30]Niccolò Machiavelli, *The Prince* (New York: Modern Library, 1940), p. 86.

[31]Allen G. Sens, "The Security of Small States in Post-Cold War Europe," in *From Euphoria to Hysteria: Western European Security After the Cold War*, ed. David G. Haglund (Boulder: Westview, 1993), p. 235.

[32]For this critique, see Thomas Risse-Kappen, *Cooperation Among Democracies: The European Influence on U.S. Foreign Policy* (Princeton: Princeton University Press, 1995), pp. 24-25; John Gerard Ruggie, "Multilateralism: The Anatomy of an Institution," *International Organization* 46 (Summer 1992): 561-98; and Steve Weber, "Shaping the Postwar Balance of Power: Multilateralism in NATO," ibid., pp. 633-35.

[33]Walt, *Origins of Alliances*, pp. 276-77.

[34]This double dilemma features in the title of Shelagh D. Grant's *Sovereignty or Security? Government Policy in the Canadian North, 1936-1950* (Vancouver: University of British Columbia Press, 1988).

[35]Desmond Morton, "Defending the Indefensible: Some Historical Perspectives on Canadian Defence, 1867-1967," *International Journal* 42 (Autumn 1987): 639.

[36]William C. Potter, "Issue Area and Foreign Policy Analysis," *International Organization* 34 (Summer 1980): 405-27.

[37]Thus David B. Dewitt and John J. Kirton can qualify their approach with the label, "complex neorealism," a curious blend of realism and complex interdependence. See their *Canada as a Principal Power* (Toronto: Wiley and Sons, 1983).

[38]Ulf Lindell and Stefan Persson, "The Paradox of Weak States Power: A Research and Literature Overview," *Cooperation and Conflict* 21 (1986): 84.

[39]See Cranford Pratt, ed., *Internationalism Under Strain: The North-South Policy of Canada, the Netherlands, Norway and Sweden* (Toronto: University of Toronto Press, 1989); and Idem, *Middle Power Internationalism: The North-South Dimension* (Montreal and Kingston: McGill-Queen's University Press, 1990).

[40]For definitions of each of these roles, see Cooper, Higgott, and Nossal, *Relocating Middle Powers*, pp. 23-27; and Kim Richard Nossal, *Rain Dancing: Sanctions in Canadian and Australian Foreign Policy* (Toronto: University of Toronto Press, 1994).

[41]Matthew Evangelista, "Issue-Area and Foreign Policy Revisited," *International Organization* 43 (Spring 1989): 147-71.

[42]See Heinz Gärtner, "Models of European Security and Options for the New 'Neutral' Members in the European Union: The Austrian Example," *European Security* 5 (Winter 1996): 604-13; Michael Handel, *Weak States in the International System* (London: Frank Cass, 1981); and Robert O. Keohane, "The Big Influence of Small Allies," *Foreign Policy*, no. 2 (Spring 1971), pp. 161-82.

[43]Escott Reid, *Radical Mandarin: The Memoirs of Escott Reid* (Toronto: University of Toronto Press, 1989), pp. 158-59. Also see David G. Haglund and Stéphane Roussel, "Escott Reid, the North Atlantic Treaty, and Canadian Strategic Culture," in *Escott Reid, Diplomat and Scholar*, ed. Greg Donaghy and Roussel (Montreal and Kingston: McGill-Queen's University Press, forthcoming 2004).

[44]See, for example, John W. Holmes, *The Shaping of Peace, 1943-1957* (Toronto: University of Toronto Press, 1982), 2: 106; Lester B. Pearson, *Mike: The*

Memoirs of the Rt. Hon. Lester B. Pearson, vol. 2: *1948-57* (Toronto: University of Toronto Press, 1973), pp. 32-33; Escott Reid, "The Creation of the North Atlantic Alliance, 1948-1949," in *Canadian Foreign Policy: Historical Readings*, ed. J. L. Granatstein (Toronto: Copp Clark Pitman, 1986), p. 171; James Bartlet Brebner, "A Changing North Atlantic Triangle," *International Journal* 3 (Autumn 1948): 318.

[45]Edna Keeble, "Rethinking the 1971 White Paper and Trudeau's Impact on Canadian Defense Policy," *American Review of Canadian Studies* 27 (Winter 1997): 553.

[46]Roy Rempel, *Counterweights: The Failure of Canada's German and European Policy, 1955-1995* (Montreal and Kingston: McGill-Queen's University Press, 1996); Michael J. Tucker, *Canadian Foreign Policy: Contemporary Issues and Themes* (Toronto: McGraw-Hill Ryerson, 1980), pp. 127-28.

[47]John G. H. Halstead, "The Alliance Road to Security: Challenge and Opportunity," in *Canada, NATO and Arms Control*, ed. Shannon Selin, Issue Brief no. 6 (Ottawa: Canadian Centre for Arms Control and Disarmament, 1987), pp. 19-27.

[48]John W. Holmes, "The Dumbbell Won't Do," *Foreign Policy*, no. 50 (Spring 1983), pp. 3-22; and Idem, "Canada, NATO, and Western Security," in *No Other Way: Canada and International Security Institutions*, ed. John W. Holmes (Toronto: University of Toronto Press, 1986), pp. 122-39.

[49]David Leyton-Brown, "Managing Canada-United States Relations in the Context of Multilateral Alliances," in *America's Alliances and Canadian-American Relations*, ed. Lauren McKinsey and Kim Richard Nossal (Toronto: Summerhill Press, 1988), p. 176.

[50]For an extensive overview of the literature, see Haglund and Roussel, "Escott Reid."

[51]J. L. Granatstein, *How Britain's Weakness Forced Canada into the Arms of the United States* (Toronto: University of Toronto Press, 1989).

[52]See Tom Keating, *Canada and World Order: The Multilateralist Tradition in Canadian Foreign Policy* (Toronto: McClelland and Stewart, 1993).

[53]For a critique of the hypothesis, see David G. Haglund, *The North Atlantic Triangle Revisited: Canadian Grand Strategy at Century's End* (Toronto: Irwin/CIIA, 2000), pp. 25-29.

[54]Risse-Kappen, *Cooperation Among Democracies*, p. 22.

[55]Ibid., pp. 201-4.

[56]See Charles C. Pentland, "Integration, Interdependence and Institutions: Approaches to International Order," in *World Politics: Power, Interdependence and Dependence*, ed. David G. Haglund and Michael K. Hawes (Toronto: Harcourt Brace Jovanovich Canada, 1990), pp. 173-96.

[57]Keohane and Nye, *Power and Interdependence*.

[58]Ibid., p. 31.

[59]Ibid., p. 206.

[60]Ibid., pp. 35-36.

[61]Keohane, "Big Influence of Small Allies."

[62]For a review of these critiques, see Pentland, "Integration, Interdependence and Institutions," pp. 188-90; and Martin Hollis and Steve Smith, *Explaining and Understanding International Relations* (Oxford: Clarendon Press, 1990), pp. 35-36.

[63]Keohane and Nye, *Power and Interdependence*, p. 166.

[64]Ibid., p. 206.

[65]Michael W. Doyle, "Liberalism and World Politics," *American Political Science Review* 80 (December 1986): 1152-54.

[66]Keohane and Nye, *Power and Interdependence*, pp. 178-93. Also see Joseph S. Nye, Jr., "Transnational Relations and Interstate Conflicts: An Empirical Analysis," in *Canada and the United States: Transnational and Transgovernmental Relations*, ed. Annette Baker Fox, Alfred Hero, and Nye (New York: Columbia University Press, 1976), pp. 367-402.

[67]Donald Barry, "The Politics of 'Exceptionalism': Canada and the United States as a Distinctive International Relationship," *Dalhousie Review* 60 (Spring 1980): 115.

[68]See David G. Haglund, "North American Cooperation in an Era of Homeland Security," *Orbis* 47 (Autumn 2003): 675-91.

[69]Joseph T. Jockel, *No Boundaries Upstairs: Canada, the United States, and the Origins of North American Air Defence, 1945-1958* (Vancouver: University of British Columbia Press, 1987).

[70]I elaborate upon these cases in chapters 6 and 7, below.

[71]Walt, *Origins of Alliances*, pp. 46-49.

[72]Robert O. Keohane, "Multilateralism: An Agenda for Research," *International Journal* 45 (Autumn 1990): 732.

[73]See David A. Baldwin, ed., *Neorealism and Neoliberalism: The Contemporary Debate* (New York: Columbia University Press, 1993); and Kenneth Oye, ed., *Cooperation Under Anarchy* (Princeton: Princeton University Press, 1985).

[74]Examples include Kalevi J. Holsti, "Governance Without Government: Polyarchy in Nineteenth-Century European International Politics," in *Governance Without Government: Order and Change in World Politics*, ed. James N. Rosenau and Ernst-Otto Czempiel (Cambridge: Cambridge University Press, 1992), pp. 30-57; Janice Gross Stein, "Detection and Defection: Security 'Régimes' and the Management of International Conflict," *International Journal* 40 (Autumn 1985): 599-627; Albert Legault, "Régimes et multilatéralisme euro-atlantique," in *Tous pour un ou chacun pour soi? Promesses et limites de la coopération régionale en matière de sécurité*, ed. Michel Fortmann, S. Neil MacFarlane, and Stéphane Roussel (Québec: IQHEI, 1996), pp. 215-32; and Roger K. Smith, "Explaining Non-Proliferation: Anomalies for Contemporary International Relations Theories," *International Organization* 41 (Spring 1987): 253-81.

[75]Robert Jervis, "Security Regimes," in *International Regimes*, ed. Stephen D. Krasner (Ithaca: Cornell University Press, 1983), pp. 182-83.

[76]See Joseph M. Grieco, "Anarchy and the Limits of Cooperation: A Realist Critique of the Newest Liberal Institutionalism," in *Neorealism and Neoliberalism*, pp. 116-40.

[77]Ole Wæver, "Figures of International Thought: Introducing Persons Instead of Paradigms," in *The Future of International Relations: Masters in the Making*, ed. Iver B. Neumann and Wæver (New York: Routledge, 1997), pp. 1-37.

[78]Robert O. Keohane, "The Demand for International Regimes," in *International Regimes*, pp. 141-71.

[79]See Andreas Hasenclever, Peter Mayer, and Volker Rittberger, *Theories of International Regimes* (Cambridge: Cambridge University Press, 1997).

[80]Barry Buzan, "From International System to International Society: Structural Realism and Regime Theory Meet the English School," *International Organization* 47 (Summer 1993): 327-52; Tony Evans and Peter Wilson, "Regime Theory and the English School of International Relations: A Comparison," *Millennium* 21, 3 (1992): 329-51.

[81]Duffield, "International Regimes and Alliance Behavior," pp. 837-39.

[82]Robert O. Keohane, "International Institutions: Two Approaches," *International Studies Quarterly* 32 (December 1988): 379-96; John G. Ruggie, "International Regimes, Transactions, and Change: Embedded Liberalism in the Postwar Economic Order," in *International Regimes*, p. 198.

[83]Sens, "Cooperation under Neorealism."

[84]Rothstein, *Alliances and Small Powers*, pp. 171-73. Also see Denis Stairs, "Change in the Management of Canada-United States Relations in the Post-War Era," in *Toward a North American Community?*, ed. Donald Barry, Mark O. Dickerson, and James D. Gaisford (Boulder: Westview, 1995), pp. 53-74.

[85]Notable exceptions include A. Claire Cutler and Mark W. Zacher, eds., *Canadian Foreign Policy and International Economic Regimes* (Vancouver: University of British Columbia Press, 1992); and Robert Wolfe, "Article 2 Revisited: Canada, Security, and Transatlantic Economic Cooperation," in *North American Perspectives on European Security*, ed. Michael K. Hawes and Joel J. Sokolsky (Lewiston, NY: Edwin Mellen, 1990), pp. 305-35.

[86]John W. Holmes, "Les institutions internationales et la politique extérieure," *Études internationales* 1 (June 1970): 20-40.

[87]Keohane and Nye, *Power and Interdependence*, pp. 170-71. Also see Livingston T. Merchant and A. D. P. Heeney, "Canada and the United States: Principles for Partnership," *Atlantic Community Quarterly* 3 (Autumn 1965): 373-91; John W. Holmes, "Merchant-Heeney Revisited: A Sentimental View," in *America's Alliances and Canadian-American Relations*, pp. 180-99; and Peter C. Dobell, "A Matter of Balance," *International Journal* 28 (Spring 1973): 315-24.

[88]A notable exception is David Leyton-Brown, who reminds us that resort to "quiet diplomacy" presupposes the sharing of certain traits, such as language, political culture, and domestic political institutions. Leyton-Brown, "Managing Canada-United States Relations," pp. 173-76.

[89]Kalevi J. Holsti and Thomas Allen Levy, "Bilateral Institutions and Transgovernmental Relations Between Canada and the United States," in *Canada and the United States*, pp. 283-309.

CHAPTER FOUR

A Liberal-Constructivist Alternative

REACTING TO THE "NEO-NEO" SYNTHESIS

The alternative to the rationalism that dominated IR theory in the 1980s (the so-called "neo-neo" synthesis, which found its expression in regime theory), gradually took shape during the same decade, as part of the intellectual camp-following of postmodernism. This latter strand of thought represented a critique of the Enlightenment tradition, positivism, the pretensions of objectivity implicit in scientific theory and, above all, of rationalism. Perceived by some as being too radical, postmodernism nevertheless served as the point of departure for the "critical" theories — feminism, neomarxism, constructivism — that questioned the epistemological bases of existing currents of thought and proposed certain corrections.

These critical theories arose from the rejection of certain logical links that were supposed to be inferred from the rationalist postulate, and which had been the basis of neo-neo calculations. In particular, the rationalist and utilitarian approach could not adequately explain the choices and interests of actors, since it considered these to be a stable, exogenously derived element, applicable to all actors regardless of time or place. For example, all states were said by rationalists to be seeking an increase in their power, their security, or their wealth, or of all of these together. These motives were considered "givens," logically immanent in the anarchical nature of the international system. As such, only the distribution of power or wealth could result in a variation of the strategies used to promote these interests.[1]

One way to get around these difficulties, it was argued, was to reintroduce such sociological variables as culture, identity, ideas, values, language, and communication. This meliorative thrust came from several institutional schools (sometimes difficult to distinguish one from the other), including the "knowledge-based" variant of regime theory[2] and, in particular, constructivism. This latter turned out to be more of a rediscovery than an innovation, given that back in the 1950s and 1960s it had been common to find social-scientific models being pieced together with such sociological building blocks as those later to be esteemed by the constructivists. Thus it came as no surprise to find that one of those earlier contributions, the idea of a "security community," should get a new lease on life — deservedly so, since the notion provides an excellent jumping-off point for any extended analysis into the utility of sociological metatheory for the study of problems in the area of defence and security. A review of that concept, security community, will lead us in turn to an inquiry into constructivism and its links with other approaches in the field — including transnationalism, institutionalism, and the theory of the liberal-democratic peace. Most importantly, it will point the way to solutions to the apparent puzzle posed by the Canadian-American security relationship.

THEORIZING SECURITY COMMUNITIES

In 1957 a group led by Karl Deutsch, inspired by work on regional integration and communication, proposed the concept of a "pluralistic security community."[3] This is formed by international actors who, linked by a sense of belonging to the same community, renounce war as a means of solving their differences. Deutsch and his colleagues studied the objective conditions favouring the establishment of a security community and, with it, the abandonment of recourse to war: communal values, behavioural predictability, and "resonance," this last being the ability to account for the interests of the other members of the group and to respond to them appropriately.[4]

The pluralistic security community is based on two central elements: identity and communication. The notion of a "sense of community" is, in the first instance, the product of a process of identification.

> The kind of sense of community that is relevant for integration ... turned out to be a matter of mutual sympathy and loyalties identification in terms of self-images and interests; of mutually successful predictions of behavior, and of cooperative action in accordance with it — in short, a matter of a perpetual

dynamic process of mutual attention, communication, perception of needs, and responsiveness in the process of decision-making.[5]

The formation of a sense of community (and thus of a kind of common identity) results from a "transactionalist" conception of international relations, that is, an approach that places the process of communication at the heart of the analysis. The community is created by the circulation of ideas and of individuals. Factors such as trade, scientific and cultural exchanges, migration, and tourism, generally discounted by the realists, here occupy a central position because they contribute to the forging of a common identity between a group of actors having a sufficiently dense and diversified set of exchanges.[6]

Communities may be identified not only by indicators relating to identity and transactions, but also by their adoption of common practices and institutions. They often have institutions aimed at managing relations between the constituent members, which are essentially norms that permit the peaceful resolution of differences. These institutions are generally the product of a convergence of ideas and values that unite the members of a community. They play a central role in reinforcing the integrative links, in particular by crystallizing a consensus around shared values and by emphasizing the degree of resonance in each of the members.[7]

Three aspects of this theory deserve attention. Firstly is its stress on the process of communication, and on ideas and values as variables that can explain decisions and strategic preferences of leaders, especially concerning choices relating to the identity of allies or partners. This aspect breaks with realist theory as far as motives of the actors and possible bases for the building of cooperation are concerned. Further, through its emphasis on the products of the society — ideas, values and the process of communication — rather than those of the state, this approach allows the analytic linking of domestic and foreign policy, areas carefully compartmentalized by the realists.

Secondly, the theory offers an innovative view of the nature of the relations between members of a community characterized by an unequal distribution of power. These relations do not exclude the pursuit of individual self-interest or the emergence of conflict or rivalry. Nevertheless, the fact that conflict is not resolved by recourse to arms reduces the heuristic potential of a variable such as military power.[8] According to Deutsch and his colleagues, banning recourse to force modifies the context in which the actors make their decisions.

Several of these pluralistic security-communities comprised states of markedly unequal power, but their existence always implied acceptance by both parties of a political situation between them which neither side expected to change by force. Small states in pluralistic security-community did not have to expect an attack by the larger ones, nor did large states have to fear that their smaller neighbors were merely biding their time while preparing to join their enemies in some future military crisis.[9]

Although the formation of a pluralistic security community tends to reduce the number of options available to secondary powers (e.g., changing alliances, or merely threatening to do so as a means of extracting concessions), it also creates an important equalization factor by eliminating one of the principal manifestations of power, the resort to armed force. Holsti introduces an important nuance in affirming, within the context of the existing North American security community, that the "great difference in military power ... is largely irrelevant in all negotiations *except those involving military matters.*"[10]

The theory is not devoid of problems, however. Although the idea of a security community is of use in describing a relationship free from war, it does not *explain* such a relationship. Deutsch and his colleagues note the presence of three characteristics in the relations between states that seem to have renounced war, but they remain vague on the causes of the renunciation. This vagueness invests the concept with the quality of circular reasoning at times when it is invoked as an independent variable.

At the root of the problem is the persistent vagueness of the idea. Concepts such as "common identity," "community of values," "confidence," or "resonance" do not easily translate into clear indicators. It is possible to use quantifiable data such as a reduction in the level of military preparedness (measured by expenditures or forces), or the growth of exchanges, so long as we can tell whether such phenomena are causes, consequences, or simply associated characteristics of a security community. Some theorists establish an implicit link with the notion of interdependence, but its nature remains indistinct. Further, it should be noted that despite the attention accorded to ideas and values, these theories remain vague on the quality of these latter. We need to go beyond the simple claim that values can serve to bind together a pluralistic security community, provided that they are shared by all the members and they are enshrined in institutions. In sum, the idea of a community offers only summary elements for reflection concerning the nature and dynamics of a cooperative relationship and, in particular, the emergence of egalitarian relations.

Deutsch's work in this area did not have any immediate effect. Although many authors would subsequently refer to the concept of a security community as one of the possible models of security institutions, the references tended to be cursory ones.[11] Not until recently, and in particular not until the resuscitation of sociological approaches to international relations during the 1990s, has the security community become the subject of a research program.[12]

There are perhaps a dozen security communities, the oldest and most stable of which, in the estimation of numerous authors, is that formed by Canada and the United States.[13] Although the roots of this community reach back to 1819, it seems to have become established only in 1871. Deutsch attributes the community's initial appearance to strategic, political, and financial factors: "[s]ince war became unpalatable to both Canada and the United States after 1815, the basic conditions were created for the demilitarization of their common border and the emergence of a pluralistic security community."[14] Deutsch does not, however, explain what led to the existence of these three sets of factors.

Kal Holsti seeks the answer to this question in the phenomenon of "transgovernmental relations."[15] Although this seems applicable for the years from 1920 or 1930 to the present, it is more problematical concerning the earlier period, characterized as it was by tenuous (to say the least) transgovernmental relations. Others find the explanation in the cultural arena: the Anglo-Saxon heritage and the use of a common language constituted an "enormous advantage" in the evolution of Canadian-American relations[16] and permitted the emergence of a common "diplomatic culture."[17] More generally, the application in the North American context of ideas linked to identity and community of values has evoked certain other concepts, such as exceptionalism and "North Americanism," both of which emphasize the homogeneity and the particularity of the region.[18]

Canada and the United States are also members of a wider security community grouping together the countries of the Atlantic region.[19] This can be comprehended in the metaphorical notion of the "North Atlantic triangle."[20] It is also manifest in the concept of a North Atlantic community that, as with Deutsch's understanding, corresponds roughly to the membership of NATO.[21] All of these sources make their contributions, but to understand why Canada joined the above-mentioned groupings, and with what consequences, we need to seek theoretical guidance from a different body of writing: the sociological metatheory associated with the approach known as constructivism.

THE CONSTRUCTIVIST CRITIQUE OF THE "NEO-NEO" SYNTHESIS

Constructivist theory currently so dominates the so-called critical approaches that some writers have not hesitated to consecrate it as the "third paradigm" in international relations, alongside neoliberalism and neorealism, and in place of neomarxism.[22] It arose, as did the other critical approaches, in reaction to the rationalism that characterizes the neo-neo synthesis, but unlike the more radical approaches (in particular, postmodernism), constructivism aims at adding a sociological dimension to rationalism, rather than replacing it.

Although the analyses of Ruggie and Kratochwil shook the convictions of institutionalist rationalists and contributed to the birth of a current called by Keohane, for lack of a better word, "reflective,"[23] it was not until the work of Alexander Wendt that constructivism gained its name and became the subject of a genuine and ambitious research program. Wendt attacked rationalism by questioning the logical and inevitable link between anarchy and the competitive nature of interstate relations, which is said to manifest itself through states' preferences for power politics and *self-help*. According to Wendt, the interest (and the identity) of actors is a function of their interaction and of their mutual perception. The interpretation by each of the actors of the quality of their interaction (especially as pertains to the perception, or lack thereof, of a threat) can no longer be taken as something exogenously "given." Competition and *self-help* are therefore no more than one set of possible outcomes among others; all depends upon the quality of the interaction and the "intersubjectivity" it engenders. Actors who do not perceive each other as threats will not necessarily establish a competitive relationship.[24]

This being the case, we need to identify the elements that determine these intersubjective relations. Wendt restricts himself to the global level and suggests the addition of a fourth element to the structure defined by

Waltz — an element designating the social fabric of an international system comprising all the interests, interactions, and institutions of the subjects.[25] Thus, the norms, ideas, and accepted values of the "international community" contribute to the definition of the identity, interests, preferences, and behaviour of the actors, as well as to their interactions.

Wendt's constructivism does not advocate a total rejection of rationalism as a means of explaining actors' behaviour. States remain rational actors, capable of making cost-benefit calculations and of elaborating strategies, but at the borders of this rationality lie vast areas where forms of subjectivity have room for action. The first of these areas is found anterior to rationality, because intersubjectivity plays a determinative role in the very shaping of identity and of interests: it is only when these are formed that states can start to develop rational policies. Subjectivity also plays a determinative role in the interpretation of the significance of the material world.[26]

The second area lies parallel to the cost-benefit calculations: confronted with a choice and in the absence of all of the information necessary to pick the option that would best allow then to maximize their benefit, actors fall back upon their values and their culture in order to select as between different avenues.[27] The constructivists, while recognizing the existence of an objective reality, believe that it is always filtered through the subjectivity of the actors (and the observers); any analysis of the relations between actors must therefore account for this intersubjectivity. Constructivism thus appears on the epistemological and ontological levels to be a compromise between the strict rationalism/positivism of the neo-neo camp and the extreme subjectivism/relativism of the postmodernists.

The large number of research projects inspired or enriched by the constructivist approach — in such areas as transnational and transgovernmental relations (i.e., complex interdependence), multilateralism, and pluralistic security communities — testifies to its fecundity. Not only has constructivism contributed to a rethinking of theoretical limits in these three more-or-less established areas, but the hypotheses stemming from this rethinking have nurtured research in a fourth area influenced by constructivism: "democratic peace theory" (DPT). The synthesis enshrined therein would constitute one of the most promising and innovative means of overcoming the paradox of the "unequal but egalitarian" relationship between Canada and the United States.

TRANSGOVERNMENTALIST AND INSTITUTIONALIST
CONSTRUCTIVISM

Although Wendt recognizes the existence and influence of many types of actors in the international system, he regards the state as always being the dominant one. Constructivist theory is in large part concerned with explaining the behaviour of the state. Some analysts, however, have turned their attention to the role of nonstate actors, in particular internal ones, as generators of the ideas, values, and norms that determine the identity and the interest of the state. They instruct us on the necessity of ceasing to consider the state as a unitary actor, and invite us to assess how the culture, ideas, and dominating values of a society can and do affect the attitude of a government at the international level.[28]

The recourse to constructivism breathed new life into certain assertions made earlier by Keohane and Nye, concerning the impact and influence of transnational and transgovernmental actors said to play an important role in the transmission of norms, ideas, and values across borders. These actors are able to contribute to the introduction of new norms in societies as well as in government, and can even assume a watchdog role concerning their application.[29] Transnational actors, by channelling values and fostering a certain uniformity among societies, effect a modification in the way states perceive each other and, in consequence, how they define their interests with respect to each other. This reduces the likelihood of their seeing each other as a threat.

If we turn things around a bit, we can ask whether societies sharing certain domestic values and norms might not, as a result, tend to develop transnational and transgovernmental relations among themselves. In other words, can it be that similarity breeds interaction? Why and how is it that transnational and transgovernmental relations seem more well-developed among certain kinds of societies? Taking things one step further, can it be that liberal-democratic ideas lend themselves more readily than other kinds to the generation of transnational and transgovernmental relations?

In many respects, constructivism started out as a critique of the "rationalist-institutionalist" approach, with regime theorists being among the principal targets. John Ruggie and Friedrich Kratochwil led the charge, in highlighting an inherent contradiction of regime theory, namely its inability to account for the preferences of actors, both as to the form and the content of institutions. Thus Ruggie advanced our thinking about "multilateralism" with his emphasis upon that phenomenon's qualitative aspects, above and beyond its merely quantitative ones (viz., the usage that had multilateralism representing interstate relations involving three or more actors). For Ruggie, what was important about the policy dispensation we call multilateralism were its normative terms, especially the principles of indivisibility and diffuse reciprocity when it came to security.[30] From this, it followed that the values and dominant ideas of actors would be what counted most.

This observation, in turn, helps us better to situate the importance of one norm in particular, that of sovereign equality in international relations. The mutual recognition that states, big and small alike, accord themselves, accounts for the hesitancy of the former to pounce upon the latter. In certain parts of the world, and thanks to certain institutions, this norm is especially entrenched. Western states are the prime illustration, with the leading norms derived from the principle of sovereign equality being consultation, the exchange of information, and the abolition of recourse to violence as a means of dispute settlement within the group. These norms, in fact, structure interstate relations for this group of countries. To understand the origins of this normative structure, we will need to identify the socio-historical characteristics that generated this kind of multilateralism. I will return to this issue later.

For the moment, however, let us revisit some rationalist accounts of the same phenomenon (i.e., the existence of behaviour that supports the notion of norms, including that of sovereign equality). We have, in the previous chapter, already glimpsed two such accounts, in the theory of hegemonic stability as well as with the neoliberal stress upon institutions. Here we need to dwell upon some of the implications of game theory. For theorists of this kidney, it is mimicry of a sort that produces norms, as through a process of trial and error, states learn to "select" those norms best adapted to guide their rational (value-optimizing) behaviour. James Rosenau speaks of the *habit-driven* actor.[31] Robert Axelrod describes an *evolutionary* process: "[w]hat works well for a player is likely to be used again while what turns out poorly is more likely to be discarded."[32] And Dan Reiter refers to the process of "historical learning."[33]

Although often criticized, the evolutionary models at least have the merit of drawing our attention to the gradual nature of the actors' assimilation of norms. The idea can be expressed in sociological terms, with evolution likened to a socialization process during which the actors integrate new norms and cast off old ones. From this perspective, evolution does not result only or even necessarily from a learning process; it is also the product of the exchange of ideas and information between actors, as well as of the pressures brought to bear on state agents by domestic civil society or international actors, or both. This perspective is able to account for possible violations of a norm, especially at the beginning of the process, without calling into question the very existence of that norm. It can also explain why certain actors appear to conform to a norm not yet explicitly formulated.[34]

Finally, Ruggie's work directly raises a question crucial to the present study and neglected by neoliberal institutionalists: what distinction should be made between the bilateral and the multilateral levels? In theory, nothing prevents the application of regime theory to relations between only two actors. For Ruggie, the major difference is that the principles of indivisibility and reciprocity apply to multilateral but not to bilateral relationships. These principles restrict the ability of the strongest member to dominate the weaker ones. As explained by one of Ruggie's supporters: "Multilateralism tends to make security a nonexcludable good. This minimizes the hegemon's coercitive power and its ability to extract payment for protection. It makes the sanctioning of free-riders difficult and threats of abandonment almost impossible."[35]

Conversely, bilateralism carries a negative meaning because it connotes a relationship of dominance between a great power and its dependency, such as existed between Nazi Germany and the different states of Eastern European. This reasoning can be applied to relations between the US and various Latin American countries (the OAS to the contrary notwithstanding), or to those between the USSR and its erstwhile allies in the Warsaw pact. Anne-Marie Burley insists that the "meaningful alternatives to multilateralism in the twentieth century can all be reduced to efforts to establish an asymmetrical set of rules favoring the dominant power."[36] But if this is so, how and why do Canadian-American relations, managed for the large part on a bilateral basis, escape from this logic? Paradoxically, in making a link between Ruggie's definition of multilateralism and liberal values, Burley herself provides an implicit answer to this question, as I discuss below.

CONSTRUCTIVIST SECURITY COMMUNITIES

As noted earlier, constructivism helped spark a renewed interest in the idea of a security community. Deutsch and his colleagues had cleared the path for scholars seeking the sociological "identity" and "sense of community" underpinning the enterprise. Identity refers to the specific "role" an actor gives himself, causing him to adapt behaviour according to the characteristics and expectations of this role. The concept makes sense only within relationships, since it has no meaning until other actors recognize that role and expect to observe a certain kind of behaviour associated therewith. "Sense of community" refers to one's feeling of belonging to a particular group, which then leads members of that group to see themselves differently from the way they see others.

These two concepts, which impel actors to establish a difference between "we" and "they," are inextricably related. The group's shared values and norms can contribute both to the emergence of a feeling of belonging and to a sense of identity, since they foster strong relations and solidarity between the members, as well as encourage them to sense what sets them apart from those who do not share these values and norms. This first characteristic of a security community (a community of values), is therefore anterior to the two other characteristics, namely predictability of behaviour, and resonance. Some argue, for example, that members of a community tend to perceive threats and ways to deal with them in a similar fashion, which reinforces their ability to cooperate.[37] Theorists after Deutsch, however, seemed not to concern themselves with defining more precisely the kinds of values and ideas that might lead to the abolition of the resort to force as between the members; as a result, they gave the (perhaps unintended) impression that a security community could thrive whenever a community of values could be deemed to exist.

The constructivist approach would come to be applied to analyses of Canadian foreign policy. Roger Epp, demonstrating that Canadian participation in the Atlantic community could not be explained entirely by realist formulations, stressed the role of progressive values associated with the notion of community within the Kantian liberal tradition; and Robert Wolfe applied the constructivist approach to a study of the economic development of the transatlantic community.[38]

But the concept of security community, within a constructivist framework, would also prove to be a useful tool for those seeking to explain the emergence and maintenance of the "long peace" in North America. Sean Shore used the assumption of war's impossibility as a starting point for his "Wendtian" account of the "undefended border" between the North American neighbours, held by him to be the product of a relationship of mutual trust. The border's irenic qualities were a resultant of the actors' interactions (viz., their mutual arms reductions) as well as of the manner in which they interpreted those interactions (viz., the expression of a feeling of trust). Thus, at the beginning of the 20th century a North American identity could emerge, one that was recognized as such by élites in both countries. Relations between the two North American states were said to be different from relations between European states because they were founded upon a common culture, an attachment to democracy and transparency, the absence of an arms race, and the peaceful resolution of differences. This common ("collective") identity would be reinforced by such phenomena as the development of transnational and transgovernmental relations, significant cross-border flows of people, economic exchanges, and cultural mixing. Like the transnationalists, Shore maintained that it was the impossibility of war that favoured the development of interdependence within the Canada-US security community.

Three objections can be made to this reasoning. Firstly, even though there exists cultural convergence and a community of values, identity itself may not merit the important place ascribed to it. Using Adler and Barnett's distinction between a "loose" community (i.e., a "transnational region comprised [sic] of sovereign states whose people maintain dependable expectations of peaceful change") and a "tight" one (i.e., a "system of rule that lies somewhere between a sovereign state and a regional, centralized government"),[39] we can see that while North America falls into the first category, it hardly makes the grade in the second. The governments of both countries have carefully avoided entering into a process of political integration. In addition, Shore's causal chain is the opposite of that postulated by Adler and Barnett, for whom demilitarization follows the development of a common identity. Put bluntly, Canadians and Americans, unlike member states of the European Union, do not behave, even episodically, like members of the same body politic, notwithstanding William T. R. Fox's claim to the contrary.[40] Although the terms, "North Americanism" and "We, North Americans," have sometimes figured in the discourse between the élites of the two countries, they have tended not to be encountered (except for during the 1920s) in utterances directed at audiences outside the continent. It may well be that words and deeds of American leaders sometimes give the impression that they consider Canadians to be just like them, but the converse is hardly true.[41] Indeed, a felt need to be different from the US has typically served as the lodestar of Canadian foreign policy, with the result being that when notions of a North American identity do crop up, they are encountered much more frequently in American than in Canadian writings.

Secondly, Shore pays little heed to political factors that might increase the potential for resonance, and with it the predictability of actors' behaviour. He considers the convergence of political values to be but a secondary factor in the formation of community: "In this case, democracy's role in producing peace was indirect.... Of course, democratic values strongly conditioned these relations, but democracy by itself was not the decisive factor."[42] Given that these two countries are among the oldest and most stable democracies in the world, this conclusion is surprising, and cries out for closer examination.

Thirdly, and lastly, Shore turns out to be like Deutsch, Adler, and Barnett, in that what he really wants to explain is the absence of war in North America, and not the reasons for the egalitarian nature of bilateral cooperation.

THE IMPACT OF POLITICAL VALUES, OR DEMOCRACY AS THE SOURCE OF PEACE AND COOPERATION

Contemporaneous with their renewed interest in sociological theories, international relations scholars engaged in a debate over the impact of institutions and liberal values upon their discipline. It became *de rigueur* for authors of a liberal bent to proclaim that democratic states do not resort to force in their dealings with each other, although they do reserve that option in respect of nondemocratic states. Exactly *why* and *how* democracy possessed this irenic property was the subject of much debate, which goes on today. One important feature of the debate is the place of liberal values as peace-keeping elements between the democracies, and reference to these values enables us to overcome the obstacles, discussed previously, that hobbled institutionalist theories. Yet despite the virtual flowering of inquiry into the causes of the democratic peace, there has been precious little application of DPT to the study of the Canadian-American relationship. It is precisely this shortcoming that I hope to remedy in this book.

Kant's seminal 1795 essay on perpetual peace[43] argued that war would disappear once individuals learned how to participate more effectively in political decisionmaking through republican (what we today call "democratic") institutions. Three conditions (or, "definitive articles") were essential for the establishment of the democratic peace. Firstly, states must possess a republican form, since republicanism is the only political system permitting the expression of the public will. Because the population always bears the brunt of war, it could not be expected to enter into such an undertaking lightly — a proposition that undoubtedly became even more logically tenable with the advent of nuclear weapons. The proposition in effect aimed at making individuals rather than the state the principal actors in international relations. The emergence of a lasting peace would therefore be dependent upon an increasing number of states adopting democracy.

Secondly, individual rights were to be enshrined and strengthened by the federation of free states. Kant believed that republics applied rules of international law in their dealings with each other that, by definition, excluded the recourse to war. Moreover, these states tended to associate in a "federation," that is, a form of decentralized union (one not necessarily possessing any supranational government) inspired by experiment underway in the United States at the time.[44]

Thirdly, "cosmopolitan" (i.e., international) law should be limited to creating the conditions of universal hospitality. Individual legal rights should aim at creating favourable conditions for peaceful exchanges, including and especially of goods. Kant attempted through this element to limit claims on territory already inhabited and to foreclose resort to legal arguments as justifications for conquests or protectorates. Peaceful intercourse would enable the circulation of ideas (and therefore encourage the development of republicanism) while at the same time increasing the wealth of citizens.

Kant's ideas, so neglected during his own era when there were precious few democratic states, began to resurface during the late 1930s and early 1940s, through the writings of Clarence Streit and Quincy Wright, among others.[45] Kant became a virtual charter member of the liberal school of international relations.[46] It would be this school that championed DPT, whose core concepts all revolve around one empirical claim, namely that states whose political system can be defined, if only minimally, as democratic have never entered into war with each other. In the oft-cited expression of Jack Levy, this claim ranks as the closest thing the discipline of international relations has to an "empirical law."[47] The claim rests upon a number of factors whose correlation is said to be both intuitively strong and statistically significant.[48] Studies comparing the hypothesis of the democratic peace with other explanations tend to corroborate the claim that the democratic variable plays an independent role.[49]

DPT makes for an interesting point of departure for studying the Canadian-American security relationship, for the good reason that these countries (along with England) have to rank among the world's longest-lived liberal democracies — if not the longest-lived. Thus, the "long peace" in North America during the 19th and 20th centuries stands out as a prime candidate for inclusion in the category of the "democratic peace."

Explanations of *how* democracy leads to peace fall into one or the other of two schools.[50] The first is often called the *structuralist* school, because it emphasizes the constraints imposed on decisionmaking by domestic political structures and institutions, among which constraints are those are said to be derivative of transparency, accountability, and the division of powers. This school also takes into account processes such as free elections and freedom of expression, which enable societal forces to express disagreement with the government and even to overturn it. What works at home is said to work abroad, such that whenever two democracies enter into a dispute it is anticipated that structures that have kept the peace *within* should also keep the peace *between* them.[51] Because this school cannot explain why the same peace-inducing constraints fail to stay any aggressive tendencies of democracies when it comes to *non-democratic* states,[52] their approach is sometimes used only as a backup weapon in the arsenal of the second school. Nor is the first group's emphasis upon structure of much use when we seek to explain cooperative relations.

The second school, called here *interactionism*, is concerned with what happens when two liberal-democracies meet. Their interactions produce two sorts of complementary phenomena that modify the dynamics of their bilateral relationship. The first type relates to the agents' (i.e., the leaders and other élites) interpretation of intentions of their counterparts in the other country; the second has to do with a process of internationalization of liberal norms that can only take place when both interacting states are liberal. The interactionism school, strongly influenced by constructivism, opens up new areas for theoretical application. Instead of being exclusively rivetted upon the absence of war between democratic states, analysts can shift their focus to other aspects and dynamics, especially those relating to interstate cooperation.[53] Constructivism is the logical link between the different approaches that employ the notion of norms: transnationalism, institutionalism, and DPT. It has the added merit of introducing into DPT the element of intersubjectivity, which enables us to refine interactionism arguments.

THE INTERPRETATION OF INTENTIONS

Because they share a political culture, leaders of democratic states are more inclined to consider each other reasonable, predictable and peaceful, to have confidence in each other, and to expect the other to treat them in a like manner (viz., the principle of reciprocity). These expectations stem from a presumption that leaders embody the will of the people, with the latter being thought to be peaceful as well as reasonable, in keeping with Kant's first article. In accordance with the principle of reciprocity, and in stark contrast to their attitude to nonliberal states, liberal states tend to be tolerant of each other and to give each other the benefit of the doubt: "Only those believed to be tolerant are tolerated."[54] This idea corresponds with, and refines, Deutsch's affirmation that a community of values fosters the emergence of a feeling of trust.

In addition, that the leaders of a democratic state know their foreign counterparts to be subject to the same constraints as they themselves face can increase mutual understanding and sympathy.[55] It is therefore not surprising that there should be a ready acceptance of justifications citing public (or legislative, or interest group) pressure as an explanation for the defence of certain positions during delicate negotiations, as has so often happened in the Canadian-American relationship. Appeals to electoral exigencies help to fend off lasting bad relations between leaders.

Intersubjectivity can also be important on another level. Because of their shared political values, it is more likely that the leaders of these different states will define their national interests in a similar fashion, frequently adopting similar positions and perceiving threats in the same manner.[56] This can help explain why democracies become allies,[57] and especially why there are rarely antagonisms between them serious enough to degenerate into violence. As Kal Holsti has observed: "In many areas, the interests of [Canada and the United States] are perceived by policy-makers as essentially identical.... Other interests, while not identical, are at least compatible.... There have been differences on details of strategy but seldom on ultimate objectives."[58]

The constructivists associate the convergence of values with the existence of a collective identity unifying the actors. This latter element is not essential, however, since different actors may perceive a menace in similar terms without sharing a collective identity.

The ability of liberal states to establish relations of trust with each other allows them to surmount what the realists consider one of the major obstacles to the establishment of cooperative relations between sovereign states. Because they can overcome the mistrust of actors in an anarchical environment, democracies are able to focus more on the absolute than the relative gains that issue from their cooperation. This logic also serves to rebut the realist contention that economic interdependence must be regarded as a source of vulnerability, and therefore as a harbinger of conflict.[59]

In keeping with the logic of Kant's third article, trade serves as a force for unity and of peace. Although rivalry and economic conflicts are still possible, they will not end in war. From the liberal standpoint, economic competition in accordance with marketplace rules is legitimate and healthy, for it produces wealth. In short, the transposition of liberal norms and the rules attendant thereupon permits the management of interdependence. Similar reasoning underlies Donald Barry's elaboration of the three principles of exceptionalism, which he argues perform the exact same function: advance notice of any policy change(s) that could affect the other state, consultation during the implementation of such change(s), and the search for compromise to lessen the impact of such change(s).[60] Although he does not make the point himself, it is obvious that Barry's three principles are themselves immanent in the liberal order.

THE INTERNATIONALIZATION OF NORMS

The internationalization of norms, the second phenomenon created by the interactions of liberal states, is the process whereby the norms and principles that govern political relations at the domestic level become social constraints at the international level. Anne-Marie Burley has demonstrated that states tend to create international institutions that reflect those existing at the national level. Thomas Risse-Kappen reasons further that states sharing the same values recognize each other as doing so, and consequently they apply norms derived from those values in their mutual dealings. Internal norms embraced by more than one state become international norms.[61]

The convergence of norms affects such other institutions as principles, rules, and decisionmaking processes that link these same actors.[62] Formal institutions (rules and decisionmaking procedures) and informal ones (customs and practices) also tend to recreate at the international level the same liberal domestic order, thus these serve to structure relations between sovereign states. Risse-Kappen explains:

> Democracies are ... likely to form *democratic institutions* whose rules and procedures are oriented toward consensual and compromise-oriented decision-making respecting the equality of the participants. The norms governing the domestic decision-making processes of liberal systems are also expected to regulate their interactions in international institutions. Democracies externalize their internal norms when cooperating with each other.[63]

At first glance, this seems tautological. But it is not, since nothing guarantees that states will follow at the international level the same path they take at the domestic one. The international norms that result from this process should, by definition, be inspired by liberal values and norms. The specific reference to liberalism thus responds to demands like those of Ruggie and Kratochwil that more attention be paid to the socio-historical context in explanations of the specific content of institutions. It enables the identification of a coherent set of values that determine both the identity and the interests of the actors as well as the nature of the institutions they share, thereby filling a gap in regime theory and alliance theory.

Several consequences follow from the internationalization of norms. Firstly, because of the transposition of internal norms governing the resolution of societal conflict, democratic states do not resort to force to resolve their differences. Instead, they tend to submit to dispute resolution mechanisms comparable to those existing at the domestic level — e.g., courts, arbitrated negotiations, and special committees of experts. It is simply not considered legitimate to threaten to resort to force or coercion to resolve disputes.

The second consequence relates more directly to the nature of cooperative relations between liberal-democracies, and offers insight into the egalitarian nature of these relations. According to Risse-Kappen, the norms governing regularized consultation and joint consensus-building are the reflection, at the international level, of domestic systems that privilege equality between the actors, authorize competition under clear rules, and attach great value to the public nature of decisionmaking.

> These norms serve as key obligations translating the domestic decision-making rules of democracies onto the international arena. The obligation to regularly consult each other can then be regarded as the functional equivalent to domestic norms regulating the publicity of the political process, its constitutionality, and the equality of the participants.[64]

Egalitarianism among states can also be taken to represent the internationalization of two norms at the heart of the liberal order: preeminence of the rule of law, and equality before the law; more generally, it also speaks to the preeminence of individual rights and freedoms. The liberal state can be considered as the embodiment of the civil society that functions according to these precepts. Liberal states are equal, because they represent equal individuals; in this way, the norm of equality completes the notion of sovereignty. The idea of equality between sovereign actors is strengthened by the norm of nonresort to coercion and violence, because the latter norm neutralizes in large part the criterion of power that gives rise to hierarchies between sovereign actors.

It is true that relations between nonliberal states can sometimes be marked by such norms as consultation, joint consensus-building and even nonhierarchy, but these latter are much more evident and more deeply rooted when it comes to relations between liberal-democracies. Since the values giving rise to these norms form the basis of the latter's domestic political systems, their leaders and élites find themselves on familiar ground as they attempt problem-solving methods similar to those used at the domestic level. Furthermore, the norms must be respected if the process is to be considered legitimate, not only by the civil society of the states concerned but also by the leaders and the public opinion of all other liberal states. The internal and external consequences of a violation of the norms can be very serious, and can lead to loss of support, image, and credibility.

Consultation, joint consensus-building and nonhierarchy are factors that diminish the importance of power asymmetries and that give small states an influence out of all proportion with their military and economic capabilities. Again, Risse-Kappen explains:

Power asymmetries should be mediated by norms of democratic decision-making among equals emphasizing persuasion, compromise, and the non-use of force or coercive power. If the norms regulating behavior in international institutions among democracies are themselves democratic, the practices following these norms should enable small allies to influence the decisions.[65]

Here, in a nutshell, we have the answer to the anomaly presented by the curiously egalitarian nature of the Canadian-American relationship. The core of the argument I develop in the following chapters, accordingly, rests upon a synthesis of constructivism and DPT, and borrows insights from interactionism theory. Simply stated, leaders who perceive each other as belonging to societies founded upon liberal-democratic values and norms will apply the same norms and values to the management of their mutual relationship as they do to managing domestic problems within their respective countries. This explains a lot about the quality of Canadian-American cooperation in the realm of security and defence, as I will endeavour to demonstrate.

INDEPENDENT VARIABLE: DEMOCRACY AND PERCEPTIONS

The method of I follow in adapting the interactionism thesis to the study of Canadian-American security relations hews rather closely, as one would expect, to the approach generally employed by the interactionists themselves. Where I part company from them is in the fashion in which I establish a link between the two elements of my independent variable (discussed below) and that which they themselves seek to explain, namely the quality of bilateral interactions in North America.

My independent variable consists of two elements: 1) the leaders' respect for the hard-core liberal values; and 2) their perception that the leaders of the other states with which they establish contacts share this respect. Both of these elements, as well as the relationship between them, deserve further analysis.

The first element is the most controversial, since it is based on an objective definition of the values associated with liberal- democracy. One of the main disputes between realists and adherents to DPT revolves precisely around how ones defines liberal- democracy. Because of the great variety of political and socio-economic systems that can and do lay claim to liberalism, it is necessary to try to identify some common ground at the outset, rather than to dwell upon the ways in which these self-proclaimed liberal-democracy differ the one from the other.

Can we say that there exists a hard core of norms and values essential to a liberal-democratic system, applicable to all members of the set of such countries during the nineteenth and twentieth centuries? To start to answer this question, let us take a close look at the generic definition supplied by Philippe Schmitter and Terry Lynn Karl: "Modern political democracy is a system of governance in which rulers are held accountable for their actions in the public realm by citizens, acting indirectly through the competition and cooperation of their elected representatives."[66]

Democracy is thus a system of governance, a set of principles that define the type of interactions between leaders and citizens. The definition is inadequate, however, in that we cannot deduce from it the values and norms attached to it. A value is a moral precept than enables one to distinguish the desirable from the undesirable, whereas a norm, generally flowing from a value, is a more specific term. It is a prescription, conceived in terms of rights and obligations, that guides the behaviour of the actors by providing a framework for their activities and structuring their expectations; it distinguishes what is acceptable from what is not.[67] There is a scholarly consensus, I believe, derived both from political theory writ large and particular works on DPT, into which we can tap to fill out the Schmitter/Karl definition.[68]

We can say, subject to certain qualifications I introduce below, that liberal-democracy centres around the following values: 1) the equality of individuals with respect to each other and before the law, meaning that each may participate in political life, all are subject to the same laws, and none has to submit to arbitrariness; 2) freedom of speech, of association, and of the press — freedoms judged essential to the exercise of civic and political rights; 3) other individual rights, including the right to private property and to free enterprise, considered the basis of the economic order and the chief mechanism for collective wealth-building; 4) tolerance, resulting from respect for the individual; 5) cosmopolitan law in the Kantian sense, which guarantees the free circulation of people, goods, and ideas between states; and 6) the sovereignty of the state, which enables it to act as the depository and agent for the realization of actions undertaken in the collective interest, as well as the guarantor of individual rights against both internal and external threats.

Norms that can be associated with liberal democracy are, obviously, those that bear upon the values enumerated above. To these can be added those norms that relate to the manner in which leaders are chosen as well as the way in which they make decisions, plus the relationships citizens have with each other. The most important of these norms is summed up in the notion of "bounded competition" as concerns the representation of interests and the choice of decisionmakers.[69] Democracy is here typically associated with an electoral system guaranteeing a free, secret ballot on the basis of universal suffrage. More than this, it also implies the right of citizens to organize to promote their interests, and the acceptance at the governmental level both of an institutionalized opposition and a separation of powers. Along the same lines, "representation" (whether by officials or groups) and "accountability" are regarded as intrinsic features of any democracy worthy of the name.

The second element of our independent variable is the *reciprocal perceptions of the actors*; this corresponds to what the constructivists call "intersubjectivity." There can, in truth, be no appeal to any objective definition of liberal democracy, due to the obvious need for objective reality to get filtered by and through the subjective consciousness of the actors; it is only in this way that the impact of liberal norms and values can be felt. For the most part, analysts of DPT take for granted the universal acceptation of liberalism, as if the concept possesses meaning in and of itself. But it does not and cannot, given the welter of different variants of this political tradition, sometimes even cohabiting within the bosom of a single state. Thus there can be and is a great degree of flexibility when it comes to imagining how liberal norms and values are supposed to work their magic. For instance, a constitutional monarchy can be expected to have a more dour assessment of the "liberal" character of a republic than would a fellow republican state.

In the case of our two countries, what is important is not that they correspond to the same model of liberal democracy (for as I have argued, objectively this makes no sense), but rather that at some moment they began to act toward each other as if they *perceived* each other to be liberal democracies. We need to know when this happened, and to determine how widespread was the perception within the two countries' political classes. The intersubjective dimension is critically important: without it, there can be no convergence of values, with all that this must imply for élite perceptions and the creation of international institutions.

But appealing to intersubjectivity can be a tricky business, for it can lead one straight into a number of logical pitfalls. One in particular bears flagging at the outset: everything said to this point suggests that our "agents" (that is, élites and elected officials) should share the same views, to such a degree that we simply do as the realists do, and conceive of the liberal state as a unitary actor. The problem is that one of the common features of democracies (liberal ones at least), is that they all worship at the altar of toleration and political pluralism. This raises some questions for those analysts who appeal to subjectivity and try to show that decisionmakers in liberal states perceived their foreign counterparts to be liberal. For instance, can we really imagine that all of a given state's key decisionmakers are going to make an identical judgement regarding the liberal bona fides of some other state(s)? Might it not be likely that the party in power sees things in quite a different way from the opposition or the media? In sum, how *can* we reconcile the divergent perceptions held by actors within the same state?

This question takes on greater significance when we recall the tremendous variety of political and socio-economic systems that can and do lay claim to the rubric, "liberal democracy." *Inter alia*, the following can be said to so identify themselves: constitutional monarchies, republics, ultraliberal economic systems, social democracies, parliamentary regimes, presidential systems, protectionist states, and free-trade ones. Seen in this light, a social democracy might be regarded by an ultra-liberal observer to be too far to the left to warrant being labelled "liberal." Many hard-core republicans would find it impossible to regard any constitutional monarchy as being within the liberal family. In a general sense, as John Owen reminds us, liberal observers tend toward skepticism even in respect of other liberal regimes if they consider them to be based upon institutions that, were they transposed upon their own state, would create a threat to their interests.[70] Truly, the lack of a commonly accepted definition of liberal democracy create analytical difficulties.

Nor is this in any way a new problem. During the nineteenth century, it was common for some decisionmakers to disqualify as being liberal those states that seemed to have many of the earmarks of liberalism (e.g., free elections and protection of individual rights) but that also possessed major defects inherited from the old order, for instance monarchy or slavery. Things began to clarify in the twentieth century, for the arrival of the scene of clearly competing political systems such as communism and fascism led liberal democracies to rally around each other, and to seek to marginalize that which set them apart from fellow liberal democracies. Thus the problem of mutual recognition (as liberals) became less challenging, at least in the West, and certainly during the era of the Cold War. Nevertheless, nodes of ambiguity continued to be found, even in that West; we recall in this respect the cases of Spain, Portugal, and a host of Third World countries that were both anticommunist and committed to the market economy, but that nevertheless came up short politically, being virtual dictatorships. This ambiguity persisted into the post-Cold War period.

Canadian-American relations were hardly immune to the definitional problem. If during the twentieth century it became an article of faith in both countries that the other was definitely a liberal-democracy, things were much different in the nineteenth century. As we shall see in chapter five, this mutual recognition of "liberalness" was neither widespread in the respective countries' political classes, nor quick to take root.

John Owen has grappled with this issue in his work on US diplomacy during the nineteenth century, a period of time when many political actors in America simply rejected outright the thought that the United Kingdom, France, or Spain might be cognate democracies. Owen's way around the problem had two dimensions. The first consisted in trying to identify and gauge the influence of those factions who practiced what we might term "democracy-denial." If such factions managed to determine policy, either directly by attaining control of the executive or indirectly by shaping public opinion, then that would tell us something important about the state of the "democratic peace" of the day. There is much to commend this approach, and in fact I am going to employ it below.

But there is also something risky about it. For if the democracy-denial crowd comes to power, what is left of the hypothesis of the democratic peace? How can DPT be applicable, if one of the countries in question is governed by individuals who do not recognize the other country as being a fellow liberal-democracy? To solve this puzzle, Owen proposes a second course of action: appeal not to perceptions but rather to domestic institutions, and make these do the heavy lifting in the preservation of peace. Such a course spirits us completely out of the realm of intersubjectivity, and obliges us to develop objective criteria for identifying the liberal-democratic state. For Owen, such a state is one that possesses an established pattern of free and fair elections and recognizes the individual's freedom of expression. This second solution of his threatens to submerge us in an epistemological swamp, because it necessitates the coexistence of subjective and objective construes of liberal-democracy; if one does not do the trick, just try the other!

For obvious reasons, I am going in this book to give a wide berth to Owen's second dimension. Instead, I will put the emphasis upon subjective construes. For sure, so long as decisionmakers in both countries regard their counterparts as being genuinely liberal, there need be and is no contradiction between the objective and subjective aspects of our independent variable. But what happens when you have both states actually playing by the rules (in the sense that they each respect core liberal norms and values), but one state's decisionmakers do not concede its counterparts in the other to *be* playing by those liberal rules? Or take the reverse: what do you do when decisionmakers continue to regard as liberal-democratic a state that clearly has no commitment to core political and socio-economic norms associated with liberal-democracy?

It is easy to imagine problematical cases. For instance, British Tories could easily draw the conclusion that America's presidential system is hardly liberal, given that cabinet members are appointed by the executive and are not, as in the British system, directly accountable to parliament. In this instance, a refusal to acknowledge America as a liberal-democracy would owe more to an assessment of institutions and less to a judgement about the country's commitment to liberal norms and values. But these same British conservatives might point to those norms and values (basically freedom of expression and free markets) as evidence of the dangers of republicanism, on the basis that the chief executive's need to be elected makes him more likely to be corruptible; ergo, the so-called democracy could be regarded as but a stepping stone to plutocracy. In this case, the core liberal values are not what is being called into question; it is their potential for being manipulated to produce non-liberal institutional outcomes.

These contradictions are difficult, though not impossible, to resolve. Their resolution must depend upon our establishing one baseline rule: our independent variable will not have the expected effect if there exists a contradiction between its objective and subjective components. In other words, we cannot speak of the "democratic peace" or of "cooperation among democracies" if a) one of the state actors in question does not adhere to the core liberal norms and values, *or* b) decisionmakers in one state do not regard their counterparts in the other as reflecting those core values. Thus *both* dimensions, objective as well as subjective, must be taken as constituting (with a qualification I explain below) a necessary condition for the application of DPT.

Stating thusly the rules of the game enables us to introduce the qualification, which comes into play in those cases where one side's ruling body practices democracy-denial. To the extent that denial flows not from any assumption about missing norms and values but rather is predicated upon assumed institutional defects, there can be room for nuance. Whenever the existence of core norms is taken as a given, there is always the chance that these will be thought capable, eventually, of remedying the institutional shortcomings, and by so doing restoring the explanatory prowess of our independent variable and giving substance to our two dependent variables, namely the interpretation of intentions and the internationalization of norms. But this cannot be expected to happen overnight; it takes time for those who would deny the other's liberal-democracy to have their suspicions allayed as a result of their basic recognition that the other's heart may be in the right place, even if his institutions are a mess.

The reason why it is necessary to introduce a qualification such as that above stems from the difficulty we would otherwise encounter when dealing with political factions within one state that refuse to accept the liberal-democratic credentials of the other. For example, pressure groups might raise a hue and cry over the other state's "true" character, without necessarily having an influence over the eventual decision taken. By the same token, we need to be aware that there will times, in the life of any pluralist democracy, when domestic political considerations make it worthwhile for those in power to downplay or otherwise deny the liberal nature of the other state(s) with which they are dealing; at these moments, it can be taken for granted that there is political payoff at home in playing the nationalist card. Luckily, liberal leaders in the "target" state themselves realize, and play by, these same rules of the game.

DEPENDENT VARIABLE: INTERPRETATION AND INTERNATIONALIZATION

The components of our dependent variable do not differ very much from those cited earlier by the "interactionists." The process of the *internationalization of norms*, as we have seen, depends upon the ability and willingness of liberal actors to project to the international level those values they cherish most at home, within their domestic political arenas. In doing so, they modify the normal dynamic of international relations in two ways. They affect the way in which leaders of other states perceive intentions. And they give structure to the content and practices of the institutions that link liberal states to each other.

The *interpretation of intentions* indicates the manner in which one actor will "read" the intentions, motivations, and behaviour of another. This is a variable that we can gauge in terms of confidence at one extreme, and mistrust at the other. A confident actor will not suspect military aggression to be in the works, and accords benign significance to what it sees its partner doing; this sets the stage for the beginning of a process of cooperation. Thus, the more a liberal actor senses its partner to adhere as well to liberal norms and values, the more it is liable to extend the benefit of the doubt to that partner, and to structure its behaviour accordingly.

Examining the causal linkage between perceptions and the interpretation of intentions is also replete with logical pitfalls. In his study on the balance of threat, Stephen Walt concludes that ideology plays a minor, or tactical, part in the formation of alliances: "The states examined here did show a slight preference for alignment with similar states, but the difference was readily abandoned in the face of significant threats or discredited by the rivalries that emerged between ideologically kindred regimes."[71] In so concluding, he provides an alternative account of the part played by perceptions in establishing the democratic peace, effectively reversing DPT's lines of causality. It is not because governments mutually recognize each other as liberal-democracies that we have peace, but rather the reverse: it is because they do not see the other state as a threat that they are prepared to regard it as being liberal-democratic. In this context, it is the interpretation of intentions that determines the perception of the nature of the regime. The discussion, then, becomes purely tactical, involving either the denigration of the political system of one's adversary or the elevation in stature of the system of one's ally.

The only way around this logical dilemma is to ensure that leaders' perceptions are not allowed merely to fluctuate according to the rhythm established by international crises, and to be driven purely by assessment of threat. On the contrary, we should look for evidence that leaders' perceptions vary according to the nature of the regime with which they are dealing. Thus, to be considered relevant, the attitude of liberals vis-à-vis a foreign government should not follow a pattern established by the coming and going of political and even military crises arising with that other government. Nevertheless, attitudes can change should the institutions or domestic political practices of that other government change. Whenever there are changes afoot that tend in the direction of liberalism within the observed state, then so too will attitudes alter in the perceiving state, whose leaders will want to regard the other as being a cognate democracy. The reverse also holds true, of course, and can lead to the aforementioned practice of democracy-denial.

The convergence of norms and values will also have an impact upon the *content* of international practices and institutions that arise out of interstate relations. Liberal democracies, in their mutual dealings, apply liberal norms and form liberal institutions. Transposed to the international level, liberal norms tend both to be reproduced and reinforced as a result of interaction. First among these norms, and most importantly, is the injunction against resort to violence and coercion as means of dispute settlement. The second in importance, and a logical sequel of the non-resort to violence, is the willingness of states to submit their differences to institutional means of dispute settlement that resemble, in large part, domestic dispute-settlement mechanisms (appertaining, for instance, to arbitration, and the reliance upon the reports of expert commissions).[72] These mechanisms might be regarded to be the application, at the international level, of the domestic practices of a political system that emphasizes equality of actors, and sanctions a practice of pluralist representation of interests within a transparent system endowed with established rules.

Certain logical traps also crop up when we study the process by which norms get internationalized; these arise in particular when attempts are made to assess the impact of norms. The first pitfall to avoid is the assumption that there can be or must be a direct and perfect correspondence between norms and the behaviour of decisionmakers. Although norms define behaviour that actors consider to be acceptable (or not), it does not follow that their violation of norms constitutes an ipso facto case for falsifying our hypothesis, and this for two reasons.

Firstly, as numerous critics of the rationalist-instrumentalist approach to regimes have made clear, it is fallacious to argue that if a norm is violated it does not exist![73] On the contrary, even the violations can testify to the existence and effective influence of norms, given their impact upon the behaviour both of the violator and the state that has to suffer the consequences of the violation. Insofar as concerns the former, the violation is often justified as being a necessary and temporary departure from the pattern of behaviour that is most of the time shaped by liberal values. Insofar as concerns the latter, the consequences of norm violation include a demand for reparation buttressed by liberal norms and values. In sum, it the motivation and the consequences of norm violation that demand our attention, and not the violation per se. The latter would be significant only if it were not attended by any attempt, on the violator's part, at expiation that was itself premised upon liberal norms and values.

Secondly, it has always to be remembered that norms and values have a progressive impact: they become reinforced over time, to the extent to which they are integrated by the actors. Thus violations will be more likely to show up at the beginning of this iterative process. To be sure, it would make a difference if the violations were to recur repeatedly, no matter that the violator sought refuge an expiatory rhetoric itself premised upon liberal values.[74] Our hypothesis would indeed face tough sledding in the event of repeated norm violations. By the same token, the reverse is true: should a violation not be repeated, we are justified in taking this as a demonstration of the hypothesis' validity.

It remains very important, however, to try to determine what forms the violation takes, for this can help us understand whether we are dealing with a dynamic derived purely from power considerations, in which there is no possibility for institutions, norms, or even counterweights to come into play.

In the context of bilateral conflict resolution, let us say that the violation of North America's liberal order could express itself in the following manner: the US imposes its preferences upon Canada, and backs this up with a threat to employ military force or political subversion, or both, against its northern neighbour. There have been any number of cases in which the US might have resorted to such means of conflict resolution on the North American continent, especially in the domains of boundary delimitation and fisheries management. Elsewhere, for instance the case of bilateral cooperation for the common defence, the negative consequences (for Canada) of the asymmetrical balance of power in North America could take a variety of forms: loss of control over the country's own armed forces stationed on its own territory; absence of any control over American forces stationed on Canadian territory; the calling into question of the very territorial integrity of Canada; the obligation for Canada to modify its policies toward third countries; the absence of any voice in defining the threat against which the common defence effort is directed; and the loss of any input into the shaping of those American policies and strategies that bear importantly on Canadian interests.

The historiography of bilateral security relations reveals that, at one time or another, each of these dire prospects loomed in Canadian consciousness.[75] Thus the manner in which such conflicts evolved should allow us to test whether norms and values — along with the institutions they did so much to shape — played a determinative part in setting the dynamic of bilateral security cooperation.

TRANSNATIONALISM AND TRANSGOVERNMENTALISM

Can we obtain some "value-added" by injecting liberalism into the related categories of "transnationalism" and "transgovernmentalism"? I believe we can, and that our doing so will enable us resolve some issues that Keohane and Nye left hanging. For them, the abjuring of a resort to force was a necessary condition for the emergence of transgovernmental relations. Yet they did not specify what it was that led the two governments to foreswear the use of force. They did take note of democracy, but did not really pursue the connection between it and relations they were trying to describe and explain. Sean Shore went a bit further, in invoking the "confidence" that had been instilled as a result of the two countries' demilitarization of their border. But as with Keohane and Nye, there was no attempt to specify the normative content of the altered regime.

Here is where reference to liberal values can help us get a better appreciation of the factors that spawn transgovernmentalism; for as Bruce Russett tells us, transnationalism is closely linked with democracy.

> Individual autonomy and pluralism within democratic states foster the emergence of transnational linkages and institutions — among individuals, private groups, and governmental agencies.... Democracies foster, and are fostered by, the pluralism arising from many independent centers of power and influence; autocracies do not. Democracies are open to many private and transgovernmental linkages; autocracies rarely are. Thus transnationalism cannot easily be considered separately from the distinction between democracies and other kinds of states. Since it is substantially correlated with the "open" institutions of

democratic politics, it cannot be treated analytically or empirically as an independent cause [of peace].[76]

Thomas Risse-Kappen is more exact in pinpointing how liberal political systems favour the emergence of transborder linkages.

Transboundary activities of societal actors largely depend on whether the domestic structures of the states involved enable governments to control these activities. Since democratic systems are based on the separation of state and society, their governments are less able to control the transnational activities of their citizens than authoritarian political systems. Transnational relations are expected to flourish in alliances among democracies. The same conditions of open structures and highly institutionalized interstate relations also facilitate the emergence of transgovernmental decisions.[77]

Certain norms associated with liberalism can also facilitate the emergence of transnationalism and transgovernmentalism, in particular those associated with the free movement of people. Moreover, individuals who work within a similar political and socio-economic environment are much more likely to establish linkages between themselves than they are with those who function in an entirely different milieu.

All these elements lead in the same direction: the likelihood that transgovernmental coalitions will form and become relevance varies in direct proportion with the incidence of liberal-democratic political cultures. This seems self-evident, and possibly because of this no one has really bothered to verify it empirically.

It is possible to go further, and to show that once they have been established, transnational and transgovernmental relations serve to reinforce a liberal interstate order, and in so doing maintain the peace. In the first place, these relations can serve as the vehicles for diffusing norms and values, which in their turn work to strengthen the transborder relations. Secondly, transborder coalitions often act as pressure groups in their own right, and in the event of conflict will have a vested interest in seeking a compromise solution. If necessary, government representatives participating in a transnational coalition with side with the political faction that recognizes the liberal character of the other state.

Thirdly, these relations serve to depoliticize problems, precisely because the presence of transnational actors can often shift the responsibility for conflicts to transnational actors, effectively taking the heat off the respective decisionmakers. By the same token, the existence of transgovernmental coalitions and networks favours the search for technical rather than political solutions, and does so by shifting the action to decisionmakers at lower levels of the state, bureaucrats who generally think of their job as consisting in "problem solving," unlike politicians and other higher-ranking officials who often fancy themselves obliged to defend the "national interest."

Finally, transgovernmental coalitions will tend to lead to a compartmentalization of conflicts, meaning that trouble in one policy area will be unlikely to spill over into another, thereby injecting an element of poison into the overall workings of the relationship. This is what transnationalists have in mind when their study of Canadian-American relations leads them to emphasize both the avoidance of linkage between issue-areas and the virtues of "quiet diplomacy."

DEMOCRATIC SECURITY COMMUNITIES AND
BILATERAL INSTITUTIONS

Deutsch and his colleagues may have been the pioneers of security-community research, but it cannot be said that they probed the phenomenon in any particular depth. Passing references may have been made to a federation of democracies, but was there any sustained inquiry into the place liberal values occupied in their "North Atlantic community"? Not really, possibly because at the time they were writing, certain members of the community — Turkey, Spain, and Portugal — could not be said to be very liberal. Despite this, analysts who followed in the footsteps of Deutsch and his colleagues did begin to theorize the evolving community in terms of a Kantian republican federation.[78]

These references to liberalism would reinforce the ongoing research program on security communities, by clearly identifying one of the likely sources of the three necessary conditions for such communities: value congruence, predictability, and reciprocity. On the other hand, the concept reinforced the perception-based hypotheses of interactionists, and enabled them to push their reasoning a bit further: it could now be said that the mutual recognition democracies accorded each other gave rise to a sense of "we-ness" — possibly even a common identity — that was founded *not* upon culture or language, but on an attachment to certain political values.

This had the advantage of reconciling what might otherwise have seemed like contradicting phenomena: the existence of a sense of belonging at the same time as members of the "in-group" insisted on maintaining differentiable identities, founded upon culture and economic particularities *within* the broader group. This is a distinction that is of special importance in the analysis of Canada-US relations.

It allows us to remedy some of the shortcomings of the approach to the North American security community developed by Sean Shore. He insisted upon economic and cultural interdependence as being constituent elements of the security community, and as a result he overlooked how the pull of identity would affect Canadians, who worried about the Americanization both of their culture and of their economy. This pull has given periodic rise to strong expressions of Canadian nationalism, making it both undesirable and very difficult for Canadians to think in terms of a "North American" identity. Given this, it remains unclear how Shore can postulate a *North American* community. On the other hand, the tension is easily resolved if what is postulated is something else — a *democratic* community. Such a grouping, founded upon adherence to liberal political values, can be and is fully consistent the existence of a distinct Canadian identity, based upon socio-economic referents. What is surprising among the plethora of studies on the Canada-US relationship is precisely how little attention gets paid to the ability of difference to persist within the context of (liberal-democratic) commonality.

There is something else that has been overlooked. It is very common for scholars to detect within *multilateralism* the presence of such values as indivisibility and reciprocity. It is also very common for these same scholars to fail to detect such values in *bilateralism*. Risse-Kappen has even gone so far as to wonder whether his own theory of "cooperation among democracies" can have any applicability at the bilateral level.[79]

The fact is, however, that insofar as concerns the *quality* both of the interaction and its consequences, there is no difference between Canadian-American relations, on the one hand, and US-European relations on the other, and this notwithstanding that the former are by definition bilateral and the latter multilateral. Nor is there anything in the theories either of Ruggie or Risse-Kappen that requires multilateralism to be part of the explanation of outcomes, even if they do not recognize this. Why is it, when we examine Canada-US relations, we do *not* see them as being determined by asymmetries of power, when all the pundits tell us that bilateralism is always an undesirable option for the smaller power in an asymmetrical relationship? How can we account for this, other than to argue that both multilateralism and bilateralism derive their inspiration from the same source?

Burley gives part of the answer when she notes that "multilateralism is nothing more than the internationalization of the liberal conception of the rule of law."[80] Seen in this light, a bilateral relationship that itself reflects this liberal conception of law can itself, paradoxically, bear the earmarks of "multilateralism." Reference to liberal-democratic values becomes the means of answering the criticism that so many multilateralists being to bear against bilateralism. Contrary to what might be claimed by structural realists, neoliberals, and even constructivists, hypotheses about the democratic peace require no distinction as concerns the number of actors involved. Whether two or ten democratic states are involved in the interaction, the result is the same — the establishment of a separate zone of peace. Logic suggests that would applies in the case of DPT should also hold when we examine the effects of liberal-democracy upon modalities of interstate cooperation.

It is that logic that undergirds the analysis in this book. The synthesis between constructivism and the hypotheses of interactionists (viz., their stress upon both perceptions and the internationalization of norms) provides the solution to the puzzle that the anomalous Canada-US security relationship poses. On the level of theory, the synthesis enables us better to understand how ideas and values structure interstate relations. Too much of the scholarship on DPT reposes upon statistical correlations. The synthesis allows us to probe the *qualitative* and not just the quantitative dimensions of the question. And it is just those qualitative dimensions that inform the next three chapters of this study.

Notes

[1]Friedrich Kratochwil and John R. Ruggie, "International Organization: A State of the Art on the Art of the State," *International Organization* 40 (Autumn 1986): 753-75; Friedrich Kratochwil, "Norms Versus Numbers: Multilateralism and the Rationalist and Reflexivist Approaches to Institutions — A Unilateral Plea for Communicative Rationality," in *Multilateralism Matters*, ed. John R. Ruggie (New York: Columbia University Press, 1993), pp. 443-74; Martha Finnemore, *National Interests in International Society* (Ithaca: Cornell University Press, 1996).

[2]Andreas Hasenclever, Peter Mayer, and Volker Rittberger, *Theories of International Regimes* (Cambridge: Cambridge University Press, 1997), pp. 136-210.

[3]Karl W. Deutsch et al., *Political Community and the North Atlantic Area: International Organization in the Light of Historical Experience* (Princeton: Princeton University Press, 1957).

[4]Ibid., pp. 66-68.

[5]Ibid., p. 36.

[6]Emanuel Adler and Michael N. Barnett, "Governing Anarchy: A Research Agenda for the Study of Security Communities," *Ethics & International Affairs* 10 (1996): 66-67, 74-75.

[7]Deutsch et al., *Political Community*, pp. 8, 66.

[8]Adler and Barnett, "Governing Anarchy," pp. 75-76; Kalevi J. Holsti, *International Politics: A Framework for Analysis*, 1st ed. (Englewood Cliffs, NJ: Prentice-Hall, 1967), p. 493.

[9]Deutsch et al., *Political Community*, pp. 65-66.

[10]Kalevi J. Holsti, *International Politics*, 4th ed. (Englewood Cliffs, NJ: Prentice-Hall, 1983), p. 446 (emphasis added).

[11]See, for example, Barry Buzan, *People, States and Fear: An Agenda for International Security Studies in the Post-Cold War Era* (Boulder: Lynne Rienner, 1992), pp. 218-19; Andrew Hurrell, "Regionalism in Theoretical Perspective," in *Regionalism in World Politics, Regional Organization and International Order*, ed. Louise Fawcett and Andrew Hurrell (Oxford: Oxford University Press, 1995), pp. 64-65; David R. Mares, "Looking for Godot: Can Multilateralism Work in Latin America This Time?," in *Multilateralism and Regional Security*, ed. Michel Fortmann, S. Neil MacFarlane, and Stéphane Roussel (Clementsport, NS: Canadian Peacekeeping Press, 1997), pp. 81-103.

[12]Adler and Barnett, *Governing Anarchy*, pp. 68-69.

[13]Deutsch et al., *Political Community*, pp. 6, 29-35; Holsti, *International Politics*, 4th ed., pp. 443-47; Sean M. Shore, "'Ready, Aye, Ready': The Impact of the North American Security Community on Canada's Decision to Fight, 1914," paper presented to the 38th annual meeting of the International Studies Association, Toronto, March 1997; Idem, "No Fences Make Good Neighbours: The Development of the Canadian-American Security Community, 1871-1940," in *Security Communities*, ed. Emanuel Adler and Michael Barnett (Cambridge: Cambridge University Press, 1998), pp. 333-67.

[14]Deutsch et al., *Political Community*, p. 115.

[15]Holsti, *International Politics*, 4th ed., pp. 443-47. See also Idem, "Canada and the United States," in *Conflict in World Politics*, ed. Steven L. Spiegel and Kenneth N. Waltz (Cambridge, MA: Winthrop, 1971), pp. 392-93.

[16]C. P. Stacey, *The Undefended Border: The Myth and the Reality* (Ottawa: Canadian Historical Society, 1973), p. 19. See also David Leyton-Brown, "Managing Canada-United-States Relations in the Context of Multilateral Alliances,"

in *America's Alliances and Canadian-American Relations*, ed. Lauren McKinsey and Kim R. Nossal (Toronto: Summerhill, 1998).

[17]John Kirton, "Canada and the United States: A More Distant Relationship," *Current History* 79 (November 1980): 117-20, 146-49.

[18]Donald Barry, "The Politics of 'Exceptionalism': Canada and the United States as a Distinctive International Relationship," *Dalhousie Review* 60 (Spring 1980): 116-18; William T. R. Fox, *A Continent Apart. The United States and Canada in World Politics* (Toronto: University of Toronto Press, 1985).

[19]Gene M. Lyons, "More than Allies: The Atlantic Community," in *America's Alliances*, pp. 52-72; Roger Epp, "On Justifying the Alliance: Canada, NATO and the World Order," in *North American Perspectives on European Security*, ed. Michael K. Hawes and Joel J. Sokolsky (New York: Edwin Mellen, 1990), pp. 89-121; Robert Wolfe, "Atlanticism Without the Wall: Transatlantic Co-operation and the Transformation of Europe," *International Journal* 46 (Winter 1990-91): 137-63.

[20]"[P]olitically, militarily, economically, and culturally, the English-speaking nations of North Atlantic developed common institutions and common patterns of behaviour." D. M. L. Farr, "Britain, Canada, the United States and Confederation: The Politics of Nation-Building during the Turbulent Years," in *Reflections from the Past: Perspectives on Canada and on the Canada-U.S. Relationship* (Plattsburgh, NY: Center for the Study of Canada, State University of New York, 1991; orig. pub. 1967), pp. 61-62. Also see also J. Bartlet Brebner, *North Atlantic Triangle: The Interplay of Canada, the United States and Great Britain* (Toronto: McClelland and Stewart, 1966; orig. pub. 1945); B. J. C. McKercher and Lawrence Aronsen, eds., *The North Atlantic Triangle in a Changing World: Anglo-American-Canadian Relations, 1902-1956* (Toronto: University of Toronto Press, 1996), pp. 184-219; and Thomas Risse-Kappen, "Collective Identity in a Democratic Community: The Case of NATO," in *The Culture of National Security: Norms and Identity in World Politics*, ed. Peter J. Katzenstein (New York: Columbia University Press, 1996), pp. 357-99.

[21]Claude Delmas published a contemporaneous essay on Deutsch, expressing similar views, *Le Monde atlantique* (Paris: Presses universitaires de France, 1958).

[22]Stephen M. Walt, "International Relations: One World, Many Theories," *Foreign Policy*, no. 110 (Spring 1998), pp. 29-46.

[23]Robert O. Keohane, "International Institutions: Two Approaches," *International Studies Quarterly* 32 (December 1988): 379-96.

[24]Alexander E. Wendt, "Anarchy Is What States Make of It: The Social Construction of Power Politics," *International Organization* 46 (Spring 1992): 391-425.

[25]Ibid., p. 401.

[26]John M. Owen IV, *Liberal Peace, Liberal War: American Politics and International Security* (Ithaca: Cornell University Press, 1997), pp. 18-19.

[27]This proposition is explored in Judith Goldstein and Robert O. Keohane, "Ideas and Foreign Policy: An Analytical Framework," in *Ideas and Foreign Policy:*

Beliefs, Institutions, and Political Change, ed. Goldstein and Keohane (Ithaca: Cornell University Press, 1993), pp. 3-30.

[28]See Yosef Lapid and Friedrich Kratochwil, eds., *The Return of Culture and Identity in IR Theory* (Boulder: Lynne Rienner, 1996); and Thomas Risse-Kappen, ed., *Bringing Transnational Relations Back In: Non-State Actors, Domestic Structures, and International Institutions* (Cambridge: Cambridge University Press, 1995).

[29]Thomas Risse-Kappen, "Ideas Do Not Float Freely: Transnational Coalitions, Domestic Structures, and the End of the Cold War," in *International Relations Theory and the End of the Cold War*, ed. Richard Ned Lebow and Risse-Kappen (New York: Columbia University Press, 1995), pp. 187-222.

[30]John Gerard Ruggie, "Multilateralism: The Anatomy of an Institution," *International Organization* 46 (Summer 1992): 561-98.

[31]James N. Rosenau, "Before Cooperation: Hegemons, Regimes, and Habit-Driven Actors in World Politics," *International Organization* 40 (Autumn 1986): 861-65.

[32]Robert Axelrod, "An Evolutionary Approach to Norms," *American Political Science Review* 80 (December 1986): 1095-1111; Idem, *The Evolution of Cooperation* (New York: Basic Books, 1984). Also see Ann Florini, "Evolutionary Models in International Norms," *International Studies Quarterly* 40 (September 1996): 363-89.

[33]Dan Reiter, *Crucible of Beliefs: Learning, Alliances, and World Wars* (Ithaca: Cornell University Press, 1996); Idem, "Learning, Realism, and Alliances: The Weight of the Shadow of the Past," *World Politics* 46 (July 1994): 490-526.

[34]Kratochwil and Ruggie, "International Organization," pp. 367-68.

[35]Steve Weber, "Shaping the Postwar Balance of Power: Multilateralism in NATO," *International Organization* 46 (Summer 1992): 637.

[36]Anne-Marie Burley, "Regulating the World: Multilateralism, International Law, and the Projection of the New Deal Regulatory State," in *Multilateralism Matters*, pp. 125-56, quote at p. 144.

[37]Thomas Risse-Kappen, *Cooperation Among Democracies: The European Influence on U.S. Foreign Policy* (Princeton: Princeton University Press, 1995), p. 32.

[38]Epp, "On Justifying the Alliance"; Robert Wolfe, ed., *Transatlantic Identity? Canada, the United Kingdom and International Order* (Kingston, ONT: Queen's University School of Policy Studies, 1997); Idem, "Article 2 Revisited: Canada, Security, and Transatlantic Economic Cooperation," in *North American Perspectives*, pp. 305-35.

[39]Adler and Barnett, "Governing Anarchy," p. 73.

[40]Fox, *Continent Apart*, pp. 57-78.

[41]David Baldwin, "The Myths of the Special Relationship," in *An Independent Foreign Policy for Canada?*, ed. Stephen Clarkson (Toronto: McClelland and Stewart, 1968), pp. 6-7.

[42]Shore,"'Ready, Aye, Ready'," p. 27.

[43]Immanuel Kant, "Perpetual Peace," in *The Theory of International Relations*, ed. M. G. Forsyth et al. (London: Allen & Unwin, 1970), pp. 200-45. Also see Michael W. Doyle, "Kant, Liberal Legacies, and Foreign Affairs," *Philosophy and Public Affairs* 12 (Summer-Autumn 1983): 225-28; Idem, "Liberalism and World Politics," *American Political Science Review* 80 (December 1986): 1157-58; and David Held, *Democracy and the Global Order: From the Modern State to Cosmopolitan Governance* (Stanford: Stanford University Press, 1995).

[44]André Tosel, *Kant révolutionnaire: Droit et politique* (Paris: Presses Universitaires de France, 1988), p. 99.

[45]Clarence K. Streit, *Union Now: A Proposal for a Federal Union of the Democracies of the North Atlantic* (New York: Harper, 1939); Quincy Wright, *A Study of War* (Chicago: University of Chicago Press, 1942).

[46]Bruce Russett, *Grasping the Democratic Peace: Principles for a Post-Cold War World* (Princeton: Princeton University Press, 1993).

[47]Jack S. Levy, "Domestic Politics and War," *Journal of Interdisciplinary History* 18 (Spring 1988): 662.

[48]James Lee Ray, *Democracy and International Conflict: An Evaluation of the Democratic Peace Proposition* (Columbia: University of South Carolina Press, 1995). But for a critiques of the statistical significance of the postulate, cf. John J. Mearsheimer, "Back to the Future: Instability in Europe After the Cold War," *International Security* 15 (Summer 1990): 5-56; and David E. Spiro, "The Insignificance of the Liberal Peace," *International Security* 19 (Autumn 1994): 50-86.

[49]Stuart Bremer, "Democracy and Militarized Interstate Conflict, 1816-1965," *International Interactions* 18 (Spring 1993): 231-49; Zeev Maoz and Bruce Russett, "Alliance, Contiguity, Wealth, and Political Stability: Is the Lack of Conflict Among Democracies a Statistical Artifact?," *International Interactions* 17 (Spring 1992): 245-67. Again, criticisms can be made of these claims; cf. Christopher Layne, "Kant or Cant: The Myth of the Democratic Peace," *International Security* 19 (Autumn 1994): 5-49.

[50]On the debate between the two schools of DPT, see John M. Owen IV, "How Liberalism Produces Democratic Peace," *International Security* 19 (Autumn 1994): 87-125; and Nils Petter Gleditsch and Harvard Hegre, "Peace and Democracy: Three Levels of Analysis," *Journal of Conflict Resolution* 41 (April 1997): 283-310.

[51]Timothy Y. C. Cotton, "War and American Democracy," *Journal of Conflict Resolution* 30 (1986): 616-35; T. Clifton Morgan and Sally Howard Campbell, "Domestic Structure, Decisional Constraints, and War," *Journal of Conflict Resolution* 35 (June 1991): 187-211; T. Clifton Morgan and Valerie L. Schwebach, "Take Two Democracies and Call Me in the Morning: A Prescription for Peace?" *International Interactions* 17 (1992): 305-20.

[52]Though this is not an uncontested assertion. See for instance, Kenneth Benoit, "Democracies Really Are More Pacific (in General)," *Journal of Conflict Resolution* 40 (December 1996): 636-57; and R. J. Rummel, "Democracies Are More

Peaceful than Other Countries," *European Journal of International Relations* 1 (December 1995): 457-79.

[53]A focus that has characterized the work of Risse-Kappen; see his "Democratic Peace — Warlike Democracies? A Social Constructivist Interpretation of the Liberal Argument," *European Journal of International Relations* 1 (December 1995): 491-517.

[54]Owen, *Liberal Peace, Liberal War*, p. 36.

[55]William J. Dixon, "Democracy and the Peaceful Settlement of International Conflict," *American Political Science Review* 88 (March 1994): 17.

[56]William J. Dixon, "Democracy and the Management of International Conflict," *Journal of Conflict Resolution* 37 (March 1993): 45.

[57]Kurt Taylor Gaubatz, "Democratic States and Commitment in International Relations," *International Organization* 50 (Winter 1996): 31-63; Randolph M. Siverson and Juliann Emmons, "Birds of a Feather: Democratic Political Systems and Alliance Choices in the Twentieth Century," *Journal of Conflict Resolution* 35 (June 1991): 285-306.

[58]Holsti, "Canada and the United States," p. 378.

[59]Katherine Barbieri, "Economic Interdependence: A Path to Peace or a Source of Conflict?," *Journal of Peace Research* 33 (February 1996): 29-49; Dale C. Copeland, "Economic Interdependence and War: A Theory of Trade Expectations," *International Security* 20 (Spring 1996): 5-41.

[60]Barry, "Politics of 'Exceptionalism'," p. 115.

[61]Burley, "Regulating the World," pp. 141-46; Risse-Kappen, *Cooperation Among Democracies*, pp. 29-34.

[62]According to one institutionalist formulation, norms are institutions, as rules and decisionmaking processes; see Stephen D. Krasner, "Structural Causes and Regime Consequences: Regimes as Intervening Variables," in *International Regimes*, ed. Krasner (Ithaca: Cornell University Press, 1983), p. 3.

[63]Risse-Kappen, *Cooperation Among Democracies*, p. 33.

[64]Ibid., p. 35.

[65]Ibid., p. 33.

[66]Philippe C. Schmitter and Terry Lynn Karl, "What Democracy Is ... and Is Not," *Journal of Democracy* 2 (Summer 1991): 76.

[67]Robert O. Keohane, *After Hegemony: Cooperation and Discord in the World Political Economy* (Princeton: Princeton University Press, 1984), pp. 57-58.

[68]For instance, see André-J. Bélanger and Vincent Lemieux, *Introduction à l'analyse politique* (Montréal: Presses de l'Université de Montréal, 1996), pp. 121-28; Georges Burdeau, *Le Libéralisme* (Paris: Seuil, 1979); Herbert McClosky and John Zaller, *Capitalisme et démocratie: L'Amérique, juge de ses valeurs* (Paris: Économica, 1990); and G. Bingham Powell, Jr., *Contemporary Democracies: Participation, Stability, and Violence* (Cambridge: Harvard University Press, 1982).

[69]Schmitter and Karl, "What Democracy Is ..."

[70]Owen, *Liberal Peace, Liberal War*, pp. 39-40.

[71]Stephen M. Walt, *The Origins of Alliances* (Ithaca: Cornell University Press, 1987), p. 266.

[72]Dixon, "Democracy and Peaceful Settlement," p. 16.

[73]Friedrich Kratochwil, *Rules, Norms, and Decisions* (Cambridge: Cambridge University Press, 1989), p. 63. Also see Risse-Kappen, *Cooperation Among Democracies*, p. 37; and Peter J. Katzenstein, "Introduction," in *Culture of National Security*, pp. 20-22.

[74]"While above a certain threshold behavioral violations invalidate norms, occasional violations do not." Katzenstein, "Introduction," p. 20.

[75]See, for examples, J. L. Granatstein, "The American Influence on the Canadian Military, 1939-1963," in *Canada's Defence: Perspectives on Policy in the Twentieth Century*, ed. Barry D. Hunt and Ronald G. Haycock (Toronto: Copp Clark Pitman, 1993), pp. 129-39; and Shelag D. Grant, *Sovereignty or Security: Government Policy in the Canadian North (1936-1950)* (Vancouver: University of British Columbia Press, 1988).

[76]Russett, *Grasping the Democratic Peace*, p. 26.

[77]Risse-Kappen, *Cooperation Among Democracies*, p. 38.

[78]Harvey Starr, "Democracy and War: Choice, Learning, and Security Communities," *Journal of Peace Research* 29 (May 1992): 207-13.

[79]Risse-Kappen, in response to a question I posed during a seminar at the University of Montreal on 26 March 1997.

[80]Burley, "Regulating the World," p. 144.

PART TWO

EVOLUTION OF COOPERATION

CHAPTER FIVE

The Beginning: From the "Long Peace" to Conflict Resolution, 1867-1914

THE LONG CANADIAN-AMERICAN PEACE

The century spanning the end of the War of 1812 and the start of the Great War witnessed an increase in the economic and military power differentials between the United States and Canada. Yet this did not seem to have had the effect expected by realists. Despite their numerous disputes, and in light of the profound asymmetry in America's favour, the two countries never fought each other again after 1814. An examination of the causes of this North American "long peace" sheds light on why such an imbalance of power did not seem to have made a major difference to the quality of the Canadian-American relationship.

It is not that scholars have been oblivious of this long peace. To the contrary, several hypotheses have been advanced to account for it, including the balance of power, economic interdependence, and "obsolescence" of war. None of these, however, depends much upon the liberal-democratic variable. Indeed, those rare authors who do consider this latter variable do so only to reject it. According to Sean Shore, democratic institutions did not play a significant role in the creation of the North American security community. William Thompson inverses the relationship, arguing that it was the peace ensuing from the strategic disengagement of Britain and the United States that facilitated the development of democratic institutions over the course of the nineteenth century — i.e., it was peace that "caused" democracy, not democracy that caused peace.[1]

The argument that the peace that prevailed after 1814 might be considered a "democratic" one is complicated by the colonial status of Canada before Confederation, and of its semicolonial status thereafter. For if we exclude Canada from our analysis of the period preceding 1867 (to say nothing of that preceding the 1931 Statute of Westminster), then it makes not a whit of difference how the country was governed during those years. Most of the disputes that threatened to develop into armed conflict during the several decades following 1814 involved Britain and the United States; the risk of war between the latter and Canada during this period was little more than an extension of the highs and lows of the British-American relationship. None of the authors who seek to apply democratic peace theory to Anglo-American crises affecting Canadian security take into account the kind of government that happened to be in place in Ottawa.[2] Thus, if there *was* a democratic peace before 1867, it was an Anglo-American affair, and as such is beyond the compass of this study.[3]

It is true that liberal institutions did exist on both sides of the border from the end of the eighteenth century, that the Canadian and American governments did establish tentative bilateral relations (viz. the Reciprocity treaty of 1854), and that liberal values and ideas did take on transborder significance at times, as happened with the rebels of 1837-38, who sought ideas and support from, and eventually refuge in, the United States. These elements constituted, nonetheless, too thin a gruel to sustain a democratic peace diet, and the most that should be said is that Canada benefitted from the Anglo-American "democratic peace" (if that is what it was), but it did not contribute much to its emergence prior to 1867.

The argument changes after 1867, as the two countries began to establish bilateral relations that took into account values and norms. But if we limit our study to the post-Confederation period we run into a major problem: given that the peace predated the democratic relations established during this period, the latter cannot explain the former. Critics can thus easily affirm that the absence of war since Confederation is nothing more than the legacy of a regnant peace whose roots are found in the pre-1867 balance of power, or in economic interdependence, or in the obsolescence of war. Although it might be countered that the Canadian-American peace, being the child of the Anglo-American peace, would therefore might qualify as a democratic peace, this seems to be more than a bit of an analytical stretch.

Heedful of this, I am not going to argue that liberal ideas and values constituted the sole, or even the principal, cause of the long peace after 1867 in North America. My aim is the more modest one of assembling some elements that might be regarded as supportive of the democratic peace argument, even if only by inference. Democracy is surely not the only cause of the long peace, but it is in part responsible for it. This statement, modest as it is, might still be considered as a contribution to the work of those who do factor Canadian-American relations into claims about the democratic peace, either in support of or in opposition to democratic peace theory.

Might we do even better than this modest claim? By this I mean to suggest that even if we cannot posit a strong causal linkage between liberal ideas and values and the long peace for the *first* two-thirds of the nineteenth century, it could turn out that the gradual rise of cooperative relations between the two countries after 1871 will sustain a more robust linkage. Most writers have treated the Canadian-American relationship as being nothing more than a story of neighbours needing and erecting "good fences." This impression, perhaps arising from the lack of formal and institutional bonds, fails to take into account the proliferation of *ad hoc,* informal, interactions from the 1870s onwards, a span of decades during which Britain's gradual disengagement, militarily and diplomatically, from North America favoured the development of a structured, formal, bilateral relationship. The interactions that developed during this period may not have been as spectacular as the formation of the bilateral "alliance" during the Second World War, but they relate to matters equally fundamental, since they concerned disputes having the potential to lead to war.

So there is a genuine puzzle here, which I make it the business of this chapter to unravel: What *has* kept the peace in North America for so long, and why?

THE EMPIRE TO THE RESCUE

The history of Canadian-American relations is studded with disputes, the "undefended border" to the contrary notwithstanding. That the US represented a genuine military threat to Canada until the turn of the nineteenth century is evidenced by invasions in 1775-76 and 1812-14, tensions between Washington and London during the Civil War (especially the Trent and the Alabama affairs), crossborder raids led by groups fighting against one or the other of the governments (viz., the rebellion of 1837, the St. Albans raid of 1864, and the Fenians in 1866), rumours of war during the Venezuelan crisis of 1895-96, and Teddy Roosevelt's threat to resort to the "big stick" over the Alaska Panhandle boundary dispute in 1903.[4] The grounds of these conflicts were manifold, and included boundary delimitation, fishing and navigation rights, American "manifest destiny" rhetoric, economic controversies, and an American desire to eradicate British influence in North America as well as to obtain "compensation" for Civil War losses.[5] Military leaders, on either side of the border, seem to have considered armed conflict to be a real possibility during this period, and it would not be until the 1930s that planning for war within the North Atlantic triangle would finally cease.[6]

Despite the recurring rumours of war, a long peace did settle in between Canada and the United States after 1814. This peace, which has subsisted for nearly two centuries, is all the more remarkable given that for more than half of its existence nothing similar existed between the US and its other North American neighbour, Mexico. How can we explain this peace, which began during an era when America was not shy about proclaiming its continental ambitions — and indeed resorted to arms to fulfil them in the Mexican War? How can we account for the fact that North American asymmetries in power did not fully manifest themselves in the Canadian-American relationship?

The reason most often advanced to answer this question is the "British counterbalance," expressed alternatively as the "balance of power between England and the United States."[7] To those who argue thusly, Canada's security was guaranteed by its membership in the British Empire, and it had been British troops, after all, who were largely responsible for stopping the two American invasions, just as it had been the British military presence that guaranteed the post-1814 status quo. One American senator, comparing the contemporaneous events of the Oregon boundary dispute and American claims to Texas, is said to have concluded in 1846: "Why all of Texas and only a part of Oregon? Because Great Britain is strong and Mexico weak."[8] D'Arcy McGee, a father of Confederation, shared the sentiment when he observed in 1867 that had Canada not had the "strong arm of England over us," it would never have known an existence separate from the US.[9]

This argument, straightforward and seductive as it is, suffers withal from some weaknesses, all the more so if we turn our gaze to the defence of Canada after 1870. It is probably true that the British supplied the bulk of the forces defending Canada between 1763 and 1870. After that time, things would change radically, with the emergence of three broad principles. First, it became apparent to the British at the time of Trent affair in 1862 that it might no longer be possible to defend their colony successfully against an American attack. The mood of the British electorate a decade later forced Gladstone to withdraw almost all of the imperial troops stationed in Canada, with the exception of those in Halifax and in Esquimalt. Ottawa had thenceforth to accept, like it or not, that the defence of Canada was primarily going to be the responsibility of Canadians, with the British providing nothing more than assistance in the organization and the training of the troops, along with an *implicit* promise of help in the case of an attack.

The second principle of early Canadian defence policy flowed from the first. The departure of British troops forced Ottawa seriously to consider forming its own army. Lack of both resources and political will resulted in the lowering of ambitions. Given the impossibility of mounting a credible defence of the country's vast territory, Ottawa adopted the "simple" policy of avoiding war altogether.[10] This meant avoiding acts and postures that could be interpreted as being hostile to or against the interests of the United States, including the mobilization of a significant army or navy.[11] Thus it came to pass that Canada's militia had as its primary function not the defence of the country's border, but instead aid to the civil authorities — it being understood that civil unrest might serve as a pretext for American intervention in Canadian affairs, just as domestic turmoil had triggered American military involvement in the affairs of its southern neighbours, including those in Central America and the Caribbean.[12]

Colonel Wolseley's expedition to the Red River in 1870 was aimed not only at reestablishing order in the Métis territory recently acquired by Canada, but also at preventing annexationist maneuvers by the Americans seeking to take advantage of Riel's uprising. A similar preoccupation was responsible for the sending of an expeditionary corps to the Yukon in 1898 to police a region swarming with gold seekers. Given the ambiguities associated with the region's border, it was important to act quickly in order to prevent the US from sending a "police force" to maintain order on territory that Canada claimed as its own. Thus was established the principle of "defence against help," though no one called it as such at that time, connoting the need to manage Canadian security problems that might affect America's security, thereby depriving the latter with a pretext for intervention.[13]

The third principle inhered in the new doctrine of "reciprocity," which resulted from the a need for Britain to increase its military investment *pari passu* with the expansion (especially in India and Africa) of imperial commitments. For Ottawa, hardly exuberant at the best of times about incurring military expenditures, this implied a new and distinctly unwelcome dispensation: henceforth, Canada and other dominions were to be expected to contribute to imperial defence by sending troops and materiel wherever imperial interests were endangered. The empire protected them; it was their turn to protect the empire.

In accordance with this doctrine Ottawa despatched troops to support the 1885 Nile expedition, to fight the Boers in 1899, and of course to combat Germany in 1914. From this standpoint, Canada's vaunted "internationalism" is a function of a simple calculation: by contributing to the defence of the empire, Canada would assure itself of that entity's support should it become necessary. Contributing to the fight against the Boers was said to serve the cause of the balance of power in North America. A similar logic has even been applied, though this gets us ahead of our story, to the period between 1949 and 1991, and extended well beyond the confines of the empire: Canada's military contribution to the defence of the "central front," it was said by some, was the price that had to be paid in order to obtain privileged relations with the European members of NATO, seen as "counterweights" to America's political influence.[14]

For these three reasons, the "empire effect" was less powerful than the counterweight (or North-American-balance) analysts imagine it to have been. One way to salvage the balance-of-power argument might be to consider the North American balance from a virtual not a real perspective, and to maintain that what really protected Canada was not so much the actual, physical, presence of British troops in the country as it was the prospect of London deploying the Royal Navy on Canada's behalf. This virtual "counterweight" would seem to pack a mighty deterrent punch, for according to a calculus detailed by Karl Deutsch

> [w]ar became unattractive because it promised to be both devastating and indecisive, as in the case of the United States and Canada after 1815: American land power could easily devastate much or all of Canada, while British sea power could easily inflict great harm upon American shipping and American seaports. But American armies could not have destroyed Britain's ability to make war, nor could British seapower have destroyed the military capabilities of the United States on the North American continent.[15]

This counterweight calculus seems to have had applicability, at least until the Venezuelan crisis of 1895, for despite the blustering of some congressional figures, American military leaders' concern about the physical and financial cost of a war with Britain looks to have persuaded President Cleveland to accept a compromise. But the calculus loses credibility the closer we draw to our own day, starting in 1898.

From the turn of the century and especially after the First World War, the supremacy of the Royal Navy had been under challenge, first by the Germans, later by the Japanese and the Americans. The 1922 Washington treaty on naval arms limitation enshrined Anglo-American parity at sea. But two decades earlier, the British admiralty had begun to appeal to the dominions for help in maintaining naval supremacy — an appeal that led to the creation of the Canadian navy.[16] The 1906 withdrawal of British troops stationed at Esquimalt and Halifax signalled a renunciation of even the symbolic British military presence in Canada.

Canadian leaders, in any case, do not appear to have put much stock in the counterweight theory. In fact, Sir John A. Macdonald thought that a strengthening of British naval power in North America would succeed only in *poisoning* Canadian-American relations. And Sir Wilfrid Laurier, contemplating Canadian participation in a British naval arms race, concluded that such participation would have little positive effect on Canada's security, since the US could easily neutralize British sea power through coastal defence measures.[17]

A more general objection to the argument of the North American balance questions the credibility of the British deterrent: would London really be willing to risk war with the US in order to protect Canada? One can well pose this question, given British attitudes during the negotiations leading to the conclusion of the Washington treaty of 1871, to say nothing of the Alaska Panhandle boundary dispute of 1903.[18] Britain appeared preoccupied more with the defence of the empire in general — which called for an improvement in relations with America — than with that of Canada in particular. Should the two aims conflict, as they did in 1871 and again in 1903, the first had a way of claiming priority over the second.

Starting in the mid-nineteenth century, some began to question whether Britain's colonies possessed any further usefulness to it. Their market value had been degraded by the adoption of free trade in 1846 and their defence costs looked like a black hole into which ever growing resources would have to be dumped. The empire, in the midst of a crisis due to strategic overexpansion, was faced with painful choices. Worse yet, money spent on the defence of Canada had little effect on the power relationship on the ground: Canada would continue to be a hostage to American intentions, forcing London always to prefer a policy of compromise with Washington.[19]

For these reasons it is difficult to claim that the British counterweight was *the* explanation of the long North American peace from 1896 to 1914 (or possible even later). William Thompson is certainly not wrong in saying that "republican institutions cannot claim all the credit [for that peace]... The geopolitical reasons that help to account for the outcomes appeared to have been maintained from 1783 to 1895."[20] But after that time, and running into the interwar period, the counterweight argument possesses declining utility.

One last point needs to be made, and it also adds to the case against the British counterweight: bilateral Canadian-American relations not only increased in frequency with the withdrawal of the British, they *improved in quality*. Britain's troop withdrawals turned out to be a means of reducing diplomatic tensions between the North Americans. As Richard Preston remarks:

> If the principle of stark *Realpolitik* and a simplistic view of the relations of foreign policy to military strength had applied after Britain's withdrawal, Canada's increasing loneliness in North America would have left her a victim of American military blackmail, or perhaps of invasion. Instead Canadian-American confrontation has become diplomatic, economic, and cultural, rather than military.[21]

This observation is particularly embarrassing from the realist standpoint, according to which the emergence of a power disequilibrium should result in instability and conflict; instead, we see the opposite occurring.

Some historians who refer to the balance of power use an ad hoc argument to explain the dynamic of Canadian-American relations after 1871, thereby reversing the causal chain: after the treaty of Washington, peace could be kept because most of the potential causes of conflict had disappeared. It was thus no longer the power relationship that permitted a climate of peace, but rather the climate of peace that enabled a change in the power relationship, without resulting in an American invasion of Canada.[22] Canadians are well aware that there has been virtually no risk of war over differences with their American neighbour since the border disputes at the start of the twentieth century; they also know that whatever risk of war existed between them and the US since that time did so because of their links with the empire. Furthermore, those links would become increasingly uncomfortable as they began to imply Canadian involvement in extracontinental wars. Such overseas interventions not only represented a military and financial burden; they also endangered national unity, given that they almost automatically divided the country along linguistic lines.[23]

To sum up this section: the theory of the British counterweight, or of the North American balance of power, provides a useful point of departure, and this for two reasons. First, it does offer a generally satisfactory explanation for the North American peace that prevailed between 1814 and 1871, and it has partial applicability at least until the Venezuela crisis of 1895. Secondly, the very weakness of the theory after the late nineteenth century leads to the conclusion that it must not have been the only factor at play. The theory, in demanding that we concentrate upon the Anglo-American balance of power as the peace-keeping element *par excellence*, causes us, however unintentionally, to look elsewhere for those factors that would enable the long peace to become even longer, as the power equilibrium became less and less credible as an explanation. In our bid to explain why the fundamental asymmetry in Canadian-American relations did not result in the sort of catastrophes for Canada that realist theorists would expect, let us examine those competing explanations.

INTERDEPENDENCE AND THE "OBSOLESCENCE" OF WAR

At the outset, it has to be acknowledged that, apart from those accounts derivative of the British-counterweight thesis, few theories have been advanced to explain the long North American peace. Among those few competing versions, we can identify at least two analytical camps, drawn from assumptions about both economic interdependence and the postulated "obsolescence" of war. In this section, I take these in turn.

The first competing category holds that increasing commercial and financial exchanges between Canada, the US, and the UK must have contributed to the maintenance of peace. The nineteenth century was characterized by ever-increasing trade between the three countries, and it would seem reasonable to assume that their governments would wish to avoid war in order to continue to enjoy the fruits of such economic intercourse. By 1870, for example, the US was already absorbing more than half of Canada's exports, and accounting for a third of its imports. A war would do more than just trouble these continental exchanges; it would also entail a blockade of American ports by the Royal Navy, thereby threatening the bulk of America's worldwide exports. The stock market crash of 1895, occasioned at least in part by the looming prospect of an Anglo-American war over Venezuela, provides a good case in point.

Furthermore, despite recurring bouts of protectionism in the US, that country's trade border with Canada was becoming more open, and this in itself deprived would-be American annexationists of an argument, for there could be "no frustrated Americans to call for annexation so that they might pursue their private interests more freely in the British colonies to the north. The incorporation of Canadian territory into the United States would have brought no more security to investors in either country than already existed."[24]

There can be little doubt that those who identify interdependence as an element contributing to the long peace have a point. Nevertheless, the argument suffers from some drawbacks. First, the outbreak of war in 1914 between two such important trading partners as Britain and Germany demonstrates that the fear of disrupting profitable trade arrangements does not in itself always constitute a sufficient deterrent to war.[25] The attitude of economic élites in the belligerent countries is best explained by the widely held belief that as the war would be short and easily won — a "cult of the offensive" dominating the general staffs at the time — there would actually be little disruptive impact upon trade arrangements.[26]

Secondly, trade relations between Canada and the United States, although important, were never completely harmonious. To the contrary, they were generally characterized by protectionism, despite a reciprocity treaty in 1854 (covering only primary resources), which the US chose to rescind in 1866. Attempts to revive reciprocity, in 1874-5 and again in 1911, resulted in humiliating and costly defeats for the two governments. The industrial development of the two countries was, in fact, more a function of protectionism than of free trade.[27] You might almost say that economic interdependence, accompanied as it so often is by mistrust, protectionism, and shattered illusions, can be a *cause* of, rather than a deterrent to, war.[28]

Thirdly, nineteenth century American thinking, influenced at the start by the ideas of Alexander Hamilton and at the end by those of Alfred Thayer Mahan, was not stamped by the conviction that liberalism and free trade favoured peace. Like Rousseau, Hamilton considered trade to be a source of conflict and recommended the adoption of protectionist measures to strengthen the power of the state and the nation. For Mahan, war was not necessarily synonymous with a loss of wealth; thus the resort to force in order to advance economic interests was not excluded, as illustrated by the numerous American interventions in Latin America aimed at protecting economic and other interests. Nothing in principle should have ruled out the same medicine being applied to Canada.[29]

Finally, it can be argued that interdependence theory is not relevant during this period because, despite significant trade with the US, the majority of Canada's exports continued to find their market in Britain; it would not be until after the First World War that the Canadian economy grew ever more dependent upon that of the US. As for the latter, commercial dependence on either Canada or Britain was limited to only a few sectors, among the most important being the cotton industry, heavily reliant upon access to European markets.[30]

The second competing account to the British counterweight is the "obsolescence of war" thesis — with obsolescence being taken either in a technical or a moral perspective, or both.[31] Technically speaking, just as the existence of nuclear weapons should logically lead to the absence of war between nuclear-weapons states (because of the prospect of mutually assured destruction)[32], so should the ability of England and the US to have significantly damaged each other led to the absence of war between Canada and the US. War had simply become too difficult to conduct, too uncertain as to outcome, and certainly too costly.

Many other issues apart from the logical and normative untenability of a North American war were preoccupations during the latter half of the nineteenth century — and these distractions, it is said, further buttressed the obsolescence-of-war explanation. Both countries were concerned first and foremost with the need to develop their vast western territories. After 1865, Washington was kept busy with the tasks of reconstructing the vanquished Confederacy. Later on, Washington would be just as distracted by the desire to enhance America's international influence, especially during the period 1890-95. In Canada, the idea was gaining ground that the country should become free of the empire and its constraints, in part inspired by a perception that British diplomatic fumbling was jeopardizing Canadian interests. The principal objective of foreign policy under Laurier's government became the gradual acquisition of the attributes of "sovereignty."

One of the paradoxes of the obsolescence argument is that war in North America *was* becoming "unthinkable" at the time, but only because some continued to think about it. According to Richard Preston, the work of those officials charged, in both countries, with planning future martial contingencies, provided a constant reminder to leaders about the dangers and folly inherent in any future conflict between Canada and the US.[33]

The technical obsolescence of war, in the North American context, seems at first glance to be a byproduct of the military balance of power between the US and the UK; if so, it merely becomes a gloss upon, not an alternative to, the British-counterweight thesis. However, although intimately linked, the balance of power and the obsolescence of war are actually distinct phenomena. This is because the "impossible war" perspective is logically congruent with the concept of security community, which of course is antithetical to the notion that peace *within a group* is kept by power balancing. Deutsch explains: "Since war became unpalatable to both Canada and the United States after 1815, the basic conditions were created for the demilitarization of their common border and the emergence of a pluralistic security community."[34]

The second definition of the obsolescence of war that Mueller proposes concerns ideas and values: it is not so much the technical impossibility of waging war that leads to its disappearance as it is the evolution of thinking about war. Instead of being romantic and morally acceptable, war becomes repugnant, immoral, and pointless. With respect to the situation between Canada and the United States, Mueller concludes that

> [p]eace came about mainly because both sides became accustomed to, and generally pleased with, the status quo. In simple fact, there no longer seemed to be any outstanding issue worth fighting over. The idea of war between these former enemies faded, like dueling, beyond the realm of conscious possibility.[35]

The acceptance of the status quo is fundamental here. Even though the US might be certain of winning a war against Canada, there is adjudged to be no point in waging one, as preserving the status quo is valued more highly than whatever might be obtained by threats or by the resort to arms. That even American annexationists could abandon the idea of a resort to force after 1870 lends strength to this hypothesis. However, Mueller's citing the long North American peace to advance his claim regarding the obsolescence of war between industrialized states suffers from one important weakness: the core of his argument really does not apply during the first century of that peace, from 1814 to 1914.

As late as August 1914, leaders and populations in the soon-to-be belligerent countries (Canada among them) still considered war to be romantic, progressive, and normal; it was only later, after becoming aware of the extent of the horror they were engaged in, that they changed their minds about war. This is as true of the Americans as of the British and the Canadians. If so, then Mueller's account seems to be missing sight of what did keep the peace in North America for that century. Why or how could it be that relations between Canadians and Americans were so irenic starting a full century before war was declared "obsolete" throughout the industrialized world?

Why not explain the long peace by an amalgam of the foregoing theories? The long peace might thus appear during the nineteenth century to have been the product of a balance of power between the British empire and the United States, whereas during the twentieth century it could be chalked up to a combination of such factors as economic interdependence and the rejection of war. Tempting though it might be to resort to this means of solving the puzzle, it is less than satisfactory, for there exists yet another alternative for us to consider — an alternative that, curiously, has been neglected in the scholarly writing on Canadian-American relations. This alternative pays heed to the setting up of democratic regimes and the institutionalization of relations affecting security problems.

NORTH AMERICA'S LONG LIBERAL PEACE

"Convergence of values" is a process often mentioned in the literature, but those who use it do so in very general terms and without saying exactly what they mean. Scholarship on security communities makes reference to the importance of the "compatibility of politically significant values," of their institutionalization at the domestic level, and of the "depoliticization of conflicting values." Yet one strains to comprehend how those who use these terms define them![36]

Historians might emphasize the "Anglo-Saxon" sociocultural heritage shared alike by British, Americans, and Canadians as being the factor enabling the mother country, its former colonies transformed into a republic, and the descendants of the Loyalists caught between them to transcend their differences. Yet surprisingly few historians (or political scientists) interested in Canadian-American relations have considered the impact of a different set of "political cultural" values, namely the specifically liberal ones associated with the broader scholarship on the "republican peace" (also known as the democratic peace). This is all the more astonishing, given that relations between the US, UK, and Canada are so often hailed as one of the most longstanding manifestation of the democratic peace.

As we have already glimpsed, some obstacles stand in the way of presenting of democratic peace theory as the solution to the puzzle posed by the long North American peace. The first of these stems from Canada's colonial (later semicolonial) status, for even if we agree that the Americans and the British gradually saw each other as liberal democratic states during the course of the nineteenth century and that this had an impact on their relationship, what can be said of the mutual perception between Canadians and Americans? To resolve this difficulty, I am only going, as it were, the "start the clock" in bilateral North American affairs from 1867, the year in which Canada was formed as an entity endowed with more or less total autonomy insofar as concerned domestic affairs. By 1867 Canada was a liberal democracy within a strict definition of the term. Moreover, after 1867 there began to develop an abundance of interactions between the North American neighbours, permitting us to attempt to measure the impact of liberal values and ideas upon their mutual perceptions.

But other obstacles loom. There can be no doubt that the United States of 1776 and the Canada of 1867 can be regarded as liberal democracies. Not only this, but it is also clear that the American political system influenced the manner in which the Canadian one evolved.[37] Nevertheless, these two liberal systems did spring from different political cultures, which led them to interpret differently the meaning and significance of these items we label liberal values.

For starters, consider that the US was born of a violent revolution whereas Canada evolved slowly in the context of a parliamentary monarchy — and, indeed, in direct reaction to some of the principles of the American Revolution.[38] The two countries had a different ethnic makeup. The principle of the rights of the individual suffuses all of American political philosophy, while Canadian leaders have traditionally been more solicitous of minority rights, initially those of the Anglophones, who were in the minority until the 1840s, and subsequently those of the Francophones. Finally, Canada's political system was unable to generate anything equivalent to the populism associated with America's Jacksonian tradition.[39]

Given these differences, how unifying could liberal values be within North America? What kind of perceptions could be supported based upon these values, "intersubjectively" contemplated and discussed as they might have been? Would not a thoughtful liberal of a critical cast of mind, no matter in which North American country he lived, conclude from the differences that his interests would be threatened should the institutions of the other variant of liberalism get a foothold in his own country?

Finally, the empirical record seems to stand as a prima facie contradiction of democratic peace theory in North America. American leaders during the period from 1870 to 1911 continued to express annexationist proclivities, while Canadian political élites exhibited a wholesale mistrust of American republican institutions.

Despite all of the above, however, it is possible to view things in a different light, and to regard liberal democracy as the indispensable element in the North American liberal peace in the decades between Confederation and the First World War. In the remainder of this section, I begin this exercise by briefly examining Americans' perceptions of their neighbour; in the longer section that follows, I turn my attention to Canadians' perceptions of the US.

American élite opinion was influenced by Manifest Destiny ideology. This was especially so for the Republicans who dominated American federal politics between 1869 and 1885. The GOP was also fond of protectionism. President Ulysses S. Grant showed little liking for the new political entity that emerged in the north in 1867. In his 1870 state of the union address he described it as a colonial authority, a quasi-independent yet irresponsible entity that exercised the power granted it by London in a manner unfriendly to the US. Passage of the British North America Act provoked scorn among some Americans, concerned that the new country might develop into a monarchy ruled by Prince Arthur. It took some time for the hostility and skepticism to pass from the American scene, and as late as 1890 one American observer could write that the "dominion government is essentially a political party government, the leader of the party in power being at once chief of the executive branch and boss of the legislative branch of the government; in a word, a partisan autocrat."[40]

As for the vast majority of Americans, things were different. Then, as now, Americans by and large tended to know very little about their northern neighbour. As Lester B. Shippee noted, "Confederation and the gradual expansion of the Dominion of Canada no longer disturbed the average American; indeed, he generally ignored the fact that a colony was disappearing and a nation was rising in its place."[41] It would take some time for American élite opinion of Canada to correspond with American popular opinion. But it would happen.

The 1871 treaty of Washington may have represented the preliminary phase in America's recognition of Canada's existence, but it did not signal the demise of annexationist aspirations.[42] Starting with Andrew Johnson and extending through Chester Allen Arthur, all presidents mentioned the possibility of the Canadian provinces and territories joining the Union.[43] This, however, does not constitute a case for dismissing the liberal hypothesis; it is rather the reverse! All depends, of course, upon the manner in which annexation was supposed to take place.

William Seward, Lincoln's secretary of state, appears to have been the last American policymaker to have promoted the idea, in 1861-62, of a *forceful* annexation of Canada. At first, Seward sought to use annexation as a means of uniting an America that was on the verge of falling apart; subsequently, he promoted the idea as a way of compensating for the loss of the southern states. Post-Civil War thinking on annexationism was different, and more in conformity with liberal principles. Canadians were invited to join the Union when they could, that is when they were able to break their ties with the mother country.

The new annexationist thinking was clearly liberal, based as it was on the primacy of the "will of the people." Unfortunately for Grant and his successors in the White House, the Canadians proved not so eager to join up. Yet in contrast with its application of the mailed fist to the southerners — not just during the war itself but also in postwar reconstruction until 1877 — America extended merely an invitation to the northerners. Why the distinction? One Canadian historian, W. L. Morton, thought he knew the answer. "The respect inherent in the American character and tradition for the self-determination of genuine nationalities played its part, despite much skepticism concerning the validity of Canadian nationality."[44]

Another reason has to be found in the nature of America's political institutions in the last decades of the nineteenth century, where playing the British card, or "twisting the lion's tail," so often characterized — and disguised — what was primarily a contest not between the American and British governments, but an internal struggle between the White House and Congress. For many Americans at this time were beginning to recognize Britain as a democracy — a "crowned republic" — and this too would have an impact upon the manner in which they perceived Canada.[45]

Just as American conceptions of what was north of them were changing, however gradually, so too were Canadian perceptions of their southern neighbour altering in the closing decades of the nineteenth century.

CANADIANS REGARD THE UNITED STATES

For most of the nineteenth century, the Canadian political class was universally critical, distrustful, and scornful of American democracy.[46] The presidency was described as being at the same time impotent and despotic, attended by nonelected ministers, and the legislative branch was considered a source of instability, especially in foreign relations. Generally speaking, American democracy was adjudged to be too "pure," and prone to majoritarian excesses. The absence of a political class (e.g., the monarchy or nobility) capable of embodying the state and remaining above partisan disputes accounted in large part for the weaknesses of a system held to be devoid of ideals and driven by materialism — a system in headlong dash toward plutocracy.

As proof of the superiority of their British system, Canadians pointed to violence-racked American labour relations, a high divorce rate in certain states, mistreatment of blacks and Indians, assassinations of three presidents (Lincoln, Garfield and McKinley). To top things off, there was the Civil War itself as evidence of the danger of American democracy. Given these fairly widespread perceptions, can it be any surprise that few in Canada's political class saw in annexationism an opportunity to improve their lot in life?

All of the above would seem to work against democratic peace theory. How could Canadian leaders, so scornful of America's political institutions, trust its government? Could anyone in his or her right mind imagine a North American democratic peace, at least at the end of the nineteenth century? The short answer is, Yes, and a nuanced examination of Canadian-American political reality of the time reveals why. Especially critical for this nuanced examination is an analysis of the *differing* parties and factions contending for power in Canada.

By far the overwhelming majority of the anti-Americans were to be found among conservative and loyalist ranks, including government officials who owed their appointments to the monarchy (i.e., governors-general and lieutenant-governors). Conservatives dominated post-Confederation politics: with the sole exception of the five-year period of Mackenzie's Liberal government (1873-78), they reigned from 1867 until 1896. Among the most well-known of the Conservative political figures were Sir John A. Macdonald (who led the party until 1891), George-Étienne Cartier, D'Arcy McGee, Stephen Leacock, along with a bevy of imperialists, including George Taylor Denison.

Federal Conservatives were supported by the interests of high finance in Montreal and Toronto (and in particular by the promoters of the Canadian Pacific Railroad and the leaders of the Bank of Montreal), by Cartier's *Bleus* and by the members of the Ontario Conservative party. The latter in particular incited anti-American sentiment, supported by the Toronto imperialists and by the Loyalist descendants, still nurturing the memories of 1776 and 1812. The hostility of the latter is not hard to grasp, and though it was attenuated somewhat by Hamiltonian inclinations in American politics, it was exacerbated by the ascension of the Jeffersonians and Jacksonians.[47] The Bleus, for their part, considered the survival of the "French Canadian race" to be riding on British institutions with their guarantee of group rights, especially as they were sen to be supportive of Roman Catholicism.[48]

A Canadian anti-Americanism founded upon political considerations was only reinforced by economic interests, among them being a financial and industrial bourgeoisie whose well-being could only be threatened by American competition. The Conservative program reflected those interests: from 1878, the commercial policy of Macdonald's government was squarely based on protectionism (the "National Policy"). This bias was reflected in foreign policy, with Conservatives trumpeting the merits of the imperial connection, in significant measure because they saw Canadian political independence as but a precursor of annexation to the US.

There was a chicken-and-egg aspect to Canadian annexation worries in the late nineteenth century. Did the peril of annexation cause Canadians to be dismissive of American institutions, as Underhill maintained?[49] Or was it rather the repugnance for America's sociopolitical system that reinforced the fear of annexation? It was a bit of both. Those who feared for their economic interests probably fell into the first camp, while in many cases, in particular those of the Bleus and the Loyalists, it was their attachment to British institutions that caused them to reject the American model. That is, it was not the *interpretation* they may have had of Americans' intentions that determined their attitude; it was the American institutions themselves.

Mistrust and criticism of the US would gradually wane between 1890 and 1910. Partly this was due to the improved state of Anglo-American relations; partly it was a result of the steady economic growth Canada had been experiencing, which generated a growing confidence among Canadians in themselves and in their country. But we should also bear in mind that the improvement in Canadian-American relations also coincided with the arrival in Ottawa of a new government, one much less distrustful of American institutions and intentions than its predecessors had been. It would be under this government that the residual disputes that had been festering since 1871 would finally be resolved, and the first permanent bilateral institutions be created.

The Conservatives, as noted, had dominated post-Confederation political life. The opposition, initially made up of Radicals, Ontario "Clear Grits," and *Rouges* from Québec, would crystallize around the federal Liberal party. The first Liberal government, that of Alexander Mackenzie, held power from 1873 to 1878. Not until eighteen years later would the Liberals be restored to power, under Wilfrid Laurier. Other major Liberal figures included Edward Blake, leader of the opposition from 1880 to 1887, and George Brown, founder and editor in chief of the Toronto *Globe*.

The Liberals inherited from the Grits and the Rouges a centrist program similar in some respects to the Jeffersonians, with an admixture of ideas stemming from the revolutions of 1848 and the British Radicals. This program centred around the defence of the interests of the middle class, the advancement of democratic practices and institutions (notably universal suffrage), and certain anticlerical measures, including the separation of church and state.

After 1878, the Liberals differed most from their adversaries in one sphere above all the others: economic policy.[50] Whether by conviction or out of pragmatism, most Liberal party members supported free trade. Their support for free trade is interesting in that it reveals a totally different attitude towards the US from that held by their Conservative colleagues. Neither Mackenzie nor Laurier ever took seriously the idea that free trade would be just the first step down the road to annexation — and this, notwithstanding that many *American* leaders would make such a causal connection!

How can we account for the Liberals' refusal to believe that free trade had to be a logical precursor of annexation? It seems insufficient to ascribe it merely to economic interest, though such was obviously at issue for a party beholden as it was to agricultural and raw material exporters. No; the source of the Liberals' confidence in the US was much more deeply rooted and appeared in a variety of ways. For instance, during the Civil War Canadian public opinion was more concerned with the possible consequences of the conflict than with its causes, and majority sentiment favoured neutrality. Among Liberal dissidents, however, a different view prevailed, as recalled by W. L. Morton:

British American opinion was hotly engaged in the war; it became steadily more anti-Northern in reaction to the attacks in the Northern press and the intermittent talk of the need to conquer Canada. But provincial governments enforced the policy of neutrality and most British Americans were content to keep out of the war. *Only The Globe and some liberals staunchly supported the North.*[51]

Liberal indifference in the face of hostile American rhetoric argues against the commonly accepted view that it was the desire to defend themselves against the US that motivated the leaders of the British North American colonies to join together in 1867. Obviously, several leaders did feel this way, but the fact that others, including George Brown, did not consider America to constitute a serious military threat is often overlooked. Liberals also challenged the Conservative and imperialist claim that a weakening of imperial ties would facilitate the process of annexation, and instead regarded American annexationist discourse as intended essentially for domestic consumption. Richard Preston relates that the Liberal Kingston newspaper, the *British Whig*, was aware that President Ulysses S. Grant and many of his countrymen might speak of Manifest Destiny, but dismissed the rhetoric as mere "electioneering claptrap." He adds that

[t]hose Canadians who thought that annexation was impossible, or unlikely, found their convictions reinforced by confidence that the United States would not attempt to bring it about by force. Canadian Liberals, conforming to the pattern of Liberal thinking in Britain, *usually assumed that constitutional democracies, by their very nature, abjured the use of force.*[52]

The same attitude was on display during the 1895-96 Venezuelan crisis, the other great Anglo-American confrontation of the second half of the nineteenth century. Some Canadians seemed remarkably unflustered by American threats to retaliate against Canada: "Many of them believed that they understood American political behaviour better than did the British. They dismissed Cleveland's message as meant for domestic consumption: there was an election in the offing."[53] The Conservative government of the day took the matter more seriously, and began planning to reform and rearm the militia. And though Laurier himself would continue to build up the militia, he did so mainly so that it might help maintain internal order and, despite his reservations, help defend imperial interests in South Africa. Significantly, he regarded it as wholly incapable of defending Canada from American invasion, and is said to have made this surprising observation — to a British official, no less — early in the twentieth century: "You must not take the militia too seriously.... [I]t will not be required for the defence of the country as the Monroe doctrine protects us against enemy aggression."[54]

This Liberal attitude drew inspiration from the Radical/Grit/Rouges coalition that had been the wellspring of the party. The Radicals, like their British counterparts, demanded profound political and socio-economic changes, inspired by the American model. After the 1837 rebellion, the British Radicals even urged the cession of Canada to the US.[55] The position found an echo in Canada during debates, in the 1840s, over what parliamentary system would be best suited for home rule. "Canadian radicals were seeking new departures in colonial government, departures based almost exclusively upon their ardent admiration for democratic republicanism as practiced in the United States."[56] Once they changed into Clear Grits, the radicals toned down their enthusiasm for the American system — due in part perhaps to the Civil War — but their political platform continued to be influenced by American ideas and they never lost confidence in the US.

The Québec Rouges had a totally different view from that of their provincial adversaries, the Bleus. They considered the British parliamentary system to be a symbol of English domination and a product of the Durham Report. Resolutely anticlerical, they were steeped in the ideas of the French revolution of 1848 and cared nothing for the religious guarantees extended to the Catholic church. They admired the American political system not only because of its intrinsic qualities but also because the principle of direct democracy would mean political emancipation for Canadian francophones. They were in many ways the spiritual descendants of the 1838 *Patriotes*, maintaining their Jacksonian ideals; they saw American democracy as a way to fight against the privileges of the Montreal upper middle class — in particular the merchants and the railroad promoters — and it was therefore not surprising to see Rouge leaders such as Jean-Baptiste Dorion publicly advocating annexation by the US.[57] Their annexationist fervour, like that of the Clear Grits, may have diminished during the 1860s, but they transmitted their admiration for the US to the Liberals, both federal and provincial.

Of course some political actors close to the Liberals had less sympathy and regard for the Americans and their institutions. Québec nationalists grouped around Henri Bourassa, for example, feared annexation as much as, if not more than, they feared a strengthening of imperial ties.[58] In general, the Liberals were more moderate in their opinions than the Rouges; although they favoured changing Canada's place in the empire, they did not question the necessity of the link. And while they did not take seriously the risk of annexation by the US, neither did they favour it: on this the *Globe* remained intransigent.

The Liberals' position on free trade could and would be diluted for electoral purposes, and Laurier's trade policy resembled in some ways Macdonald's National Policy. The Liberals in power proved disinclined to undertake major institutional reforms inspired by the American model, and the reforms they ultimately did make were modest, even by British standards. Their borrowing from the US was much more in terms of practices (on the logic that "similar problems called for similar solutions") than of institutions, which remained resolutely British.

Nuanced as it turned out to be, the Liberal record is stable enough to enable us to draw certain conclusions. They did not consider American ideas and institutions threatening to Canada's political order, and for this reason they not only refused to take annexationist rhetoric seriously, but they showed themselves ready to trust their neighbours. That they differed from the Conservatives in assessing American intentions stemmed from their differing perception of American institutions. This very stability of their opinion undermines the thesis of the "balance of threat," according to which the interpretation of intentions determines the perception of the regime. Liberal opinion not only did not vary with crises, but it manifested itself well before the marked improvement in Canadian-American relations that occurred at the end of the nineteenth century.

The Conservatives' position would itself evolve once they regained power in 1911, following the Liberal defeat on the issue of reciprocity. The perceptible improvement in Anglo-Canadian-American relations over the course of the previous fifteen years seems to have soothed their fears of the US. The rapid industrialization of Canada brought with it socio-economic problems similar to those facing American leaders. Although they maintained a skeptical attitude toward the Americans, the Conservatives grew preoccupied by internal, imperial and, in 1914, international problems. The First World War did away with many of their older worries about American institutions, and though fighting in a common cause facilitated a rapprochement, it was above all the ideological characterization of the war — i.e., as a struggle for the triumph of freedom and democracy, as well as a counter to communism — that reduced the importance of the older, intra-liberal, differences.

The war therefore accelerated and deepened a tendency already discernible in the last decades of the nineteenth century. The butchery of the combat gave credence to the emerging belief (timidly held at the beginning of the century, more robustly felt after 1914) that the relationship between the two North American states was something "special," and qualitatively distinguishable from international relations in Europe. In the wake of the celebrations attending the centenary of the peace of 1814, leaders as well as policy intellectuals of the period began to refer to a "North American community," founded upon a common political, cultural, and linguistic heritage, and to "North-Americanism" and the "North American idea" as a model for the peaceful management of interstate relations elsewhere.[59]

The long peace may have grown up, but we still cannot label it with certitude as having been a democratic peace. There are two reasons for hesitating. The first is familiar enough: the North American peace may largely have been a byproduct of Anglo-American relations. Secondly, and related to this, the American perception of the nature of the *Canadian* regime remains difficult to assess because it was, and had to be, influenced by Canada's status as a member of the empire (subsequently to be called, starting in the 1920s, the Commonwealth). Although the convergence of values and political ideas certainly played a role in establishing a climate of peace in North America, it is difficult to measure their relative importance compared to military, economic and socio-cultural factors.

What we can establish at least, from the discussion to this point, is the link between the manner in which another regime is *perceived* and the interpretation given to the *intentions* of those who lead that regime. Moreover, this perception varies according to the political convictions of the perceivers. Those who, as did many Conservatives, considered American institutions inimical to their interests, adopted a critical approach to American democracy and attributed aggressive intentions to American leaders, regardless of the real state of relations between the two countries. Conversely, those who admired (or who considered benign) American institutions were more likely to attribute peaceful intentions to American leaders, even in periods of crisis or when American leaders voiced annexationist rhetoric.

In order to develop the analysis further, we need to introduce a new set of variables that might help us decide whether the long North American peace really was a democratic one. We need to look at some procedural and institutional aspects of bilateral relations.

"PRACTICES" AND "RECURRENCES": COOPERATION PRIOR TO INSTITUTIONS

It is both true and false to claim that cooperation and bilateral institutions were nonexistent in the security domain before the 1940 Ogdensburg meeting between the American and Canadian leaders, which I discuss in the following chapter. True, because Canada had no competence in the realm of foreign policy until the end of the nineteenth century, thus relations with the US could only be determined by London. True, because no institutions for the common defence of the two countries would be created until the Second World War had already begun. But in another sense, false, because the joint institutions created after 1940 did not arise out of a void; their form and content resulted from a lengthy process of evolution going back to the previous century.

Following the end of the War of Independence, the British and the Americans established practices and conflict-management measures that would serve to constitute an important marker in North American security cooperation. The period 1871-1909, leading to the creation of the International Joint Commission (IJC), witnessed the gradual replacement of British representatives by Canadians, accompanied by the growth of strictly bilateral relations between the two North American countries. The Commission charged in 1871 with drafting what would become the treaty of Washington may have included only one Canadian (Prime Minister Macdonald); approximately thirty years later, however, a similar commission (struck to settle the location of parts of the Alaskan-British Columbian boundary) featured two Canadians among the "British" side's three representatives. And six years later, in 1909, no British members would have a seat on the newly established International Joint Commission.

Canadians inherited and further developed practices and mechanisms put in place by the British. They also began to innovate: in 1909, Laurier established a secretary of state for external relations charged *inter alia* with handling questions that directly affected Canada but had only a secondary importance for the empire.[60]

Although no permanent bilateral institutions existed before 1909, diplomatic practices and behaviour were recurrent enough to provide the actors with reference points, in effect making their relations somewhat more predictable and thereby creating "habits of cooperation." Such recurrence cannot be considered the simple result of a rational process of trial and error or of chance; instead, the practices and mechanisms reflected the presence and importance of certain precise norms and values: in a word, as I show below, "liberal" norms and values.

There are at least two security areas in which Canada, either directly or through British representatives, and the United States cooperated episodically but frequently enough to enable the development of a habit of cooperation: border dispute settlement, and arms control.

As noted earlier, Canadian-American relations during the period between 1840 and 1940 were marked by numerous conflicts. Some of these quarrels (e.g., those associated with the *Patriotes*) simply subsided on their own, without any need for the two governments to try to "solve" them. Other disputes (the *Alabama* claims or the Venezuelan crisis) arose from Anglo-American differences and thus affected Canada indirectly, if still importantly, given that it might have become the stage upon which the disputants might have sought to project the dispute. The quarrels that were most significant for our purposes here — e.g., border and fishing disputes — directly implicated Canadians, and in so doing permit us to observe of the presence of principles and practices with applicability to the bilateral relationship. Two considerations stand out when we contemplate these disputes: 1) they were effectively settled by negotiation , as opposed simply to being put on hold or resolved unilaterally; and 2) their resolution was often the result of *both* parties following similar procedures.

This recurrent nature of the settlement of conflicts is well illustrated by the history of border disputes. Between 1794 and 1903, at least ten such quarrels, some of which led to tense situations, were settled by treaty.[61] The methods used not only enabled the definitive solution of the conflict at hand, but also offered implicitly the bases for future relations between the countries. The first method, that of negotiation and the search for compromise, resulted in such notable successes as the saw-off known as the Webster-Ashburton treaty of 1842.[62] The second method, which became the norm during the nineteenth century, was a form of arbitration that consisted in delegating the task of reaching a solution to a joint commission comprising experts named by each side.

These two methods set the tone for the Canadian-American relationship from the nineteenth century on. The regulation of border disputes was more often done via negotiation, while commissions dealt with matters considered to be less controversial (and often involved fine-tuning what had broadly been settled by treaties). Nevertheless, the work of the commissions tells us a great deal about the evolving character of bilateral relations. Most importantly for Canada, it was through commissions that the country took its first steps as an autonomous international entity. Moreover, it was the commissions that would set the pattern for the future, so we look to them when we wish to comprehend the phenomenon of recurrences.

The joint commissions date from articles 4 and 5 of the Jay treaty of 1794, calling for the creation of four commissions, one of which would be charged with determining the boundary between the US and the British colonies.[63] The model was followed in the treaty of Ghent of 1814, ending the War of 1812: article 6 stipulated that a commission, composed of two commissioners and two government representatives, be set up to draw the border in the Niagara region. This marked an important step in the evolution of the commissions, for rather than regarding the bodies as tribunals before which the parties would plead their cases, the American commissioner, Peter Buell Porter, considered the commission to be a place for negotiation and agreement, where strictly technical considerations would mix with pragmatism and diplomacy. His view prevailed, and the commission, instead of becoming a forum of confrontation, was effectively depoliticized.[64] This would set the tone for future conflict-resolution between the two neighbours: depoliticization of problems, pragmatism, and a search for compromise based on technical considerations, with specialists being chosen for their expertise rather than for their partisanship. As such, we can regard the phenomenon as the forerunner of what would later be called "transgovernmental" relations.

The method would be applied often in subsequent dispute-settlement efforts. The results would not always be pleasant, and Canada sometimes found to its chagrin that if the interests of the empire and the dominion did not happen to coincide, British commissioners would be prepared to side with the US against Canada. The most painful such reminder, for Canadians, came with the settlement of the Alaskan boundary, in the early 1900s.

In 1898, Laurier had missed an opportunity to clean the slate of contentious issues with the US, by referring all such matters to an omnibus commission on which Canada would have four of the six "British" seats. Even though Washington agreed to the commission, Laurier decided not to proceed in this manner.

This proved to be a blunder, for upon the assassination of William McKinley, the president who had agreed to the omnibus commission, a new chief executive came to power, with a different view on dispute settlement procedures. Theodore Roosevelt, in no doubt as to the legality of America's claim to parts of Alaska's "panhandle" that had recently attained crucial economic importance to Canada as a result of the Yukon gold rush (and the desire of Ottawa to have untrammelled access to the Pacific coast), agreed to the creation of an arbitration commission composed of three Americans, two Canadians, and one Briton. Though he may have accepted the process, he did so only reluctantly and in a Pickwickian manner, for Roosevelt made it clear that in the event of a decision unfavourable to the US, he would deploy troops and engineers to establish the border where it should be. This turned out to be unnecessary, for the British commissioner sided with the American position.[65]

Although this outcome might seem to run counter to the practices established back in 1794, it does not negate the existence and importance of liberal norms in bilateral dispute- resolution. Instead, what it illustrates is the folly of either side flouting the norms — as both sides did, with Laurier being the first, through his refusal to accept an arbitration commission during the McKinley administration. Once the first misstep had been taken, others followed, on both sides. Roosevelt appointed three political figures to that was supposed to be a body of impartial jurists. Laurier issued a public demand that the Canadian representatives support his position. Roosevelt responded accordingly, and then upped the ante by hinting that he would be willing to use force to settle the matter.

Despite this tit-for-tat, and notwithstanding Laurier's profound bitterness at the outcome, relations with the US would improve markedly in ensuing years. Between 1905 and 1909 most of the residual contentious issues were resolved, during what two historians have called the "slate-cleaning" era in bilateral relations.[66] Ever since, both countries have continued to make use to commissions, even vesting the process with the quality of permanency. The trend began with the 1905 establishment of a joint commission on boundary waters, which attained permanence in 1909 as the International Joint Commission, and is charged with a wide range of recommendatory, supervisory, investigatory, and regulatory functions. Other institutions followed.[67]

In addition to formalizing practices in existence for more than a century, these new institutional dispensation would prove innovative in a couple of respects. Firstly, as permanent institutions intended to deal with future problems, they were qualitatively different from the previous ad hoc bodies. At the insistence of the Canadian delegation, provisions to this effect were included in the Boundary Waters treaty, and the International Joint Commission was created in large part to ensure their application.[68] Secondly, the new institutional order signified the emergence of a truly autonomous Canadian foreign policy, and therefore the birth of genuine bilateral relations. The settlement of the Alaskan boundary dispute had left scars, and Canadians found themselves no longer willing to rely upon the British to defend their interests. Britain's fading into the background could bode will for Canadian interests, argued George Gibbons, head of the Canadian delegation, in September 1907.

> Once the Americans come to deal directly with us they will play the game fairly. It is only because we have John Bull along that they bully us. Once get him out of the game and there will be no prestige in tackling a little fellow who will kick their shins.[69]

The permanent nature of the IJC and other institutions allowed Canadians to develop a strategy that would permanently mark their foreign policy: the norms and working procedures of these international institutions were seen to be capable of structuring and rebalancing the asymmetrical power relationship with the US. As two students of the issue have put it, the "smaller of the two nations ... opted for a strong treaty with strong methods of implementation, a natural position for the smaller power, which gains from any formula equalizing sovereign powers."[70] Good-bye, balance of power.

The "North American way" of settling disputes peacefully would become a popular notion among historians, pacifists, and quite a few Canadian politicians (including the young Mackenzie King) during the decade starting in 1910. The "North American idea" had at its core the resolution of conflicts by conciliation and arbitration commissions. Norms and practices developed gradually and often implicitly over the course of the previous century would henceforth possess a formal and explicit body of doctrine, one to which more and more Canadian diplomats adhered, viz. their penchant for recommending to their European counterparts the North American model as an example for the world.

The settlement of differences by negotiation and arbitration has continued to be the privileged method of resolving disputes ever since 1910; the norm has become so well-established that it is no longer held to be exceptional, as it had been during the century of its gradual emergence.

The British, Americans, and Canadians were also noteworthy, in the nineteenth century, in defining and putting into place effective arms-control measures. The Rush-Bagot agreement of 1817 specified the number, tonnage, and armaments of war vessels on that can be deployed on the Great Lakes. This agreement has remained in force down to the present, with the exception of a brief period related to the St. Albans raids of 1864, though it has been violated on more than one occasion.[71] Even so, Washington and Ottawa have chosen to maintain this symbolic agreement, the spirit of which is more important than its letter, for it buttresses the conviction that the Canada-US border *should* be demilitarized.[72]

To summarize this section: the establishment of norms in the Canadian-American relationship was anything but linear, and it was marked by violations, impasses, dead-ends, and even temporary regressions — in short, with all the baggage of the typical evolutionary dynamic. Despite these difficulties, the recurrent nature of the dispute-settlement methods supports the thesis that a process of norms development was clearly taking place, and a "habit of cooperation" flourishing. That this evolution was not reflective of the power relationship between the two North American countries is evidenced by the fact that their relations improved once the British were removed from the equation, as Gibbons had predicted in 1907. Canadians, it is true, continued to prefer settlement by negotiation rather than by arbitration, in large part because of the lasting bitterness over the Washington treaty of 1871 and, especially, the Alaska boundary dispute.[73]

LIBERAL NORMS AND PRINCIPLES

Two questions are raised by the finding of recurrence in the way that Britain, the United States, and Canada resolved their disputes during the nineteenth century and into the twentieth. Firstly, why was the governments choose this form of conflict resolution instead of something else?

Secondly, what explains the results? Each question can be answered in large part by reference to the states' adherence to "hard-core" liberal values.

Liberal states, as William Dixon has demonstrated, are particularly likely to resort to negotiation, arbitration, or to seeking the opinion of experts, because these are precisely the approaches employed in dealing with domestic conflicts.[74] *Mutatis mutandis*, what Dixon says applies to the record of Anglo-American-Canadian conflict resolution, characterized as it was by a propensity either to refer the problem to a quasi-judicial body or to resort to negotiation. Another hallmark of their relationship was the ability of these states to find mutually acceptable solutions of a generally permanent nature; the same conflicts did not continually crop up. It is more difficult, however, to establish a causal link from this case study. Dixon does not maintain that such conflict-resolution methods are only used between democracies, or that they are the product of a liberal order; he simply affirms that democratic states are more likely to have resort to them. An examination of Anglo-Canadian-American relation provides some insight as to why this should be so.

The norms, practices, and institutions structuring the Canadian-American relationship doubtless owe their existence to the convergence of particular political, military, and socio-economic factors. But *why* did they follow the path they did? To answer this, we need not only to observe the emergence of norms; we also have to know the origin of their content. Studies dealing with the peaceful resolution of conflicts and the development of legal and political practices between Canada and the US largely avoid the issue, at most making vague reference to factors such as economic interdependence and a common legal, cultural, linguistic and political heritage.[75]

The states' divers bilateral treaties manifest a desire to submit their relations to the principles of law and equity. This indicates an agreed definition of the rule of law, as well as a willingness to adhere to certain common principles. It is not possible, though, to explain the resort to arbitration by reference to international law. In fact, it is arguable that the advance of international law is more the *result* than the cause of Canadian-American harmony, given that the latter, more than anything else, led to a rebirth for the principles of arbitration and conciliation, abandoned as they had been since the emergence of the modern international order.[76] After all, by the time, 1899, that the Hague Convention codified the rule that states should arbitrate their differences, the practice had already been in use in North America for more than a century.

Most authors explain the recourse to joint commissions by pointing to the precedent established by the Jay treaty of 1794. This method created therewith cannot easily be explained by reference to contemporary British or American institutions; it would appear that it was an original idea advanced by the American representative, John Jay, but its origins are unclear.[77]

It is unlikely that the treaty's shapers intended to effect a revolution in international jurisprudence. More likely, despatching a committee of experts to study matters was an expedient, resulting from the simple fact that so little really was known about the location of borders in the sparsely settled region under dispute. Existing maps proved useless to the task. At Jay's suggestion, negotiators agreed to defer to the expertise of three commissioners, one chosen by each side and a third jointly named.[78]

Britain may not have been a democracy, but it boasted at the time a liberal-economic order corresponding to America's own, and the Jay treaty reflected this community of values. The treaty's distinction between private and public property illustrated the great importance attached to freedom of trade and private property, and paved the way to negotiations aimed at the legal settlement of a plethora of disputes arising from the Revolution. The sociopolitical context needs to be considered at two levels: the internal level, where the legal and political similarities of the two countries fostered a relationship of trust; and the international level, where the practices and norms structuring conflict management developed in parallel with such other liberal norms as the principles of equality and consultation.

Britain (and therefore Canada) and the US were among the first countries to found a legal system on the preeminence of the rule of law, and a political system permitting structured and regular competition for office. The similarity of the two legal systems played an important role, for as Corbett noted, the "original identity and continued similarity of legal systems, coupled with confidence on both sides in the common judicial process, add[ed] another motive for resort, not to force, but to investigation and to adjudication."[79] Because each state recognized that the other could legitimately arbitrate conflicts arising within its own society in conformity with the principles of law and equity, both were able to expect that the same principles would be applied in their mutual dealings. This convergence of political and legal values gave rise to an expectation of reciprocity.

The success of their dispute-resolution methods also owed something to the flexibility that was a byproduct of their confidence in the process adopted. Joint commissions are quasijudicial bodies that may rely upon international law, but which nevertheless possess a certain discretion. Unlike with the later permanent arbitration mechanisms created by the International Court of Justice, the Canadian-American "litigants" named on their own those who were to decide the outcome. The commissioners were expected to act as "judges" who made their decisions on the basis of technical and legal imperatives, rather than as diplomats pleading their countries' cases. Thus the commissions more resembled *internal* administrative tribunals than they did international courts. And the actors recognized this difference.

The ability of these organs to mix pragmatism with respect for principles of law can probably be explained by the depoliticized and nonpartisan nature of the commissioners' work. Corbett is correct in noting that the "remarkable success of arbitration between Canada and the United States is due to the fact that these two countries have sufficient respect for judicial methods and their common legal tradition to endow their joint tribunals with the power of deciding according to 'law and equity', and then to accept, in the main with no more discontent than the losing litigant may be expected to manifest, a liberal interpretation by the arbiters of what constitutes equity in the matter at issue."[80]

The part played by public opinion is another indication of the importance of the domestic sociopolitical context in accounting for the recurrence and elaboration of the two states' conflict-resolution methods, as well as the egalitarian relationship that developed through them. As much as the political leaders were able to distinguish between rhetoric aimed at a domestic audience and that truly reflecting foreign policy priorities, they did remain conscious of the influence public opinion could have on decisionmaking. In 1907, for example, Gibbons considered that the weight of public opinion might oblige the US to submit to the decisions of the international joint commission he was trying to get set up: "My own idea, growing stronger every day, is that there is only one way in which we will get fair play, and avoid a conflict with them, and that is by a permanent joint Commission which will play the game fairly, and whose conclusions will be so justified by public opinions, even in the United States, as to compel their acceptance."[81]

We can also see this dynamic at work in the parallel between the respective countries' approaches to industrial relations, significant because it is often remarked that how they dealt with domestic conflicts resulting from industrialization within their own societies had a great deal to do with how the two countries dealt with each other; more than a few policy intellectuals at the turn of the nineteenth century believed that practitioners of international relations could learn a great deal from practitioners of the "other IR" — industrial relations.

> What was significant about the twentieth-century Canadian-American approach to the outstanding points of contention was the effort to institutionalize and depoliticize the mechanisms of conflict resolution.... The preference to avoid diplomatic disputes that might become hotly debated public issues paralleled the emergence of a more bureaucratic and "scientific" approach to conflict management during the years of progressive reform. Whether it was the creation of a Bureau of Corporations under Theodore Roosevelt ... or the attempts by John D. Rockefeller, Jr., to [develop] a new industrial relations system that would eliminate strikes, the thrust of the Progressive era was toward organization, systematization, stability, and conflict reduction. This approach found a harmonious echo in Canada: Rockefeller's expert consultant on industrial relations was William Lyon Mackenzie King, former Canadian minister of labour and future prime minister. It was thus not surprising that the United States and Canada sought to establish bilateral bureaucratic institutions to deal with contentious common problems.[82]

The creation of three permanent international commissions between 1909 and 1923 not only manifests the transposition of domestic, and liberal, socioeconomic constructs to the international level, it also marks the adoption of two important principles in the establishment of a North American liberal order. First of these is the principle of equality. Although this principle would apply as a matter of course between two great powers such as Britain and the US, it is remarkable that it continued to apply when Canada took the place of Britain. Donald Barry, writing about the IJC, observes that "Canada enjoyed legal and operational parity with the U.S., so that the actual disparity between the two countries did not become an issue in the Commission's operation."[83]

Secondly, the permanent commissions introduced the principle that there should be regular consultations between the representatives of the two states. Although the IJC more often concerns itself with private rather than public initiatives, these regular meetings do allow high-level civil servants of both countries to exchange viewpoints on common problems. And equality and consultation are both essential to the development of an international liberal order.

The depoliticization of problems, the resort to nonpartisan commissions generally composed of members chosen for their competence, confidence flowing from shared legal and political values, and the adoption of the principles of equality and consultation: these are all factors that permit us to draw a link between the domestic liberal orders of each country and the international order that emerged in North America. The norms and institutions arising first in the Anglo-American relationship, then in the Canadian-American one, reflected accurately, and strikingly, those liberal-inspired norms, institutions, and mechanisms at work *domestically*. This process of externalization of norms was so entrenched by the early decades of the twentieth century that one commentator, writing in *Foreign Affairs*, could confidently predict, apropos the bilateral relationship, that

> [t]here will be nothing to fight about because there is developing in each country with respect to the other the habit of arbitration and peaceful settlement. So true is this that when differences now arise there is a tendency to regard them almost as domestic matters and to apply to them domestic procedures based on inquiry into facts followed by an award based on that inquiry, which is to be accepted as a domestic award is accepted — with obedience even if with grumbling.[84]

The period from the end of the war of 1812 until the eve of the First World War developed into a period of peaceful coexistence, during which efforts to improve relations alternated with times of tension and rumours of war. Considered as a whole, it was a time when the actors defined, assimilated, and refined norms that forbade the resort to force, and offered alternative methods to settle differences. Although numerous military, political, and economic factors contributed to this long peace and to the emergence of peaceful conflict-resolution methods, there can be no denying the central part played by the community of norms and liberal values as between the two countries. These norms and values helped to fashion the way in which the actors perceived each others' intentions and to determine the content of the practices and the institutions. In so many respects, the international order that came gradually into being in North America over the course of the nineteenth century was a liberal order.

That said, it also needs emphasizing that the security cooperation between the two states throughout this period was rather limited, in the event to the management and resolution of conflicts; there had yet to develop a sense of the "common defence" of North America. The passage from peaceful coexistence to common defence would not be made until the era of global conflagration that began in 1914. It is more than a bit ironical that the passage would once again highlight the negative implications (for Canada, at least) of the vast power differential in North America, and while there may no longer have been any risk to Canada of American territorial aggression, problems relating to its sovereignty (and therefore independence) would come to the fore in this new era.

Notes

[1]Sean M. Shore, "'Ready, Aye, Ready': The Impact of the North American Security Community on Canada's Decision to Fight, 1914," paper presented to the 38th annual meeting of the International Studies Association, Toronto, March 1997; William P. Thompson, "Democracy and Peace: Putting the Cart Before the Horse," *International Organization* 50 (Winter 1996): 141-74.

[2] John M. Owen IV, "How Liberalism Produces Democratic Peace," *International Security* 19 (Autumn 1994): 110-19; Christopher Layne, "Kant or Cant: The Myth of the Democratic Peace," *International Security* 19 (Autumn 1994): 16-28.

[3]On the Anglo-American democratic peace, see John M. Owen IV, *Liberal Peace, Liberal War: American Politics and International Security* (Ithaca: Cornell University Press, 1997); and Michael W. Doyle, "Liberalism and World Politics," *American Political Science Review* 80 (December 1986): 1158.

[4]Desmond Morton, *A Military History of Canada: From Champlain to the Gulf War*. 3d ed. (Toronto: McClelland and Stewart, 1992); John Herd Thompson and Stephen J. Randall, *Canada and the United States: Ambivalent Allies*, 2d ed. (Athens: University of Georgia Press, 1997), chap. 1.

[5]D. M. L. Farr, "Britain, Canada, the United States and Confederation: The Politics of Nation-Building during the Turbulent Years," in *Reflections from the Past: Perspectives on Canada and on the Canada-U.S. Relationship* (Plattsburgh, NY: Centre for the Study of Canada, State University of New York, 1991; orig. pub. 1967); Peter J. Parish, *The American Civil War* (London: Eyre Methuen, 1975), p. 394.

[6]Richard A. Preston, *The Defence of the Undefended Border: Planning for War in North America, 1867-1939* (Montreal and Kingston: McGill-Queen's University

Press, 1977); James Eayrs, *In Defence of Canada*, vol. 1: *From the Great War to the Great Depression* (Toronto: University of Toronto Press, 1964), pp. 70-78; Gwynne Dyer and Tina Viljoen, *The Defence of Canada: In the Arms of the Empire* (Toronto: McClelland and Stewart, 1990).

[7]See, for this claim, Kenneth Bourne, *Britain and the Balance of Power in North America* (London: Longmans, Green, 1967); Donald Barry, "The Politics of 'Exceptionalism': Canada and the United States as a Distinctive International Relationship," *Dalhousie Review* 60 (Spring 1980): 116-18; and J. L. Granatstein, *How Britain's Weakness Forced Canada into the Arms of the United States* (Toronto: University of Toronto Press, 1989).

[8]Cited by Robert Lacour-Gayet, *Histoire des États-Unis* (Paris: Fayard, 1976), 1: 312.

[9]Quoted in S. F. Wise and Robert Craig Brown, *Canada Views the United States: Nineteenth-Century Political Attitudes* (Seattle: University of Washington Press, 1967), p. 109.

[10]Desmond Morton, "Defending the Indefensible: Some Historical Perspectives on Canadian Defence, 1867-1967," *International Journal* 42 (Autumn 1987): 630.

[11]William T. R. Fox, *A Continent Apart: The United States and Canada in World Politics* (Toronto: University of Toronto Press, 1985), pp. 45-51.

[12] Morton, *Military History*, p. 149.

[13]See Nils Ørvik, "Canadian Security and 'Defence Against Help'," *Survival* 42 (January/February 1984): 26-31. To this day, the principle continues to resonate among some Canadians, for whom it constitutes a chief justification for the maintenance of armed forces. The Second World War resuscitated this principle in a different context, one in which Canada's military concern was no longer the maintenance of internal order but rather the alleviation of American worries about poorly defended Canadian territory serving as a staging ground for an attack against the US (an argument to which I return in chapter 6.)

[14]Michael Tucker, *Canadian Foreign Policy: Contemporary Issues and Themes* (Toronto: McGraw-Hill Ryerson, 1980), p. 4: "Great Britain from the mid-19th century ... has never been a natural counterweight for Canada to the United States, nor have the European powers, simply because they have not shown a disposition to play this role. Thus it has been necessary for Canada to develop and sustain a European connection. It has attempted to do this through military commitments, to Great Britain in the past and to NATO Europe in the present era." I will have more to say about this contention in chapter 7.

[15]Karl W. Deutsch et al., *Political Community and the North Atlantic Area: International Organization in the Light of Historical Experience* (Princeton, NJ: Princeton University Press, 1957), p. 115.

[16]Barry Morton Gough, "The End of Pax Britannica and the Origins of the Royal Canadian Navy: Shifting Strategic Demands of an Empire at Sea," in *Canada's Defence: Perspectives on Policy in the Twentieth Century*, ed. Barry D. Hunt

and Ronald G. Haycock (Toronto: Copp Clark Pitman, 1993), pp. 19-30. See also Aaron L. Friedberg, *The Weary Titan: Britain and the Experience of Relative Decline, 1895-1905* (Princeton: Princeton University Press, 1988).

[17]Fox, *Continent Apart*, p. 45.

[18]C. P. Stacey, *Canada and the Age of Conflict: A History of Canadian External Policies*, vol. 1: *1867-1921* (Toronto: Macmillan, 1977), pp. 98-99.

[19]Samuel Flagg Bemis, *A Diplomatic History of the United States*, 5th ed. (New York: Holt, Rinehart, Winston, 1965), pp. 794-95.

[20]Thompson, "Democracy and Peace," p. 163.

[21]Preston, *Defence of the Undefended Border*, p. 4.

[22]Samuel F. Wells, "British Strategic Withdrawal from the Western Hemisphere, 1904-1906," *Canadian Historical Review* 49 (December 1968): 335-56.

[23]Ironically, some authors reverse the counterweight hypothesis in underscoring the negative implications of the country's imperial connection. "[T]he United States was a proven good neighbour, a striking contrast to the warlike Europeans and a useful counterweight to the British connection, a connection which threatened to pull them into another great war." John English and Norman Hillmer, "Canada's Alliance," *Revue internationale d'histoire militaire*, no. 54 (1982), p. 40.

[24]Fox, *Continent Apart*, p. 35.

[25]See Richard N. Rosecrance et al., "Whither Interdependence?" *International Organization* 31 (Summer 1977): 432-34; and Paul A. Papayaonou, "Interdependence, Institutions, and the Balance of Power: Britain, Germany, and World War I," *International Security* 20 (Spring 1996): 42-76.

[26]See Jack Snyder, *The Ideology of the Offensive: Military Decision Making and the Disaster of 1914* (Ithaca: Cornell University Press, 1984); and Stephen Van Evera, "The Cult of the Offensive and the Origins of the First World War," *International Security* 9 (Summer 1984): 58-107.

[27]Richard Arteau, "Libre-échange et continentalisme: récapitulations," in *La Politique économique canadienne à l'épreuve du continentalisme*, ed. Christian Deblock and Arteau (Montréal: GRÉTSÉ/ACFAS, 1988), pp. 169-95.

[28]Dale C. Copeland, "Economic Interdependence and War: A Theory of Trade Expectations," *International Security* 20 (Spring 1996): 5-41.

[29]See, for Hamilton's views, Walter Russell Mead, *Special Providence: American Foreign Policy and How It Changed the World* (New York: Alfred A. Knopf, 2001), pp. 103-38. For Mahanian economic doctrine, see John Mueller, *Retreat from Doomsday: The Obsolescence of Major War* (New York: Basic Books, 1989), p. 28.

[30]Peter Trubowitz, *Defining the National Interest: Conflict and Change in American Foreign Policy* (Chicago: University of Chicago Press, 1998).

[31]A distinction drawn by its leading proponent, John Mueller, *Retreat from Doomsday*, p. 9.

[32]Kenneth N. Waltz, "The Origins of War in Neorealist Theory," *Journal of Interdisciplinary History* 18 (Spring 1988): 624-27.

[33]Preston, *Defence of the Undefended Border*, p. 7.

[34]Deutsch et al., *Political Community*, p. 115. Also see Walter Lippman, *U.S. War Aims* (Boston: Little, Brown, 1944), p. 69.

[35]Mueller, *Retreat from Doomsday*, p. 22.

[36]A good illustration of this scholarly imprecision is given by Deutsch et al., *Political Community*, pp. 46-47, 66-67.

[37]Mildred A. Schwartz, "American Influence on the Conduct of Canadian Politics," in *The Influence of the United States on Canadian Development: Eleven Case Studies*, ed. Richard A. Preston (Durham: Duke University Press, 1972), pp. 102-5; Frank H. Underhill, *In Search of Canadian Liberalism* (Toronto: Macmillan, 1960), p. 22.

[38]Seymour Martin Lipset, *Continental Divide: The Values and Institutions of the United States and Canada* (New York: Routledge, 1990).

[39]Underhill, *In Search of Canadian Liberalism*, pp. 13-15.

[40]Cited in Sean Shore, "No Fences Make Good Neighbours: The Development of the Canadian-American Security Community, 1871-1940," in *Security Communities*, ed. Emanuel Adler and Michael Barnett (Cambridge: Cambridge University Press, 1998), pp. 333-67, quote at p. 364.

[41]Lester Burrell Shippee, *Canadian-American Relations, 1849-1874* (New York: Russell and Russell, 1970; orig. pub. 1939), p. 476.

[42]W. L. Morton, "British North America and a Continent in Dissolution, 1861-1871," in *Interpreting Canada's Past*, vol. 1: *Before Confederation*, ed. J. M. Bumsted (Toronto: Oxford University Press, 1986), pp. 389-405; J. Bartlet Brebner, "A Changing North Atlantic Triangle," *International Journal* 3 (Autumn 1948): 309-19.

[43]Lawrence Martin, *The Presidents and the Prime Ministers* (Toronto: Doubleday, 1982).

[44]Morton, "British North America," p. 402.

[45]Owen, *Liberal Peace*, pp. 158-59.

[46]Wise and Brown, *Canada Views the United States*; Carl Berger, *The Sense of Power: Studies in the Ideas of Canadian Imperialism, 1867-1914* (Toronto: University of Toronto Press, 1970), pp. 153-76.

[47]Jane Errington and George Rawlyk, "The Loyalist-Federalist Alliance of Upper Canada," *American Review of Canadian Studies* 14 (Summer 1984): 157-76; J. L. Granatstein, *Yankee Go Home? Canadians and Anti-Americanism* (Toronto: HarperCollins, 1996), pp. 18-19.

[48]Richard A. Jones, "French Canada and the American Peril in the Twentieth Century," *American Review of Canadian Studies* 14 (Autumn 1984): 334.

[49]"Inevitably, because of geographical proximity and the mutual interpenetration of the lives of the two North American communities, the urge towards greater democracy was likely to appear in Canada as American influence; and since the survival of Canada as a separate entity depended on her not being submerged

under an American flood, such influences were fought as dangerous to our Canadian ethos." Underhill, *In Search of Canadian Liberalism*, p. 15.

[50]Robert Craig Brown, ed., *The Illustrated History of Canada* (Toronto: Lester and Orpen Dennys, 1987).

[51]Morton, "British North America," p. 398 (emphasis added).

[52]Preston, *Defence of the Undefended Border*, p. 80 (emphasis added).

[53]Ibid., p. 126.

[54]Quoted in Roger Frank Swanson, "The United States as a National Security Threat to Canada," *Behind the Headlines* 29 (July 1970): 11.

[55]Owen, *Liberal Peace*, p. 192.

[56]Wise and Brown, *Canada Views the United States*, p. 53.

[57]Ibid., pp. 61-62.

[58]Jones, "French Canada and the American Peril," p. 334.

[59]Carl C. Berger, "Internationalism, Continentalism, and the Writing of History: Comments on the Carnegie Series on the Relations of Canada and the United States," in *Influence of the United States on Canadian Development*, pp. 37-40; James A. Macdonald, *The North American Idea* (Toronto: McClelland, Goodchild and Stewart, 1917).

[60]John Hilliker, *Canada's Department of External Affairs*, vol. 1: *The Early Years, 1909-1946* (Montréal and Kingston: McGill-Queen's University Press, 1990), pp. 54-55.

[61]Thompson and Randall, *Canada and the United States*, pp. 25-30.

[62]Howard Jones, *To the Webster-Ashburton Treaty: A Study in Anglo-American Relations, 1783-1843* (Chapel Hill: University of North Carolina Press, 1977).

[63]P. E. Corbett, *The Settlement of Canadian-American Disputes* (New York: Russell and Russell, 1979; orig. pub. 1937), pp. 5-6.

[64]Michael F. Scheuer, "Peter Buell Porter and the Development of the Joint Commission Approach to Diplomacy in the North Atlantic Triangle," *American Review of Canadian Studies* 12 (Spring 1982): 65-73.

[65]For a good assessment of the affairs, see Norman Penlington, *The Alaska Boundary Dispute: A Critical Reappraisal* (Toronto: McGraw-Hill Ryerson, 1972).

[66]J. L. Granatstein and Norman Hillmer, *For Better or for Worse: Canada and the United States to the 1990s* (Toronto: Copp Clark Pitman, 1991).

[67]William R. Willoughby, *The Joint Organizations of Canada and the United States* (Toronto: University of Toronto Press, 1979).

[68]Kenneth M. Curtis and John E. Carroll, *Canadian-American Relations: The Promise and the Challenge* (Lexington, MA: Lexington Books, 1983), p. 53.

[69]Quoted in Allan O. Gibbons, "Sir George Gibbons and the Boundary Waters Treaty of 1909," *Canadian Historical Review* 39 (June 1953): 128. Also see Harriet Whitney, "Sir George C. Gibbons, Canadian Diplomat, and Canadian-American Boundary Water Resources, 1905-1910," *American Review of Canadian Studies* 3 (Spring 1973): 65-73.

[70]Curtis and Carroll, *Canadian-American Relations*, p. 52.

[71]Alvin C. Gluek, "The Invisible Revision of the Rush-Bagot Agreement, 1898-1914," *Canadian Historical Review*, 60 (December 1979): 466-84.

[72]Freeman Dyson, *Disturbing the Universe* (New York: Harper and Row, 1979); Mueller, *Retreat from Doomsday*, p. 22.

[73]Ironically, they might rather have preferred arbitration to negotiation, for according to Keohane and Nye, results of negotiations during the period 1920 to 1939 lent support to the realist expectation that power would win out: in six out of the nine cases studied, the US was deemed the "victor." Conversely, Erik Wang's study of arbitrations over the period 1794 to 1965 reveals that the Anglo-Canadian position was upheld in thirteen of the twenty-eight cases studied, compared with only nine victories for the US (the remaining six cases being draws). Robert O. Keohane and Joseph S. Nye, *Power and Interdependence: World Politics in Transition* (Boston: Little Brown, 1977), pp. 180-81, 193, 211; Wang, "Adjudication of Canadian-United States Disputes," pp. 178-80, 220-22.

[74]William J. Dixon, "Democracy and the Management of International Conflict," *Journal of Conflict Resolution* 37 (March 1993): 42-68; Idem, "Democracy and the Peaceful Settlement of International Conflict," *American Political Science Review* 88 (March 1994): 14-32.

[75]See Don Courtney Piper, *The International Law of the Great Lakes* (Durham: Duke University Press, 1972); and Corbett, *Settlement of Canadian-American Disputes*.

[76]Thomas A. Bailey, *A Diplomatic History of the American People*, 6th ed. (New York: Appleton Century Croft, 1958), p. 77; Jones, *To the Webster-Ashburton Treaty*, p. 7.

[77]Samuel Flagg Bemis, *Jay's Treaty: A Study in Commerce and Diplomacy* (New Haven: Yale University Press, 1962).

[78]A. L. Burt, *The United States, Great Britain, and British North America: From the Revolution to the Establishment of Peace after the War of 1812* (New Haven: Yale University Press, 1940), pp. 148-51.

[79]Corbett, *Settlement of Canadian-American Disputes*, p. 3.

[80]Ibid., pp. 128-29.

[81]In a letter to Laurier of 15 February 1907; quoted in Gibbons, "Sir George Gibbons and the Boundary Waters Treaty of 1909," p. 127.

[82]Thompson and Randall, *Canada and the United States*, p. 72.

[83]Barry, "Politics of 'Exceptionalism'," p. 119. A seasoned diplomatic observer wrote, in the same vein, that the IJC was an "inspired mechanism for equitable relations between unequal states." John W. Holmes, "Crises in Canadian-American Relations: A Canadian Perspective," in *Friends So Different: Essays on Canada and the United States in the 1980s*, ed. Lansing Lamont and J. Duncan Edmonds (Ottawa: University of Ottawa Press, 1989), p. 20.

[84]R (anon.), "Neighbors: A Canadian View," *Foreign Affairs* 10 (April 1932): 417-30, quote at p. 430.

CHAPTER SIX

From Coexistence to Cooperation: The Common Defence of North America, 1914-1945

BEYOND PEACEFUL COEXISTENCE

Until 1914, Canadian-American security relations were limited to managing what we might call (using the terminology of the Cold War) "peaceful coexistence." Europe might be well along the road to war as a result of the brutal dynamics associated with alliances, but in North America peace reigned, as Canada and the United States prepared to celebrate the centennial anniversary of the ending of the last armed struggle between them. Never had the spectre of war in North America seemed more distant.

Notwithstanding the Mexican schemes of Germany's Arthur Zimmermann, the Great War unfolding in Europe would not touch North American shores. And even though they would be co-belligerents for some twenty months on European battlefields, Canada and the United States saw little need at the time to coordinate defence arrangements. As for the interwar period, the emphasis then was decidedly elsewhere, as both North American countries basked in the certitude of living in their respective "fire-proof houses," the metaphor invoked by Raoul Dandurand in his celebrated address to the League of Nations in 1924.[1] Nevertheless, a closer look at the period reveals, if ever so faintly, traces of profound change lying ahead: North American security was about to exit the era of conflict management, and enter that of the common defence. It would, however, take another world war for the transition to be completed.

Historians have typically construed the Second World War as a major turning point in Canada's political and military development, for several reasons. In the first place, the country's contribution to victory in 1945 probably did more to establish it as an independent actor in world affairs than such legal reforms as the Statute of Westminster, which nominally made Canada "sovereign." What the soldiers who took Vimy Ridge in 1917 began, would be completed by their successors a generation later, at Dieppe and in Normandy. Secondly, the war put an end to the experiment with isolationism — which had characterized Canadian foreign policy during the interwar years[2] — and ushered in an era of internationalism. Canadian leaders and diplomats discovered not only that they could exercise an autonomous international presence (this was the onset of the "Middle Power" role), but that there could also be international interests deserving of promotion via an activist foreign policy. By the same token, they appreciated more than ever how vulnerable Canada could be to violent convulsions in the international system, and this recognition put paid to any thought of reverting to isolationism.

Beyond the discovery of a national identity and of the country's openness to the world, there was the recognition of how traumatic the war had been for Canada. For if there had arisen any physical threat to Canadian territorial sovereignty, it did not stem from U-boats prowling in the St. Lawrence estuary or from Japanese balloons drifting across the Pacific with bombs tied to them, but rather from the presence of well-meaning — but unsettling nonetheless — American forces. Bilateral defence measures that had been put in place hurriedly, under the pressure of extraordinary events, would turn out to have serious implications for Canadian sovereignty.

From the standpoint of Canadian-American security relations, the Second World War era formed a distinct period, resembling neither the years preceding nor those following. The challenge of the earlier period had been to avert the risk of conflict between Canada and the US; that of the later one would be to normalize relations on a more or less egalitarian basis. But during the war itself, Canadians had to learn how to manage necessary cooperation with the Americans in such a way as to mitigate what were clearly unequal roles and responsibilities.

On the face of it, the Second World War years would appear to confirm the validity of realist hypotheses predicated upon the balance of power: problems in the bilateral relationship welled up precisely because the British "counterweight" of yore had ceased to be a factor in North American defence and security. Now there would be nothing to stand in the way of an untrammelled operation of the balance in America's favour. Seen in this light, Canadian military ties with the US look to be the perfect example of what lies in store for minor powers forced to link up with greater ones. The experience of this period would also lend support to a complementary realist thesis, regarding the "balance of threat," which holds that since alliances and other forms of military cooperation take shape in response to perceived threat, considerations of sovereignty must necessarily take a back seat to those of security.

Yet there is another way of regarding this period — as one of apprenticeship, difficult to be sure but also necessary, a training period for two states learning how to develop norms and institutions that would later come to govern their bilateral security and defence relations. Thus, liberal-constructivists would have a decidedly different way of interpreting events from that of the realists. They would start by recognizing the near-total absence of norms and institutions at the start of the period, but they would also stress the qualifier, "near-total," for it has to be said that prior to 1939 conditions supportive of institutionalization had begun to come into existence. What the war did was to bring into sharp relief, and then to refine, conceptions that heretofore had been inchoate; and during the war years the normative-institutional foundations of bilateral cooperation would be established, appearances to the contrary notwithstanding. And it would be upon these foundations that a healthier structure of cooperation would get built after the war. This explains why the problems encountered during the 1941-44 period never reappeared after the war.

To appreciate this evolutionary logic, we need to back up a bit and study the evolution of Canadian-American relations during the interwar period, for it is in those years that we glimpse the passage from a bilateral regime primarily focused upon conflict management to one whose main objective had become promoting the common defence. By looking at the interwar experience, we will better be able to come to grips with what occurred during and after the Second World War.

THE CONSEQUENCES OF THE GREAT WAR

From the strictly bilateral point of view, the First World War did not bring about any great changes, especially on the institutional level, in North

America. Direct cooperation between the two states' militaries remained relatively undeveloped until America entered the war in April 1917, and what few ties did exist were chiefly in the domain of munitions and food-stuffs, as well as in respect of training of pilots and prosecution of anti-submarine warfare.[3] But the expansion of contact with the Americans would lead the Conservative government of Robert Borden to assign Canadian diplomatic representation in Washington, which had heretofore been the exclusive preserve of the British embassy. In February 1918 a "Canadian war mission to the United States" was created, whose function was essentially to manage munition purchases for Canada. The prime minister had envisioned the mission becoming a permanent legation following the armistice, but time and circumstances did not allow him to pursue this goal.[4]

The blood bath of 1914-18 probably reinforced the sentiment, already widespread before the Great War, that North America constituted a unique case in international relations, a happy model whose adoption elsewhere would assure the spread of peace and the disappearance of war. The discourse surrounding this notion was buttressed by copious and explicit references to democracy and liberalism as factors conducive of peace. For example, during the war James Alexander MacDonald, editorialist with the *Globe* (Toronto) and author of several books, proposed erecting upon the Canadian-American model a commonwealth of nations reflective of liberal ordering principles, i.e., respect for liberty, democracy, and equality.[5]

Such concepts would come increasingly to form part of the vocabulary of world leaders, who employed them as means of justifying their countries' participation in the conflict. This was as true for Canada in 1914 as it would be for the US in 1917, when President Woodrow Wilson announced that America's goal was to "make the world safe for democracy." A priori, we should have every reason to believe, as did certain historians looking back at the Great War from the coign of vantage of the 1930s, that at the end of a lengthy period of evolution, Canada and the US had "united in defense of a common liberal democratic tradition."[6] The war certainly did display an ideological dimension not seen since the wars of the French revolution and Napoleonic empire. And it is also probably true that the fighting did stimulate the development of a collective consciousness on the part of the Western democracies confronting autocratic foes and, after 1917, communist Russia.

That said, it is hard to assess the impact such sentiments might have had upon Canadian-American relations. The rhetoric of a "common cause" and of a community of political values was indeed employed, at times, by leaders, as is evidenced in a letter sent by Canada's finance minister to his American counterpart in 1917.

> We have in your time and mine always been good neighbors. Occasionally a verbal brickbat has been thrown across the fence but we have always sympathized with each other when brickbats have come from any foreign source. *In our attitude towards constitutional liberty and all social problems our people are very much alike and understand each other better I think than any other two peoples in the world today.* The struggle in a common cause will I am sure greatly cement our friendship and respect for each other.[7]

According to C. P. Stacey, with the onset of the Great War, fewer and fewer Americans continued to look upon Great Britain as being little changed from the days of George III, and more and more came to sympathize with it as a fellow democracy.[8] The same effect could be seen in respect of American attitudes toward Canadians: "American neutrality, 1914-1917, tended to antagonize the Canadian people against their neighbors to the south notwithstanding an inveterate admiration by the people of the United States for the gallant qualities of Canadians and for their highly successful democracy."[9]

As for the Canadians, they considered America's crusade for democracy as having been far too slow getting launched, especially coming as it did in the wake of numerous displays of friendship between Washington and Berlin. Added to this was the recognition that Canadians had paid a price in blood on Europe's battlefields far exceeding, relatively, that made by the Americans. The result was that in the immediate aftermath of the war there was much ill-will directed by Canadians southward, a mood that was not lightened by Hollywood films portraying the Americans as having won the war nearly single-handedly.[10] Not only this, but the Senate's refusal to ratify the Versailles treaty foreclosed the possibility of the US joining the League of Nations, in the process dashing the hopes of those Canadians desirous of committing American democracy to the service of world peace.

Thus was a certain amount of anti-Americanism perpetuated in Canada, among elites at least. Significantly, this sentiment rested on arguments that deviated considerably from those dear to anti-Americans of the previous century. The words may have been just as harsh as before, but the grammar was different. Part of the new critique was directed against certain perceived cultural attributes, especially commercialism but more broadly the regnant superficiality of so much of what America was exporting culturally to Canada (and elsewhere) at the time. But the critics saved most of their ammunition for economic targets, of which there was no shortage, given the galloping pace of interdependence between Canada and the US. The spectacular growth in American investment, remarked early on in the postwar period by elite commentators, eventually became a preoccupation of the man in the street, no more so than during the Depression of the 1930s.[11]

Thus, interdependence would take on a significance, for some, it could never shake, namely as a Trojan Horse whose ultimate aim was to serve as a means of Canada's enslavement, albeit by nonviolent methods. This image was a carry-over from the previous century's omnipresent worries about annexation, save that after the Great War there were far fewer analysts who were prepared to conclude that with economic dependence would necessarily come formal *political* subjugation. Those who did so conclude tended to do it implicitly, and rarely could they support their thesis with any overtly annexationist declarations made on the part of American officials. So not only did annexation drop out of the list of Canadian phobias but, during the 1930s, numerous American figures would try to reassure Canadians that growing economic interdependence was actually beneficial to Canada (as it was, as well, to the US).[12]

One of the biggest — albeit generally unremarked — differences between 19th and 20th century anti-Americanism in Canada is that the sentiment discarded its former criticism of American political institutions. No one seemed ready, any more, to lambaste America because of its liberal political order, or to seek in that order the prime source of perceived American imperialism. In short, if the socio-economic gravitational field associated with US capitalism might be a cause for concern, the same could not be said of US political institutions.

Throughout the interwar period it was still possible to detect an aftertaste of the former century's political divisions in Canada, even if it is true that the import of those cleavages had diminished. Conservatives continued to advocate maintaining tight links with the Empire, and party ranks were not short on critics of the US. The Conservative governments of Robert

Borden (1911-20) and Robert Bennett (1930-35) had one important aspect in common: each had come to power thanks to an anti-American advocacy directed in particular against trade deals with the US proposed by Liberal governments. Nevertheless, in both cases, Conservatives once in power found that the pressure of external circumstances would oblige them to alter their policies vis-à-vis the US, and to adopt measures that would hasten Canada's economic interdependence with its neighbour.

The war in Europe forced Borden to turn to the American market for cash and manufactured goods essential to the war effort — so much so that by 1918 American investments in Canada exceeded, for the first time ever, British ones.[13] As Granatstein explains, "wartime necessity showed irrefutably that the Conservative Party's anti-americanism was simply words. It would linger, but the force was gone."[14]

For Bennett, the Depression had a comparable effect. After having gained victory in 1930 thanks to his denunciations of the trade talks conducted between the Canadian prime minister, Mackenzie King, and the American president, Herbert Hoover, and after having tried to strengthen economic bonds within the Empire in 1932, Bennett had to reconcile himself, two years later, to the necessity of seeking a reciprocal agreement with the Americans to lower tariffs. He never did get the agreement, but the Liberals would, when they returned to power the following year. As had Borden before him, Bennett knew how to deploy anti-American rhetoric, but he also understood as well as his Conservative predecessor how important it was to maintain good relations with Canada's powerful neighbour.[15] As for the Americans, they understood the game well enough, and were aware that Bennett was trying to shore up a domestic constituency with his rhetorical flourishes. A State Department memo to the president summed it up nicely: "For political reasons ... Mr. Bennett frequently finds it advisable to criticize us despite the fact that he personally is friendly to this country."[16]

Unlike the Conservatives, the Liberals were actually well-disposed, and overtly so, toward the US. Led by William Lyon Mackenzie King, this party formed the government from 1921 to 1930 (with the exception of a three-month period in 1926), and again from 1935 to 1957, though for most of the final decade without King, who retired in 1948. Having studied in Chicago and subsequently having worked as labour-relations advisor for the Rockefellers, King certainly knew America and the Americans much better than most Canadian prime ministers had.

Unlike the Conservatives, the Liberals (and King in particular) were not fervently attached to the Empire. He made it the dominant theme of his foreign policy during the 1920s and 1930s to stake out more autonomy for Canada vis-à-vis Great Britain; this had been a Liberal objective since the late 19th century. Throughout his career, King never hesitated to block British initiatives aimed at coordinating the foreign policies of the various dominions, or at orchestrating a common imperial defence. Anything smacking of subordination to London he systematically fought, in large measure because he dreaded the national-unity implications of Canadian intervention in overseas conflicts (the experience of 1918 had left deep wounds), but also because the Liberals wanted to establish equal relations with Washington and London. All in all, King and his most important advisor, the undersecretary of state for external affairs, Oscar D. Skelton, distrusted the British more than the Americans, to such an extent that they were even willing to countenance invoking the latter as a "counterweight" against the former![17]

What applied to the Liberals also applied to the Canadian progressive left, incarnated in the Cooperative Commonwealth Federation (CCF). To it members, the US of Franklin Roosevelt's New Deal represented a model well worth emulating in Canada, all the more so as Britain seemed to be a conservative, indeed retrograde, place. In the eyes of Canadian social democrats, the New Deal's social and economic policies constituted an ideal third way between communism and unrestrained laissez-faire economics. Also exemplary, to the left, was American foreign policy: Roosevelt's isolationism held out for Canada the best prospects both of loosening the bonds of Empire and of staying out of another European war.[18]

Loosening those imperial bonds was, in any event, a general thrust of Canadian foreign policy at the time, irrespective of which party was in power in Ottawa. The Liberals, obviously, approached the goal with more zeal than their Conservative rivals, partly because they worried less than the latter did about the negative consequences of heightened economic interdependence with the US.[19] And because they were in power for such a long period of time during the interwar years, it is natural that the trend away from Empire should primarily be associated with the Liberals; hence the debate among English-Canadian historians over King's responsibility in this matter, with conservative writers such as Donald Creighton, George Grant, and W. L. Morton blaming him for placing Canada into the American orbit.

Relations with London and Washington constituted, by far, the two principal foci of Canadian foreign policy in the interwar years.[20] It is interesting to examine, from two different perspectives, the manner in which Canadians perceived their role and their position vis-à-vis both London and Washington. The first perspective is that of the North Atlantic Triangle; the second is of bilateral Canadian-American relations.

THE NORTH ATLANTIC TRIANGLE

Making the rounds with some frequency during the interwar years was the idea of an alliance between liberal democracies, although proponents of such an alliance rarely made an explicit, reasoned, linkage between alliance and the political culture we know of as democracy. Still, we can regard these advocacies as early instances of contemporary visions of what Kant had labelled, back in the 18th century, "republican federations." The most fervent proponents were to be found in Britain, a country that also took seriously the potential peril posed by Germany and Japan. It was there during the 1920s and 1930s that Sir Alfred Zimmern published a series of articles in which he foresaw the emergence of a community of Western states.[21]

Zimmern was followed, in 1939, by Clarence K. Streit, who was one of the first analysts to remark, in a book entitled *Union Now*, that democratic states had been living peacefully with each other for a century.[22] It is true that Streit was not British but American, yet he was one of those policy intellectuals in the US who identified strongly with Britain. Shaken by the manifest aggression being committed by the "Autocratic Triangle" of Germany, Italy, and Japan, Streit urged the creation of a "federation of democracies." Responsibilities of the federation would include citizenship, defence, trade, currency, and communications. Unlike visionaries of "world government," Streit would leave to the member-states their political institutions and their sovereignty, devolving to them authority over national and local affairs. However, he really did have in mind a vast project of political integration, and even though he was not advocating a "government of governments," he did foresee a political entity having direct links with citizens. And he was nothing if not Kantian in his expectation that the proposed Union would be bound to expand *pari passu* with the spread of democracy. Once totalitarianism had been overthrown, we could expect to see a true world government emerge. Streit was confident not only that their Union would enable the democracies to achieve security, but it would also stimulate their prosperity, allowing them to slash military spending and increase mutually beneficial economic exchanges.

Despite, or perhaps because of, the grandiosity of Streit's vision, it was not that easy for policymakers on either side of the Atlantic to determine any practical means of putting into place his suggestions, even had they wished so to do. This is not to say that he lacked supporters.[23] And it has to be acknowledged that he seemed to be reflecting, given the geopolitical context, a widespread sentiment for change.

Throughout the period 1919-45, two sociopolitical factors combined to attract the attention of leaders as well as analysts to the relationship between democratic values and issues related to security and defence. First was the heterogeneity of the international system itself: not since the days of the French Revolution had there been such a plethora of political regimes aspiring to serve as models for mankind — republics and parliamentary monarchies had to share political space with various species of authoritarians and totalitarians, not least of whom were the fascists and the communists. This heterogeneity, put into stark relief by the excesses of Nazism and Stalinism, had the effect of reinforcing among the liberal democracies a sensation of belonging to a community of values. Thus the looming conflict, as seen from the vantage point of the late 1930s, took on a significance heretofore unknown, because the stakes this time were not "merely" defence against military aggression but instead the protection of values, lifestyles — indeed, of a "civilization."

Secondly, the evolution of warfare, in particular the emergence of "total war," had the effect of linking liberal socio-political and economic values to security issues. Unlike the totalitarian states, democracies could not rely on coercion to mobilize a state's military potential; after the Great War and the Depression, the majority of liberal governments recognized they had an obligation to rethink the "social contract" between state and citizen. It became a matter of necessity to improve the average person's standard of living if that person was to be called upon to defend the established democratic order. Thus it was not only the economic crisis that accounted for the emergence of the welfare state of the pre-Second World War period, with its panoply of social policies touching upon employment, pensions, housing, working conditions, and suchlike.

This intellectual and socio-economic movement was also evident in Canada during those years. One of the first advocates of a "democratic alliance," as we have seen, was a Canadian, James Alexander MacDonald. Nevertheless, the concept received its fullest Canadian treatment from those who elaborated policy prescriptions premised upon the existence of something called the "North Atlantic Triangle," an entity that was so dubbed by James Bartlet Brebner in 1945, but that had had a lengthy intellectual gestation period.[24] What the metaphor conveyed was the notion that Great Britain, Canada, and the United States enjoyed as between themselves a privileged relationship, one founded upon a common language and culture, but also upon a common attachment to liberal political and economic values.[25] And if the concept had to wait until 1945 to find its name with Brebner's book, its existence dated back to the interwar period if not earlier.[26]

Canadian leaders saw their country playing the role of "linchpin" in this triangular setting, dedicated to sustaining Anglo-American rapprochement. Other images associated with this function were "interpreter," "mediator," and "honest broker." Always, the objective was to reconcile the old and the new world, or in a later guise, to serve as a transatlantic bridge. It was Robert Borden who first invoked the role, during the Great War.[27] Following that conflict, the spirit of transatlantic alliance began quickly to dissipate, and instead of amity, a period of Anglo-American animosity set in, marked by disagreements over the pending (in 1921) renewal of the Anglo-Japanese alliance and the prospect of a naval arms race between the British and the Americans. Pressure exerted by Canada at the 1921 Imperial Conference probably convinced the British to abandon their alliance with Japan, which went some distance in improving the Anglo-American relationship. In exerting this pressure, Canada was acting for strategic reasons, given the negative impact upon its own security of significant tension between the US and Britain. Potential conflict between the Americans and the British, triggered by the latter's having to honour alliance commitments to a Japan at war with the United States, constituted a nightmare scenario for Canadian leaders.

Despite the oft-times dubious presumption of a "privileged relationship" with the two Anglo-Saxon powers, King "clung tenaciously to the dream of Ottawa's special role as a 'linchpin'," and longed to foment a democratic alliance between Canada and its partners.[28] In November 1940, the prime minister boasted in the House of Commons of the important part

Canada had has in bringing about Anglo-American friendship, and said that this was not simply a Canadian conceit he was expressing, but rather a viewpoint shared by leaders in Washington and London.[29]

Despite the prime minister's optimism, the mediator's role remained more a wish than a deed during the interwar years, for relations between the three states of the Triangle never did develop as warmly as linchpin idealism suggested they should have, such was the enduring legacy of diverging national interests. These divergences were most highlighted in the isolationist policies of the two North American countries, at a time when Britain was trying to find allies to combat rising menaces in Europe and elsewhere. In this respect, David Haglund is probably correct in stressing that the three countries' convergent political values proved insufficient to lead them to form a multilateral alliance in the absence of a commonly perceived threat: "Despite everything they had in common, the United States, Canada, and Britain still required the great fear generated by powerful adversaries to convince them of the wisdom of pooling their defences multilaterally."[30] To be sure, by the 1930s it was possible to speak of a "security community" within the North Atlantic Triangle; it was another thing altogether, however, to imagine that the three states had formed a tripartite alliance. For dynamics within the Triangle simply did not correspond to what John Ruggie insists are the defining characteristics of the institution known as "multilateralism": indivisibility of security, nondiscrimination, and diffuse reciprocity.[31] Instead, Canada, the US, and Britain continued to develop unilateral approaches to their security challenges.

Notwithstanding the obvious strain of "realism" that prevailed within the North Atlantic Triangle, we should not overlook the presence therein of another strand of thought, one steeped in "idealism." The gap between the idealism implicit and explicit in the proposals for a democratic alliance and the reality of isolationist foreign policies does give support to realist contentions regarding the indispensability of threat for the formation of alliances. It is eminently possible that such a qualitative leap as represented by the transition from security community to alliance required the stimulus of an external menace. This said, it need not follow that the link between alliances and democracies must be a spurious one. For instance, Haglund claims that Thomas Risse's theory of the "democratic alliance" requires that democracies necessarily ally, even in the absence of an objective threat, and that they do so on the basis of their convergent political values (these latter, in effect, generating a threat perception premised on the "collective identity" of an in-group needing an out-group to know its own self).[32]

This seems to me to push Risse-Kappen's argument too far; what the liberal theorists are instead saying is that democracies are more susceptible than are non-democracies to form alliances with their political kith and kin, and that when they do, the alliances are more durable.[33] Moreover, there really is no *domestic* political norm, in liberal systems, obliging members toward mutual assistance, although there is one directing them toward the peaceful resolution of conflict. Therefore it is more sensible to assert that what liberal constructivists are really saying is that the formation of a collective identity facilitates or encourages the definition of common interests, and that when liberal states do decide upon extending mutual assistance, the manner in which they will do so will reflect liberal norms. In other words, *once* they have taken the decision to ally, democracies will form democratic alliances.

Identifying what it was that prevented the North Atlantic security community from transforming itself into a collective defence system during the interwar years is beyond the purview of this monograph. Still, we may get a glimpse of those constraints by analyzing the evolution of Canadian-American relations during this period.

THE EMERGENCE OF BILATERAL COOPERATION IN NORTH AMERICA

The declaration of war issued by the King government against Germany on 10 September 1939 constituted a dual paradox. On the one hand, it looked to be unconditional support to the Empire on the part of a government that had endeavoured for the better part of two decades to undercut every British initiative aimed at strengthening collective defence of the Empire/Commonwealth. On the other hand, it was issued at the very same time that the American government, with which Ottawa was seeking to forge ever closer mutual-assistance linkages, was proclaiming its own intention to remain neutral in the conflict about to engulf Europe.

King's obstinate refusal to endorse Commonwealth defence projects at the imperial conferences of 1923 and 1926, coupled with his isolationist attitude in the face of a series of crises that shook the Empire (from the Anglo-Turk dispute of 1922 to the Italian invasion of Ethiopia in 1935), did not constitute a total refusal to play a part in imperial foreign and defence policy. On the contrary, the connection with the Empire remained strong, albeit non-institutionalized; and it is only because of the powerful sentimental attachment to Great Britain that Canada entered the war at all, given that there existed in 1939 no greater threat to Canada's physical security than had been apparent years earlier. In fact, what Canadian leaders during the interwar years feared was not only assuming an obligation to head off, once again, to European battlefields; they also worried about losing autonomy over Canada's foreign and defence policies. Despite the 1926 Balfour Declaration, imperial defence projects were always seen in Ottawa as the reinsertion of British control over dominion affairs. In other words, the Empire connection was not seen to be based on a relationship of equality. Things would go differently with Canada's bilateral relationship with the US.

The Canadian-American relationship developed, to be sure, a dynamic that was affected by the other two legs of the North Atlantic Triangle, those linking Ottawa and London, and Washington and London. But it also developed a dynamic of its own. In terms of Canadian-American affairs, the most remarkable occurrences during the first few decades of the 20th century were the development of strictly bilateral relations and the growth of cooperation, the latter defined as an adjustment process by which political conflicts can be resolved.[34] Cooperation between the two states was not exactly new, as we saw in the previous chapter. But it was taking on a different aspect as the 20th century progressed. In a general sense, we can detect an expansion of the domains to which adjustment measures were being applied, as well as a deepening of preexisting cooperative spheres. In the issue area of security especially, we can observe the beginnings of a transition from conflict-management toward collective defence.

Seen in this light, the bilateral defence relationship was showing evidence, at one and the same time, of discontinuity and continuity, with both elements possessing equal significance. The effect of norms inherited from the 19th century was felt, even though in a variety of new spheres — and collective defence was one of these — established norms were incapable of contributing much to the smooth workings of the relationship; they either had to be adapted, or replaced by new norms. This process of adjustment and creation thus entailed some difficulty, given that the absence of preexisting norms rendered it easier for either state to develop policy oriented exclusively to the defence of its own interests.

Ottawa's search for greater autonomy from Britain led it to strengthen its ties with the US. Ever since the signing of the Boundary Waters Treaty in 1909, Britain had ceased to exercise anything but pro forma oversight of Canada's relationship with the US. And even that function disappeared in 1923, when Canada and the US signed a fisheries treaty without any British participation. Another boundary was crossed in January 1927, when Skelton, despite reservations on the part of President Calvin Coolidge, the British, and a few Conservative members of parliament in Canada, succeeded in having a Canadian legation opened in Washington. A half-year later, the US would open an embassy in Ottawa.

Notwithstanding the rule, in Ottawa, of a government that was well-disposed toward the US, the era of bilateral cooperation with the US began on a bad footing. Even though he was personally convinced of the wisdom of reducing tariffs, King found himself having to engage, on two occasions (1922 and 1930) in tariff wars touched off by American protectionist gestures. The latter tussle took place following the collapse of negotiations that saw President Hoover seek to link tariff reductions with the opening of a seaway connecting the St. Lawrence with the Great Lakes, an initiative that King had to oppose for fear of alienating the all-important Québec vote. There were other disputes, among them being various chapters of the never-ending saga of the fisheries. As well, bootleggers and rumrunners made their mark on Canadian-US cordiality (or the lack thereof), as they sought to make hay while the Prohibitionist sun continued to shine in American skies.

Taken together, these conflicts illustrated Canada's "structural" weakness vis-à-vis the US. This is why Robert Keohane and Joseph Nye would later conclude that the dynamic of bilateral relations during the 1920-39 period corresponded with the expectations of realist models: they found the US to be the clear winner in six of the nine case-studies drawn from those years.[35] They attributed the difference between these outcomes and those of cases drawn from the period 1950-69 to the formation, following the Second World War, of a regime that effectively put an end to the practice of issue linkage.

King did not cede easily to US pressure when conflicts arose. His government's relationship with Washington was based on an improvement in bilateral ties, but not at any cost, and certainly not when it meant abandoning Canadian national interests. Nor was the improvement in bilateral ties an end in itself; instead, it was part of a logic project aimed at affirming

Canadian national identity. Thus King strove to find a means to guarantee Canada's sovereign, legal equality with the US even in the face of a tremendous power imbalance on the North American continent.

Although King himself was no longer in power when it took place, Franklin D. Roosevelt's election as president in November 1932 would facilitate a marked improvement in bilateral economic relations. So too would the appointment of Cordell Hull as FDR's secretary of state. Apart from the fact that Roosevelt was familiar with and liked Canada, his party was less enamoured than its Republican foes of high tariffs, and this presaged a relaxation in trade tensions with Canada and America's other commercial partners.[36] In November 1935 King, recently returned to power after five years in opposition, was able to bring to a successful end trade negotiations begun by his predecessor, and reached with Hull an agreement for a reciprocal reduction in tariffs.[37]

If trade was not a new topic for the two states to be discussing, the same could not be said for collective defence. Until the middle of the 1930s no one, on either side of the border, was giving much thought to the prospect of a Canadian-American alliance against an external threat. This neglect appeared to please Canadian officials.

> Our relations with the United States after the Washington Conference were perhaps the most satisfactory of all. Our Pacific front was as secure as our Atlantic front; the United States was unconcerned about our strategic situation, or the state of our defences. There were indeed no indications that we had any obligations, legal or moral, to co-operate in the defence of the continent.[38]

This view was reminiscent of the perspective Dandurand had sketched during the mid 1920s. And it was not without substance: in terms of physical security, Canada enjoyed a most enviable situation. Not only did it face no external threat, but in a pinch it could always invoke its membership in the British Empire and — more discretely — the Monroe Doctrine should it feel the need for protection. In the bargain, it even got to vaunt to all and sundry its newly established legal sovereignty. Not for nothing did one writer observe in 1932 that "Canada is one of the few states that can have its cake and eat it."[39] More cynically, an American diplomat, Norman Davis, would note five years later that Canada "wished to get all the benefit out of the protection afforded to her by geography, by membership in the British Empire, and by friendship with the United States without assuming any responsibilities."[40] Assuredly, the gathering momentum in bilateral cooperation was going to change things, and get Canada to assume those "responsibilities."

The first signs of a transformation in bilateral security relations, by which I mean the transition from a conflict-resolution to a collective-defence regime, became evident in the 1930s. The impetus was provided by the expansion of the imperial Japanese navy and the gradual, but unmistakable, deterioration in US-Japanese relations. It remained an article of faith on Canadians' parts, and reflected a conviction dating from the turn of the century and given voice by the then prime minister, Wilfrid Laurier, that Canada benefited from an implicit American guarantee of its physical security; this position was restated in by a Canadian writing in 1932 in *Foreign Affairs*: "It appears to be a fact that the United States would not allow a foreign invader to set foot on the shores of her northern neighbor."[41]

What had been implicit for decades was made explicit for the first time in 1936. During a visit to Québec City on 31 July, Roosevelt employed in respect of Canada terminology that heretofore had been reserved for the Latin Americans, when he extolled the policy of the "good neighbour." Canadians and Americans, said the president, did not regard each other as foreigners. Among the factors that reinforced their amicable relations was the fact that "the United States and Canada, and, indeed, all parts of the British Empire, share a democratic form of government which comes to us from common sources. We have adapted these institutions to our own needs, and our special conditions, but fundamentally they are the same."[42] In the private talks that followed, however, Roosevelt hinted at some of the more problematical aspects of good neighbourliness, when he made allusion to a possible US intervention in British Columbia, should the province be threatened by Japanese forces, and stressed the importance of beginning work on a land route linking Alaska with the lower forty-eight states.

Two weeks later, in an address delivered in Chautauqua, New York, Roosevelt strongly intimated an American willingness to go to Canada's defence. The president emphasized that the US was determined to remain at peace, come what may in the Old World. At the same time, he felt it imperative to remind any foreign leader who wished it evil that America was confident in its strength, and that it knew how to and was prepared to defend itself as well as its neighbourhood.[43] In case anyone missed the intimation, Roosevelt spelled it out clearly in a speech delivered at Queen's University, in Kingston, in August 1938, during the midst of the Sudetenland crisis.

The Dominion of Canada is part of the sisterhood of the British Empire. I give to you assurance that the people of the United States will not stand idly by if the domination of Canadian soil is threatened by any other Empire.... We as good neighbors are true friends because we maintain our own rights with frankness, because we settle our disputes by consultation and because we discuss our problems in the spirit of the common good. We seek to be scrupulously fair and helpful, not only in our relations with each other, but each of us at home in our relations with our own people.[44]

The central passages in these Rooseveltian addresses have been cited frequently by historians and political scientists. Here I wish simply to draw attention to two aspects of the president's speeches that have been relatively neglected, largely because the oft-quoted passages are usually, and probably necessarily, taken out of their immediate context.

Firstly, it is striking to consider that Roosevelt made such repeated and direct links between democracy, domestic political orders, and the international application of liberal norms and principles. The cynic might say that the president was simply availing himself of some cost-free rhetorical dodges, in the process disguising his real agenda, which was to promote American interests and those only. Yet, without at all denying that Roosevelt was indeed advancing American interests (it would an odd chief executive who did *not*), we could more fruitfully interpret his words as indications of the way in which he conceptualized Canadian-American relations. Pushing this point a bit farther, we might say that the alliance that was in the process of being created was, from the outset, a "democratic alliance," born under the star of liberal democracy.

The second aspect relates to the reactions elicited by the president's words. In the US, the idea of an alliance with Canada began to gather momentum. Back in the 1920s, a study undertaken by the US Army noted that, from the strictly military point of view, Canadian neutrality would be unwelcome were the US involved in a conflict: "Our interest would demand that we compel her [Canada] to come out squarely or as an ally."[45] In April 1938 (i.e., before Roosevelt's Kingston speech), several American newspapers had underscored the wisdom of a mutual security pact between the North American neighbours. Nevertheless, the American reaction to the Kingston address was mixed, with isolationists in the US worrying about the president drawing the country into a "European" war via the back door. Significantly, references to Canada were increasingly being made in a global, or at least transatlantic, context. And if the president's opponents fretted about America pulling British imperial chestnuts out of the fire, his supporters interpreted his Queen's address as intended for global consumption, putting aggressors everywhere on notice.

In Canada, reaction to Roosevelt's words was overwhelmingly positive. Nevertheless, once the euphoria of the moment had passed, some began to wonder whether it was such a good idea for Canada to rely upon the US for security as much as, if not more than, it did upon the Empire. Old cleavages began to reappear. Among those who felt Canada's future security prospects rested more with the Americans than with the British were the Liberals, most members of the CCF, and Québec nationalists such as Henri Bourassa. Mackenzie King and his team, however, drew back from endorsing the idea, being spread by more than one commentator, that henceforth the Monroe Doctrine applied to Canada.[46] As King saw it, "no self-respecting Government could countenance any such view."[47] Much better, it was felt, simply to regard it as a case of the US serving Canadian interests by serving its own interests, via what would later become known as the "involuntary guarantee." Those who were troubled by the US guarantee, involuntary or otherwise, were the supporters of imperialism, largely clustered in the Conservative party. Apart from the fact that, to them, the tilt toward the US looked like an abandonment of a mother country in distress, the new security order in North America threatened to strip Canada of autonomy every bit as much as they believed growing economic interdependence had.

But the alternative to tying up with the US, namely neutrality, was also fraught with risk, and some observers stressed the concept of "defence against help," meaning that if Canada did not take steps to assure the defence of northern North America, the US assuredly would. In this context, Roosevelt's words, however reassuring they sounded, could also be interpreted as a veiled threat — or at least as a not-so-disguised hint.[48]

That Canada should receive American support *when it asked for it* was judged to be a very good thing. But ever since 1933, Gen. A. G. L. McNaughton, at the time chief of the defence staff, had been growing concerned about the prospects of America becoming a difficult partner should Canada prove itself to be incapable of stopping a foe of the US from using Canadian territory to launch an attack southward. In that event, Canada could well find itself being occupied by the very same US troops who were supposed to be defending it, effectively making a mockery of the pretence of sovereignty. This worry would recur regularly among Canadian military and diplomatic figures throughout the 1930s — and we see echoes of it even in our day of "homeland security," when analysts raise the sovereignty implications of Canada's being unable to reassure Americans it is not a "safe haven" for terrorists.

In practice, the first, timid, steps toward a common defence of the North American continent went well enough. They would have implications mainly, though not exclusively, for the West Coast. In the event of war in the Pacific, Alaska looked to planners to be a very weak link. Beginning in the early 1930s, American officials had begun to search for a means to assure an overland line of communication to the territory; this meant using a Canadian route. From 1933 to 1940, three themes would recur whenever Roosevelt and King discussed the problem.

The first concerned aerial navigation between Alaska and Washington state, implying the use of Canadian airspace. Even before Roosevelt took office, Washington had been sounding Ottawa out on an arrangement by which the Army Air Corps could obtain overflight privileges in Canada. Ottawa was amenable, on the condition that the US grant Canada similar privileges over the state of Maine, thereby facilitating aerial communication between Québec and New Brunswick. In September 1932, an exchange of notes resulted in an agreement that would be in effect until 1937.[49]

The second theme related to reinforcing Canadian defences on the West Coast. As the Japanese began to appear more and more as a potential adversary, American planners grew concerned not only about Alaska but also British Columbia. In fact, given the deplorable state of the latter's defences, they were even more worried about it than about Alaska. Roosevelt himself, after a visit to Victoria in September 1937, shared this concern.[50] McNaughton needed no convincing on the state of BC defences, and he feared unilateral American action if Canada did not take steps to shore things up. Ottawa did take some measures to that effect, including raising defence spending from the miserly sums — $13 million in 1933-34! — that had been allocated annually in the early 1930s. It did so, as the prime minister would tell the House of Commons in 1938, in part because of its obligations as a "good neighbour."[51]

The theme that really grabbed the attention of Americans was the third one, appertaining to the building of a highway linking Washington and Alaska. The topic had, in fact, been appearing regularly on the bilateral agenda ever since 1929, at which time it became an issue not because the

Americans made it one, but rather because the government of British Columbia raised the prospect of attracting US assistance in building a north-south highway through the province. Despite its ostensive economic inspiration, the project's military significance did not escape the prime minister's attention, and he dragged his feet so long that not until after Pearl Harbor would work actually begin on what became known as the Alaska Highway. Neither an American offer to foot most the bill (which raised the hackles of the otherwise notoriously frugal King) nor Roosevelt's repeated entreaties could shake the prime minister and his principal advisor (Skelton) from their inertia. Their reluctance was due to a fear of Canada's being dragged, willy-nilly, into a war between the US and Japan.[52] Given the interest Roosevelt consistently showed in the project, Canadian resistance is noteworthy, to such a degree that Keohane and Nye should have adjudged the episode as one of Canada's rare "victories" in its bilateral dealings with the US during the 1930s.[53]

What can we conclude regarding these early steps toward collective defence, halting as they may have been? First, it is obvious beyond any dispute that each country understood that it was dealing with a cognate democracy; these mutual understandings we can consider to be the "independent variables" in our analysis. As for the "dependent" variables — i.e., the implications of their mutual recognition as democracies — here there must be more room for uncertainty, as it is not clear exactly *what* responses were supposed to eventuate in the sphere of collective defence. In general, the vast majority of Canadians felt no *immediate* mistrust of American actions in matters appertaining to security. As for those few who did profess disquiet about the new linkage with America, their concern was premised upon what might happen in some future crisis, and not on the situation in the here-and-now. For them, the crisis around the corner would be the decisive marker in bilateral relations.

Throughout the 1930s, the bilateral relationship did not fulfil Ruggie's criteria for "multilateralism" — and not just for the obvious reason, to wit the logical absurdity on purely quantitative grounds (after all, how can a relationship involving two partners be deemed to be "multilateral"?). More to the point, the qualitative tokens — i.e., the norms — of the institution known as multilateralism were not fully present in the Canada-US relationship. Specifically, and importantly, there was an absence of reciprocity, as Roosevelt's commitment to Canadian security went unmatched by any reciprocal Canadian obligation to American security, notwithstanding what

King had seemed to promise in response to the president's Kingston address.[54]

And while some observers professed to be witnessing the emergence, during this period, of a community of interests between the two states, it is premature to conclude that at this stage the two had arrived at a common assessment of their security requirements. That said, we can assume that their mutual recognition of possessing similar *political cultures and values* predisposed them to deducing that they would face a common threat. In other words, we are not talking about a "collective identity" on the part of the two states; rather, we are seeing them move toward a shared threat assessment founded upon their respective, but similar, domestic political orders.

So long as there was no immediate crisis, the King government really did not have to take the next step in its security dealings with the Americans. After September 1939, however, it no longer had the luxury of temporizing; and by mid-1940 it felt an urgency that would brook no further delay. No longer could it be a question of *whether* to form an alliance with the US; it was now simply a question of deciding *how* this was going to function.

THE RISE OF INSTITUTIONALIZED COOPERATION

The ending of the Phoney War in the spring of 1940 radically altered Canada's security setting. The *Blitzkrieg* made it all too obvious that physical isolation was no guarantee of safety. Even if Ottawa had no immediate anxieties about an Axis invasion of Canada, it was thought that the possession of bases on the Atlantic would enable German forces to strike at ports and other military objectives in eastern Canada. Even more worrisome were the direct and indirect consequences of a German invasion of Britain, which looked in late June 1940 to be in the offing, with France out of the war. Should Britain succumb, it would mean the virtual elimination of Canada's mobilized combat forces, which had been hastily assembled and despatched overseas. Even worse, the capture or destruction of the Royal Navy would have cleared the way for further German attacks — against British colonial holdings and those French territories that had been rallied to the side of Charles de Gaulle's Free French, and possibly even against

Canada itself.[55] Then there were the serious economic and financial implications of a British defeat.

With the benefit of hindsight, it is easy to see how exaggerated these divers threats really were; at the time, they looked to be anything but, and they had a profound impact upon the calculations of King and his colleagues. One of the most important impacts was to sweep away any remaining concerns the King government might have evinced about formalizing and strengthening security ties with the US. On 16 June the cabinet's war committee recommended that Ottawa sound out Washington on the desirability of convening a meeting to discuss matter of relevance to continental security.[56] At the same time, H. L. Keenleyside, one of the prime minister's advisors, considered it inevitable that Canada would be cooperating with the US to defend the continent, and suggested the negotiation of an alliance with both defensive and offensive objectives.[57]

A decisive step in this direction was taken on 17 and 18 August 1940, in Ogdensburg, New York, where King and Roosevelt met and decided, apparently in an impromptu manner, to create a bilateral Permanent Joint Board on Defence (PJBD).[58] The new entity's mandate would include immediate "studies relating to sea, air and land problems" of continental defence. Composed of civilian and military officials from the two countries, the PJBD's role was to serve as a vehicle for consultation and negotiation, and its task was to submit to Ottawa and Washington its "recommendations." If the Ogdensburg declaration did not constitute an alliance in the formal sense, it certainly laid the foundation for defence integration on the continent. With this agreement, Canada developed a set of bonds that would increase its own security, and in the process also contribute to an American rapprochement with the British. The accord was complemented, on 20 April 1941, by the Hyde Park declaration, which marked the onset of an era of cooperation in defence production between the two states, and in doing so solidifying the economic integration of North America. Five provisional committees were put in place to oversee the various aspects of defence industrial integration.[59]

Much has been written about the Ogdensburg declaration and the creation of the PJBD. The first wave of studies, dating from the 1950s, tended to view the construction in a positive fashion. By the 1960s, however, a revisionist wave had crested, in which the PJBD was held to be an instrument in America's domination of Canada. Retrospectively, Ogdensburg and Hyde Park were said to mark Canada's passage from dominion to "protectorate" status.[60] Canada seemed voluntarily to have left the British orbit, and to have "thrown itself into the arms" of its powerful neighbour. We now know, however, that Canadian decisionmakers were well aware of what they were doing, and why they had to do it. They certainly had a keen sense of the risks inherent in the new structures of continental defence.[61]

Without getting bogged down in the dispute over whether the new bilateral defence arrangements boded well or ill for Canada's long-term prospects, let us look instead at those elements that enable us to draw a connection between the PJBD's founding and the existence of a liberal order in North America. Ogdensburg did not establish an alliance, at least in the formal sense associated with reciprocal military assistance; but it certainly reflected the spirit of alliance-building, and as such was simply an extension of verbal commitments already proffered, in 1936 and 1938, by President Roosevelt. Ogdensburg was a curious hybrid: it enabled a neutral state to cooperate militarily with a belligerent, all the while reconciling strategic imperatives of North American defence with America's power isolationist sentiment. In many ways, it paved the way for an ongoing integrative process in defence that would prove to be much more difficult to unravel that an alliance properly considered.[62]

During the course of the war, the PJBD issued 33 recommendations, the vast majority of them concerned with elaborating combined military planning. Many of these military projects would be put in place on Canadian territory, and concerned such things as roads, bases, airports, and antiaircraft defences. Eventually, once the US entered the war, the cooperation would extend on occasion to real or potential combat operations, whether in Alaska, on the Atlantic, or in Europe.

Given the relatively informal manner by which the negotiations had proceeded at Ogdensburg, and the absence of detailed records of what went on there, a good deal of speculation must attend any analysis of the PJBD's founding. But we do not need documentary evidence to remark upon the similarity between the latter's form and functions and those of previous commissions such as those set up to deal with boundary waters and the fisheries.[63] Just as with the International Joint Commission (IJC), established to manage the boundary waters, the PJBD had a problem-solving mandate that would be implemented by a membership consisting of equal numbers from each country. The members were, in principle, independent actors, but in reality they served basically, in Willoughby's words, as "spokesmen for their respective governments."[64]

In this respect, we can say that the PJBD was probably more influenced by political considerations than the IJC — not surprisingly, in view of the more sensitive issues with which the former would have to deal. Nevertheless, as the war progressed, what was interesting was the development within the PJBD of cleavages reflecting not differences of national interest but rather differences between technical experts. With only one exception, every recommendation advanced by the PJBD was the product of consensus.[65] And even though these consensual decisions might have been taken only after very "frank" discussions, it is noteworthy that the debates were structured along technical not national fault-lines (e.g., diplomats versus military officials, or airforce versus naval officers).[66] The ties established in the PJBD, along with those in the organizations with a more clearly defence-economic function, constituted the first good examples of "trans-governmental" coalitions between the two countries in the issue area of defence.

The approach to problem-solving exemplified by institutions such as the PJBD resembled the way in which conflicts were handled *within* the respective liberal federations, Canada and the US. Shelagh Grant has remarked upon the similarity.

> In addition to the PJBD, a number of civilian co-ordinating institutions also survived into peacetime, with many retaining the basic infrastructure set down in 1909 with the creation of the International Joint Commission. In essence, the precedent for negotiated agreement was already in place; World War II simply accelerated and expanded the process by which the two countries were quickly moving towards an executive confederated-style relationship.[67]

The PJBD's functioning was unlike that of most other international institutions of this period. In addition to its informal operating procedures and its irregularly scheduled meetings in varying locales, the Board's members had precious little contact with government departments other than their own, so as to optimize the organization's independence. This did not detract from their effectiveness: far from it, for some 30 of the Board's 33 wartime recommendations got implemented. That they did constitutes further reason to claim that there existed a "liberal order" in North America by this time, for it is hard to see how such an outcome would otherwise have been possible.

Willoughby implies as much, in his analysis of the concept "joint."

The use of the word "joint" was, no doubt, intended to emphasize the reciprocity of the defence interests and obligations that had been avowed and accepted by the two leaders. What was being established, they wanted to affirm, was not a selfish, one-sided arrangement, but rather a mutually advantageous, cooperative enterprise, freely entered into by true partners striving towards common objectives. Although the population of the United States was approximately ten times that of Canada, each country was to have the same number of representatives and the board was to operate *on the democratic principle of the legal equality of the participating countries.*[68]

One way of judging how egalitarian the enterprise really was is resides in the reciprocal obligations: how seriously were these taken by policymakers? John Holmes reminds us that, reciprocity was a relative concept.

The provision had to do with the defence of the northern part of North America but not even all of the United States. In practice it involved the United States in the defence of Canada, but it did not involve Canada in the whole of United States strategy. While this might appear as an asymmetry dictated by the larger power, Canadians had no more desire to get mixed up in the United States commitments in the Caribbean, for instance, than the Americans had to share their policies.[69]

And yet the wording of the Ogdensburg declaration is such as to leave open another possibility. That the idea of Canadian forces defending American territory strikes us as so improbable has less to do with any policy declarations than it had to do with strategic realities. In this respect, we can detect a parallel with the contents of the North Atlantic treaty of 1949, establishing the Atlantic alliance; for political reasons whose inspiration fundamentally was owing to Canadians, this latter pact was explicitly premised upon *mutual* assistance rather than being a simple unilateral guarantee extended to its European allies by the US.[70] Obviously, no one interpreted this to mean a likely deployment of Belgian or Norwegian forces to defend Oregon or Maine.

In 1940, Mackenzie King went even further than he had two years previously, in recognizing that the course of events had led policymakers in both countries to realize that the best way for them to defend their own country was to participate in the defence of the other.[71] To be sure, reciprocity would always be conditioned by objective conditions: the US by and large did not need to rely upon Canadian troops for its territorial defence, while Canada did not have enough military capability to defend its own vast terrain. And even in respect of US might, it is not completely facetious to register the qualification that for the defence of Alaska, Washington availed itself of some locally stationed Canadian troops, whom Cordell Hull would call the first foreign nationals since La Fayette to ally themselves with Americans in defence of the latters' soil.[72]

Less facetiously, a glance at the 33 recommendations issued by the PJBD during the war reveals that the topics covered reflected far more than an American undertaking to defend Canada. Many of the recommendations related to Alaskan security, to Newfoundland (at the time not a Canadian province), and to such frontier zones as Sault-Ste-Marie. This means that the Board's efforts were not so unidirectional as some authors would have us believe. From this, we can state that there did exist a form of genuine reciprocity, and not just in the spirit of the 1940 declaration, but also in fact.

Most analysts will concede that the Board's efforts did result in an increase in North American security, even if the imagined threats never did materialize. Nevertheless, it does not appear that Canada was able to take from this institution the *political* benefits it had envisioned. It has been remarked that the will was present to use the wartime bilateral entities for the construction of a "special relationship" between the US and Canada, in the process enhancing the latter's diplomatic stature.[73] King had for some time nourished the hope of Ottawa's serving as intermediary between Washington and London, but it was not possible for him to play the part, due early on to the nature of the messages he was being asked by Roosevelt to convey to Churchill (as, for instance, the explosive — and to Churchill insulting — suggestion that the British fleet be withdrawn to ports in the Western hemisphere in the event of a German victory). After Pearl Harbor, the window of opportunity (to the extent there ever was one) would close definitively for this role.[74]

In fact, Canada would find itself between a rock and a hard place whenever its leader got together with his American and British counterparts throughout the war. But these frustrations were as nothing compared to what King was soon going to experience, as a result of one particular feature of Canada-US military cooperation.

INSIDE FORTRESS AMERICA

In 1940, at the time the rapprochement with the US was becoming fixed in policy, Canadian leaders were conscious of what the new flirtation with a great power might imply for the smaller partner. But the analyses concerning the precise nature of the problem, as well as the proposed solutions, varied from one group to another.

First off the mark in stressing the downside risks of the rapprochement were the Conservatives, as was to be expected, given that for some years the party had been denouncing the excessively "pro-American" Liberals. Probably the most virulent attacks were those launched by the new leader of the opposition, Richard B. Hanson, and the senator and former prime minister, Arthur Meighen, who claimed to have lost his breakfast upon learning of the news of Ogdensburg. The reason for their mistrust was as it had always been: for the Conservatives, any reinforcement of ties with the US had to come at the expense of Canada's commitment to the Empire.[75]

Analysts who sympathized with the Liberals saw matters differently. Forming an alliance with the US only made good sense, given the peril that confronted Canada in 1940. Nor was there any danger in the process backfiring, so long as the project could be begun at a time when the US itself perceived no clear and present danger to its own physical security. In the event that American elites did sense their backs were to the wall, there would have been many more problems for a Canada seeking to get inside fortress America; but this was not the situation in the summer of 1940. Had it been, the US would have proceeded with defending the continent in an clearly unilateral fashion, setting the rules of the game for and by itself.

On 27 June 1940, H. L. Keenleyside, judging the henceforth Canada might as well recognize the preponderant role of the US in defending the Western hemisphere, and cooperate on the basis of this recognition, recommended that London and Ottawa grant Washington access to defence infrastructure in the Caribbean and British Columbia.

> An offer of these facilities at the present time would be accepted as a free and generous offer. It would be in line with suggestions that have been made by certain Americans and other officials and publicists. It would dampen the ardor of the anti-British elements in the United States who have been advocating the seizure of British bases in the Caribbean. If steps of this nature are postponed

until they are forced by rapidly changing circumstances or by United States pressure they will lose their good-will value.[76]

This idea was restated in a report entitled, *Program for Immediate Canadian Action*, prepared following a meeting held on 17-18 July, under the sponsorship of the Canadian Institute of International Affairs (CIIA). Among those attending were Liberal members of parliament Paul Martin, Sr., and Brooke Claxton, and King advisors J. W. Pickersgill, O. D. Skelton, and H. L. Keenleyside. According to the document, "[i]f Canada allows this opportunity to go by default and the United States is consequently obliged to require us to cooperate, we might as a result be unable to maintain our independent identity."[77] It seemed only reasonable for the Canadian government to seize the opportunity to negotiate an accord with the US before conditions changed for the worse. Besides, did not Mackenzie King have it from Franklin Roosevelt himself that something like this logic of preemptive seizure might propel US policy, in the event of a worsening of the situation? The prime minister would later remark that the president had tried to convince the British ambassador to allow America to use British bases in the Antilles, on the basis that "as a matter of fact, if war developed with Germany and [Roosevelt] felt it necessary to seize [the bases] to protect the United States, he would do that in any event. That it was much better to have a friendly agreement in advance."[78]

The conviction that the Americans would be called upon to take over the defence of the entire hemisphere was widespread at the time, not only in Canada but also, and especially, in the US.[79] In this perspective, certain observers imagined constructing something more ambitious than a simple "friendly entente." Escott Reid, at the time second secretary of the Canadian legation in Washington, pushed the logic to its furthest point. In March 1941, convinced that the exigencies of war were going to impel the US to reorganize the political and economic life of all hemisphere states, Reid wrote to Loring Christie that

> Canada's best chance of maintaining a fair degree of real autonomy after the war is to push as hard as possible for a federalization of matters which are of joint concern to Canada and the United States.... The more joint organs for the administration of common interests, the better are our chances of having some influence over United States policies which affect us.[80]

Consistent with the logic of his argument, Reid recommended in July 1941 that Canada join the Panamerican Union,[81] something that would not happen until 1990, by which time the organization had evolved into the Organization of American States. As for the "federalization" notion, it would reemerge eight years later, in the context of the founding of the transatlantic alliance, of which Reid had been a fervent advocate.

Apart from the apprehension generated by the potential measures America might have to take to repel an invader from hemispheric soil, another worry could be detected: that of America having to adopt authoritarian methods in order to mobilize resources needed to defeat the Axis. This was an inference drawn by both Reid and Keenleyside from conversations they had with American officials.[82]

Retrospectively, from Canada's perspective, Roosevelt's timing in proposing the PJBD was perfect. Between its establishment and the attack on Pearl Harbor, the Board had the time to issue 21 recommendations. Throughout that period, bilateral cooperation in defence proved to be effective, and the tone of the discussions was consistently good, indeed cordial. Keenleyside was convinced that having constructed the framework of cooperation well in advance of America's entry into the war enabled Canada to resist better than some other US partners "neo-imperialism" engendered by the "psychosis of wartime," which following the Japanese attack could sometimes lead the US to act in a cavalier manner. As he phrased it, Washington has "recently shown a tendency in dealing with foreign countries to act first and seek approval afterward — if at all."[83]

And however cordial the tenor of discussions might be among colleagues on the PJBD, there was no disguising the reality that in some cases, the two states were going to find themselves articulating and defending different interests. In those cases, asymmetry would constitute a problem for Canadian sovereignty. Three kinds of "encroachments" were feared: 1) an American claim to control Canadian forces stationed in Canada, 2) the sheer size of the American military presence in the country, and 3) implications of the above for Canada's territorial claims in the Arctic.

The basic asymmetry in the bilateral relationship showed up in the very first defence discussions of the PJBD, which led to recommendations vesting the overall "strategic direction" of Canadian forces in American commanders in the event Britain were invaded ("Basic Plan 1").[84] Nevertheless, fearful of conceding too much to their partners, and believing that Washington was asking for "greater control than London ever had,"[85]

Canadian officials rejected the demand, and held out for an arrangement based on "mutual cooperation." It took some hard negotiating, but in the end it was agreed between the two countries that

> [c]oordination of the military effort of the United States and Canada shall be effected by mutual co-operation and by assignment to the forces of each nation of tasks for which they shall be primarily responsible.... Each nation shall retain the strategic direction and command of its own forces, except as hereinunder provided.[86]

Therewith was established what would be a cardinal principle throughout the war: Canadian control of Canadian forces stationed in the country. Washington would discover just how seriously Ottawa took this when it found, a month after Pearl Harbor, that Canada refused to allow Canadian forces based in British Columbia to be included in the command structure set up to defend the West Coast.[87] In light of the psychological mood of the time, it was little short of extraordinary that Canada should have been able to press its case successfully with its powerful partner.

The second bone of contention was occasioned by the presence of American troops on Canadian soil. Ever since 1940, when Washington began to eye the prospect of acquiring British bases in the Antilles and Newfoundland, as well as Canadian bases in Nova Scotia and British Columbia, Canadian policymakers and diplomats strove to avoid giving Americans the impression that any short-term concessions could be extended into the long term. This, too, became a fundamental Canadian principle, the defence of which would require tough bargaining.

In April 1942 Canadian officials were already expressing concern about the implications attending the stationing of US troops in Canada. There was, in particular, worry that in view of

> a growing American tendency to take action affecting Canadian interests, and even in some cases involving the use of Canadian soil without prior notification to the Canadian Government, we are justified in feeling that our relations with the United States have entered an unsatisfactory phase, and one which should be ended just as quickly as possible.[88]

Ending this phase would require, according to the drafter of this note, the elaboration of norms governing US military activities in the country. The situation would, in fact. evolve rapidly. The new sense of urgency after Pearl Harbor resulted in Washington's solidifying defences on both coasts, an undertaking that brought home to Americans the strategic centrality of Canadian territory.

> The Dominion of Canada, with which we have a common land frontier three thousand miles long, is in the geographic center ... The only land highway to Alaska passes through Canada. All the short airways to Europe and Asia pass over Canada. To fly to the United Kingdom and to Iceland, to Scandinavia, to Berlin and Moscow, to Siberia, Japan and China, the shortest airways are over Canada. Thus the geography of airpower links the leading dominion in the British Commonwealth of Nations inseparably with the United States.[89]

Notwithstanding the PJBD and the institutional presence it gave Canada, the latter's room for maneuver was going, in the strategic circumstances, to be slight. Canadian leaders understood very well the significance of Canada's territory for America's physical security. Incapable of defending that territory by its own devices, Canada would need the help of the US, if only to avert America taking unilateral measures in Canada in defence of its own interests. Those latter measures would amount, for all practical purposes, to an American military occupation. In April 1942, Hume Wrong, assistant undersecretary of state for external affairs, would revisit the issue of life in fortress America, in the event of a German-Japanese victory. This would necessarily result in Washington's having to impose a "hemispheric imperialism," which would leave America's neighbours in an awkward position.

> For protection, according to this concept, the United States must control the approaches to her territory. For them the position of Canada is altered from a good neighbour with a lauded undefended frontier to a menace to American security whose territory must be protected by the United States in her own interest. Some of the former isolationists now seem to look on Canada almost as an undeclared colony of the United States. The logic of this imperialism is, if Canada will not freely let her destinies be controlled from Washington, she must be made to do so; failure to meet any demands from the United States becomes a sort of rebellion.[90]

In 1945, when members of the advisory committee set up to investigate postwar problems looked back on some of the difficulties of wartime cooperation, they recalled this Canadian fear.

> It is possible that if Canada had not been able to carry out the defence measures required on Canadian territory the United States would have done so, even

though the United States was not then at war. This attitude of the United States became more apparent after the entry of that country into the war. If Canada had refused or failed to undertake projects which formed part of United States plans ..., or measures in Canadian territory for the special protection of the United States ..., the United States was willing and even anxious to proceed alone.[91]

There is no question but that Canadians were disturbed by the off-hand way in which Americans proceeded to organize continental defence after Pearl Harbor. Several bilateral defence projects intended to be put into place on Canadian soil were developed even before formal consultations between the two countries had been completed. It was as if the projects were being designed for American territory.

> The American authorities tend to consider us not as a foreign national at all, but as one of themselves ... They make sudden demands on us, for some concession or co-operation which they consider to be required by the war emergency, and they do not understand why we should not respond as a Governor of a State would.[92]

By late 1941, Washington was starting to have less and less time for Canada, and gave Canadians the impression they would second everything it proposed.[93] Canadian disquiet would mount during the next few years, once the government became aware, thanks in particular to a series of reports prepared by the British high commissioner, Malcolm MacDonald, of the scope of the US military presence on Canadian territory.[94] By June 1943 the American presence (including civilians) in the Canadian north numbered some 33,000 persons, engaged in a variety of activities related to the provision and protection of transportation and oil-supply infrastructure.[95] The military personnel among them even considered themselves to be part of an "occupation army."[96] Ottawa's principal concern with all of this related not to wartime exigencies but rather to what would happen after the war, when it was felt that the US might simply invoke its *droits acquis* and remain, using as it saw fit the territory and installations. Nothing, however, indicates that this was Washington's intention.[97]

Starting in 1943, the level of US activity on Canadian soil began to taper off, *pari passu* with both the reduction of the threat and the completion of some of the major projects, the most important being the Alaska highway. Ottawa nevertheless sought to find a way that would allow US troops to continue building and running military installations on Canadian territory for the duration of the war, while at the same time guaranteeing that once the conflict had ended, control would pass to Ottawa. The PJBD was the place where solutions would be sought.

Accordingly, the Board's 28th recommendation proposed a series of rules that would provide for the transfer of the US installations to Canada after the war. Issued on 13 January 1943, this recommendation would be approved by both governments within two weeks.[98] One of the solutions advanced would have Canadian reimbursing the US for the cost of such permanent installations as airfields, but at a price well below the cost of construction (some $93 million, for facilities that cost $211 million to build). One Canadian proposal, made in December 1943, called for there to be an end to construction of all installations unless Ottawa had a role both in their financing and their functioning. Other initiatives were taken by Ottawa to safeguard its sovereignty, including the refusal to negotiate an accord allowing the US military rights on the Alaska highway during the postwar period.[99] This, along with further measures adopted in 1944, enabled Canada to position itself fairly well for the postwar period.

WAR AND DEMOCRACY

The Second World War certainly had its share of trauma for Canadian policymakers. It is hardly surprising that so many historians and other analysts should have highlighted the dilemmas attending the country's close defence relationship with the US. And it is no less the case that the vaunted "special relationship" King so sought to effect with Washington remained, in large part, a will-o'-the-wisp; Canadian ties with the US accorded it very little influence over the development of American security policy (and even less over the way in which Washington chose to conduct the war).

Still, there is another way of regarding matters. Canada could have fared much worse, especially in view of the crisis engendered by Pearl Harbor and the ensuing American desire to take those measures it deemed necessary for its defence. The PJBD played a signal role as an "equalizer" of sorts between Canada and its powerful neighbour, reducing the pressure that the latter would otherwise have been able to apply to Canada.

Nor is the Board's role overlooked, notwithstanding the above-noted penchant of some writers to stress the downside of bilateral cooperation. Thus in 1945, the consultative committee on postwar problems recommended that the PJBD be kept in existence, affirming the conviction that "through the Board, representatives of two countries (the one great and the other relatively weak) meet together on an equal footing."[100] Committee members thought that in the event the world organization that was in the process of being born (i.e., the UN) should fail to thrive, the PJBD would be an invaluable backstop for the two countries, providing "an opportunity to discuss difficult problems frankly and openly in an arena where a tradition of equality has been established ... The PJBD is a practical working model of a regional defence system where weight of counsel is dependent on function rather than on net power."[101]

John Holmes would emphasize the equalizing effect of the PJBD. He held it to have been "useful in planning for common purposes and protecting the interest of the minor partner. Furthermore, as it was based roughly on the same principle as the IJC, it did not challenge Canadian sovereignty."[102] No one has expressed this thought better than Galen Perras:

> Given the realization that Roosevelt would have organized continental defense with or without Canadian approval, King gained Canada at least a voice, and possibly an important one, in the formulation of hemispheric defense, no small achievement for a nation only one-tenth as large as its neighbor ... As the unhappy argument over West Coast unity-of-command demonstrated, Canada could hold its own sometimes against the United States when viewpoints did not converge, although one might conclude that the story might have been very different had [Fiorello] LaGuardia been able to convince Roosevelt to intervene more forcefully, or had more vital American interests been at stake. Fortunately for Canadians, the Americans have possessed for some time "a strong conscience that restrains them from forcing their will on us." Many other people bordering great powers — the Finns, the Poles, or the Latin Americans for example — have not been so fortunate.[103]

We might simply wonder whether Canada just happened to have been lucky. In other words, we need to have more than just these positive assessments of the PJBD's consequences: we need to inquire into how and why it could have them in the first place. "First-image" accounts focusing upon the personalities of leaders — King and Roosevelt above all — provide part of the answer, to be sure. So, too, do "third-image" accounts stressing the existence of threat, with the unifying power it is known to command. But there is something more to it: we also need to invoke a "second-image" explanation, centred upon the North American liberal order, to complete the analysis and to account fully for the egalitarian features of Canadian-American relations during wartime.

Causal connections are never easy to establish, if they are even possible at all. Nowhere in the toolbox of liberal values and ideals are we going to find ready-to-use norms that can be applied to the "natural" structuring of cooperation between states confronting a threat from a third party. This is so, even if we *can* say that such norms do exist when the job description is otherwise, to wit, the task of conflict prevention. Nevertheless, it is not stretching things to claim that actors can apply norms developed for the latter mission to the pursuit of collective defence, and this, even if there exists no automatic passage from regimes dedicated to the peaceful settlement of disputes to those concerned with the common defence. In other words, there are no liberal norms for collective defence, but...

In 1940, norms and institutions required for framing the common defence remained to be invented. The pressure of events filled the gap. The most important institution extant in 1940, the IJC, provided a basis for transiting from conflict prevention to collective defence. In the most general sense, we can say that bilateral defence relations evidenced a similar pattern of intense and continuous consultations, and it is this patter that Thomas Risse considers to be proof of the existence of a liberal order. By the same token, we can state that major irritants that might otherwise have poisoned the bilateral defence relationship were mitigated, often eliminated altogether, thanks to compromises and negotiations. Unilateral American initiatives and imposed solutions — which are what we should have expected based upon the distribution of power in North America — proved to be the exception, not the rule. Finally, the bilateral relationship was also conditioned by factors that are in and of themselves particularly important in liberal democracy, above all public opinion.[104]

This does not warrant our touting the Second World War years as the apogee of liberalism in North America. There were still too many instances of countervailing trends, with either state showing a tendency to act not in accordance with liberal norms and values but with what passed for the typical standards of international society at the time. How can this backsliding be reconciled with the existence of a liberal order? The way to answer this is to draw a link between what happens *domestically* in liberal societies that find themselves fighting a war and the relationship *between* liberal democracies both of whom are involved in hostilities against a non-liberal foe. Citizens living in liberal states are prepared to tolerate fairly easily certain limitations of democratic norms when they are in the midst of a crisis; we have seen this recently, both in Canada and the US in the wake of the terrorist attacks on New York and Washington.

Magnify the current concerns about "homeland security" by about a hundred times, and you get some idea of the impact on the home front of the Second World War. Security measures restricting travel and communications of citizens, the bestowal of extraordinary powers upon law enforcement agencies, the replacement of a market economy by a managed one reliant upon rationing and wage and price controls, the suspension of important civil liberties and the imposition of conscription — these and more characterized life, even in liberal-democratic North America, during the war years. Needless to say, these measures flew in the face of the hard core of liberal values.

Canada's War Measures act, drafted in 1918 and only scrapped in 1988, is a sterling example of the divergence between norms and practices within liberal states in wartime. Citizens will be prepared to put up with these restrictions on their liberties to the extent that they see the cause as worthwhile. But they will want assurances that the restrictions are only temporary.

It flows from the above that the restrictions and constraints experienced by each of the North American liberal democracies domestically were bound to have an effect upon the manner in which they dealt with each other. We can further assume that once life internally got more or less "back to normal," we should have expected to see the bilateral relationship come more under the sway of liberal norms and values. And if the Second World War led to the establishment of a new set of defence and security norms, appertaining this time to collective defence, we can expect to observe their conditioning effect at a time when, despite the ending of wartime restrictions, there continued to exist a common external threat. The Cold War was such a time, and constitutes a critical test for the claim that there exists a North American liberal order.

Notes

[1]See "The Geneva Protocol (Dandurand, 2 October 1924)," in *Documents on Canadian Foreign Policy, 1917-1939*, ed. Walter A. Riddell (Toronto: Oxford University Press, 1962); and Joseph T. Jockel and Joel J. Sokolsky, "Dandurand Revisited: Rethinking Canada's Defence Policy in an Unstable World," *International Journal* 48 (Spring 1993): 380-401.

[2]See David G. Haglund, "Le Canada dans l'entre-deux-guerres," *Études internationales* 31 (December 2000): 727-43.

[3]R. D. Cuff and J. L. Granatstein, *Canadian-American Relations in Wartime: From Great War to Cold War* (Toronto: Hakkert, 1975), pp. 3-42. Also see Stanley W. Dziuban, *Military Relations Between the United States and Canada, 1939-1945* (Washington: Department of the Army, Office of the Chief of Military History, 1959), pp. 1-2; and J. L. Granatstein and Norman Hillmer, *For Better or for Worse: Canada and the United States to the 1990s* (Toronto: Copp Clark Pitman, 1991), pp. 64-69.

[4]John Hilliker, *Canada's Department of External Affairs*, vol. 1: *The Early Years, 1909-1946* (Montréal and Kingston: McGill-Queen's University Press, 1990), pp. 75-81. Also see John Herd Thompson and Stephen J. Randall, *Canada and the United States: Ambivalent Allies* (Montreal and Kingston: McGill-Queen's University Press, 1994), pp. 96-103; and Lawrence Martin, *The Presidents and the Prime Ministers* (Toronto: Doubleday, 1982), pp. 88-89.

[5]James A. MacDonald, *Democracy and Nation: A Canadian View* (Toronto: Gundy, 1915); Idem, *The North American Idea* (Toronto: Fleming H. Revell, 1917).

[6]Carl C. Berger, "Internationalism, Continentalism, and the Writing of History: Comments on the Carnegie Series on the Relations of Canada and the United States," in *The Influence of the United States on Canadian Development: Eleven Case Studies*, ed. Richard A. Preston (Durham: Duke University Press, 1972), p. 48.

[7]Thomas White, minister of finance, to the American treasury secretary, 21 June 1917, cited in J. L. Granatstein, *Yankee Go Home? Canadians and Anti-Americanism* (Toronto: HarperCollins, 1996), p. 70 (emphasis added.)

[8]C. P. Stacey, *The Undefended Border: The Myth and the Reality* (Ottawa: Canadian Historical Society, 1973), p. 15.

[9]Samuel Flagg Bemis, *A Diplomatic History of the United States*, 5th ed. (New York: Holt, Rinehart and Winston, 1965), p. 802.

[10]Thompson and Randall, *Canada and the United States*, pp. 93-98; Granatstein, *Yankee Go Home?*, pp. 73-75.

[11]Granatstein, *Yankee Go Home?*, pp. 76-80; Richard A. Jones, "French Canada and the American Peril in the Twentieth Century," *American Review of Canadian Studies* 14 (Autumn 1984): 339-41.

[12]Peter C. Kasurak, "American 'Dollar Diplomats' in Canada, 1927-1941: A Study in Bureaucratic Politics," *American Review of Canadian Studies* 9 (Autumn 1979): 61.

[13]During the 1920s, most economic indicators were registering the country's shift from the British to the American economic orbit. See Richard Arteau, "Libre-échange et continentalisme: récapitulations," in *La Politique économique canadienne à l'épreuve du continentalisme*, ed. Christian Deblock and Richard Arteau (Montréal: GRÉTSÉ/ACFAS, 1988), pp. 169-95; Gregory A. Johnson and David A. Lenarcic, "The Decade of Transition: The North Atlantic Triangle during

the 1920s," in *The North Atlantic Triangle in a Changing World: Anglo-American-Canadian Relations, 1902-1956*, ed. B. J. C. McKercher and Lawrence Aronsen (Toronto: University of Toronto Press, 1996), pp. 98-99; and Michael Hart, *A Trading Nation* (Vancouver: University of British Columbia Press, 2002), pp. 85-124.

[14]Granatstein, *Yankee Go Home?*, p. 72.

[15]Thompson and Randall, *Canada and the United States*, pp. 132, 144-45.

[16]Quoted in ibid., p. 132.

[17]Kenneth McNaught, "From Colony to Satellite," in *An Independent Foreign Policy for Canada*, ed. Stephen Clarkson (Toronto: McClelland and Stewart, 1968), p. 174; David G. Haglund, "The North Atlantic Triangle Revisited: (Geo)Political Metaphor and the Logic of Canadian Foreign Policy," *American Review of Canadian Studies* 29 (Summer 1999): 215-39.

[18]I wish to thank the historian, Greg Donaghy, for drawing my attention to the left's fascination with Rooseveltian foreign policy.

[19]Chandler Bragdon, "Reactions to the Canadian-American Rapprochement of 1935-1939: A Summary," in *Reflections from the Past: Perspectives on Canada and on the Canada-U.S. Relationship* (Plattsburgh, NY: State University of New York, Center for the Study of Canada, 1991; orig. pub. 1967), pp. 64-69.

[20]See, as evidence of this focus, Escott Reid's 1937 essay, "Canada and the Threat of War," in *Canadian Foreign Policy: Historical Readings*, ed. J. L. Granatstein (Toronto: Copp Clark Pitman, 1986), pp. 118-24; and the anonymously authored "Neighbors: A Canadian View," *Foreign Affairs* 10 (April 1932): 417-30.

[21]For these liberal-democratic advocacies, see Roger Epp, "On Justifying the Alliance: Canada, NATO and World Order," in *North American Perspectives on European Security*, ed. Michael K. Hawes and Joel J. Sokolsky (Lewiston, NY: Edwin Mellen, 1990), pp. 96-98.

[22]Clarence K. Streit, *Union Now: A Proposal for a Federal Union of the Democracies of the North Atlantic* (New York: Harper Bros., 1939).

[23]For one favourable assessment of his vision, see William P. Maddox, "The Political Basis of Federation," *American Political Science Review* 35 (December 1941): 1124-26.

[24] James Bartlet Brebner, *North Atlantic Triangle: The Interplay of Canada, the United States and Great Britain* (Toronto: McClelland and Stewart, 1966; orig. pub. 1945); Idem, "A Changing North Atlantic Triangle," *International Journal* 3 (Autumn 1948): 309-19.

[25]B. J. C. McKercher and Lawrence Aronsen, "Introduction," in *North Atlantic Triangle in a Changing World*, p. 3.

[26]Some say as early as 1871. For a study that traces the origins of the concept, see David G. Haglund, *The North Atlantic Triangle Revisited: Canadian Grand Strategy at Century's End*, Contemporary Affairs no. 4 (Toronto: CIIA/Irwin, 2000), pp. 18-19.

[27]Thompson and Randall, *Canada and the United States*, p. 92.

[28]Ibid., p. 146.

[29]W. L. Mackenzie King, *Hansard*, 12 November 1940, 4:61.

[30]Haglund, *North Atlantic Triangle Revisited*, p. 43.

[31]John G. Ruggie, "Multilateralism: The Anatomy of an Institution," in *Multilateralism Matters*, ed. Ruggie (New York: Columbia University Press, 1993), pp. 3-47.

[32]See David G. Haglund, "The Case of the Missing Democratic Alliance(s): France, the Anglo-Saxons, and NATO's "Deep Origins" (forthcoming); and Thomas Risse-Kappen, *Cooperation Among Democracies: The European Influence on U.S. Foreign Policy* (Princeton, NJ: Princeton University Press, 1995), p. 204.

[33]On the relationship between alliances and democracy, see Kurt Taylor Gaubatz, "Democratic States and Commitment in International Relations," *International Organization* 50 (Winter 1996): 31-63; and Randolph M. Siverson and Julian Emmons, "Birds of a Feather: Democratic Political Systems and Alliance Choices in the Twentieth Century," *Journal of Conflict Resolution* 35 (June 1991): 285-306.

[34]Robert O. Keohane, *After Hegemony: Cooperation and Discord in the World Political Economy* (Princeton: Princeton University Press, 1984), p. 52.

[35]Robert O. Keohane and Joseph S. Nye, *Power and Interdependence: World Politics in Transition* (Boston: Little, Brown, 1977), pp. 180-81, 193, 209, 211.

[36]Bragdon, "Reactions to the Canadian-American Rapprochement," p. 64.

[37]Thompson and Randall, *Canada and the United States*, pp. 144-45.

[38]R. A. MacKay, "Canada and the Balance of World Order," *Canadian Journal of Economics and Political Science* 7 (May 1941): 229-43.

[39]"Neighbors: A Canadian View," p. 418.

[40]Quoted in Galen Roger Perras, *Franklin Roosevelt and the Origins of the Canadian-American Security Alliance, 1933-1945* (Westport, CT: Praeger, 1998), p. 38.

[41]"Neighbors: A Canadian View," p. 420.

[42]Quoted in Roger Frank Swanson, *Canadian-American Summit Diplomacy, 1923-1973* (Toronto: McClelland and Stewart, 1975), p. 51.

[43]Cited in James Eayrs, *In Defence of Canada*, vol. 2: *Appeasement and Rearmament* (Toronto: University of Toronto Press, 1967), p. 177.

[44]Quoted in Swanson, *Canadian-American Summit Diplomacy*, p. 53.

[45]Quoted in Richard A. Preston, *The Defence of the Undefended Border: Planning for War in North America, 1867-1939* (Montreal and Kingston: McGill-Queen's University Press, 1977), p. 223.

[46]Canadian official caution on this score is reflected in a memorandum drafted shortly after the Kingston address, "Points to Be Considered Re: President Roosevelt's Kingston Speech," 19 August 1938, in *Documents on Canadian Ex-*

ternal Relations, vol. 6: *1936-1939*; ed. John A. Munro (Ottawa: Department of External Affairs, 1972), pp. 606-7. (Hereafter this source is cited as *DCER*.)

[47]Cited in Perras, *Roosevelt and the Origins*, p. 44.

[48]Claude Beauregard, "La coopération militaire et les relations canado-américaines vues par un groupe d'éminents Canadiens en 1940," *Canadian Defence Quarterly/Revue canadienne de défense* 21 (Summer 1992): 34.

[49]*DCER*, 6: 612-13.

[50]16 October 1940, *DCER*, 7: 941-42.

[51]*Hansard*, 30 March 1939, p. 2459.

[52]*DCER*, 5: 264-67.

[53]Keohane and Nye, *Power and Interdependence*, p. 181.

[54]Not all authors agree on this point. For a different perspective, see William T. R. Fox, *A Continent Apart: The United States and Canada in World Politics* (Toronto: University of Toronto Press, 1985), p. 13: "[T]he *mutuality* of commitment [after Kingston] meant that something like a North American security union was in the making" (emphasis added).

[55]H. L. Keenleyside, "Report of a Discussion of Possible Eventualities," 26 May 1940, *DCER*, 8: 67-71. So concerned was Roosevelt with the prospect of the Royal Navy's coming into German possession that he asked King to press with Churchill the case for dispersing the fleet to ports in the Canada and the other dominions in the event of a British surrender. Canada remained at the heart of a series of exchanges on this topic between Washington and London. See ibid., 8: 87-100.

[56]"Telegram 111, Secretary of State for External Affairs to Chargé d'affaires in United States, 16 June 1940," *DCER*, 8: 105-10, 117, 153-56.

[57]Archives of the Department of External Affairs, volume 781, file 394, "An Outline Synopsis for a Reconsideration of Canadian External Policy with Particular Reference to the United States," 17 June 1940; cited in Cuff and Granatstein, *Canadian-American Relations*, pp. 100-1.

[58]The quite informal circumstances attending this meeting are recounted in William R. Willoughby, *The Joint Organizations of Canada and the United States* (Toronto: University of Toronto Press, 1979), pp. 106-7.

[59]Donald Barry, "The Politics of 'Exceptionalism': Canada and the United States as a Distinctive International Relationship," *Dalhousie Review*, 60 (Spring 1980): 117.

[60]Cuff and Granatstein, *Canadian-American Relations*, p. 101; see also John W. Warnock, *Partner to Behemoth: The Military Policy of a Satellite* (Toronto: New Press, 1970).

[61]For more recent assessments, see Christopher Conliffe, "The Permanent Joint Board on Defense, 1940-1988," in *The U.S.-Canada Security Relationship: The Politics, Strategy, and Technology of Defense*, ed. David G. Haglund and Joel J. Sokolsky (Boulder: Westview, 1989), pp. 145-65; and J. L. Granatstein, "Mackenzie King and Canada at Ogdensburg, August 1940," in *Fifty Years of*

Canada-United States Defense Cooperation, ed. Joseph T. Jockel and Joel J. Sokolsky (Lewiston, NY: Edwin Mellen, 1993), pp. 10-29.

[62]As was sensed by some contemporary observers, for instance MacKay, "Canada and the Balance of World Order," p. 235.

[63]See, for the similarity with the earlier structures, John W. Holmes, *The Shaping of Peace: Canada and the Search for World Order*, vol. 1: *1943-1957* (Toronto: University of Toronto Press, 1979), pp. 160, 164.

[64]Willoughby, *Joint Organizations*, p. 115.

[65]The exception was recommendation 22 of 10 November 1941; see Dziuban, *Military Relations*, p. 41.

[66]H. L. Keenleyside, "The Canada-United States Permanent Joint Board on Defence, 1940-1945," *International Journal* 16 (Winter 1960-61): 55.

[67]Shelagh D. Grant, *Sovereignty or Security? Government Policy in the Canadian North (1936-1950)* (Vancouver: University of British Columbia Press, 1988), p. 241 (emphasis added).

[68]Willoughby, *Joint Organizations*, p. 108 (emphasis added).

[69]Holmes, *Shaping of Peace*, 1: 164-65.

[70]Escott Reid, "The Creation of the North Atlantic Alliance," in Granatstein, *Canadian Foreign Policy*, pp. 163-66.

[71]King, 12 November 1940, *Hansard*, 6: 61.

[72]Cited by Stacey, *La frontière sans défense*, p. 16.

[73]Joseph T. Jockel, *No Boundaries Upstairs: Canada, the United States, and the Origins of North American Air Defence, 1945-1958* (Vancouver: University of British Columbia Press, 1987).

[74]John Alan English, "Not an Equilateral Triangle: Canada's Strategic Relationship with the United States and Britain, 1939-1945," in *North Atlantic Triangle in a Changing World*, pp. 147-83.

[75]J. L. Granatstein, "The Conservative Party and the Ogdensburg Agreement," *International Journal* 22 (Winter 1966-67): 73-76.

[76]H. L. Keenleyside, "The United States, the War, and the Defence of North America," 27 June 1940, *DCER*, 8: 155-56.

[77]Cited in W. A. B. Douglas, "Democratic Spirit and Purpose: Problems in Canadian-American Relations, 1939-1945," in *Fifty Years of Canada-United States Defense Cooperation*, p. 33.

[78]Cited in Granatstein, "Mackenzie King and Canada at Ogdensburg," p. 21.

[79]See David G. Haglund, *Latin America and the Transformation of U.S. Strategic Thought, 1936-1940* (Albuquerque: University of New Mexico Press, 1984).

[80]Escott Reid, *Radical Mandarin: The Memoirs of Escott Reid* (Toronto: University of Toronto Press, 1989), p. 140.

[81]Ibid., pp. 157-58.

[82]26 May 1940, *DCER*, 8: 69-71. Reid would later recount, "the fear at the time that the United States would cease to be a democracy if it had to face a

Germany which had been victorious in Europe was common." Reid, *Radical Mandarin*, p. 137.

[83]Keenleyside memo of 14 April 1942, *DCER*, 9: 1136.

[84]A. D. P. Heeney memo of 27 May 1941, *DCER*, 8: 215.

[85]O. M. Biggar, 3 May 1941, *DCER*, 8: 205.

[86]Maurice Pope, memo of 5 June 1941, *DCER*, 8: 222.

[87]Maurice Pope, "Southern British Columbia-Puget Sound U.S. Request for Institution of Unity of Command," 16 January 1942, *DRREC*, 9: 1149-50.

[88]Memo of 13 April 1942, *DCER*, 9: 909.

[89]Walter Lippmann, *U.S. Foreign Policy: Shield of the Republic* (Boston: Little, Brown, 1943), pp. 119-20.

[90]Wrong, quoted in Grant, *Sovereignty or Security?*, p. 72.

[91]"Final Report of Advisory Committee on Post-Hostilities Problems — Summary," January/February 1945, *DCER*, 11: 1570. The advisory committee on post-hostilities problems was created in 1943 by the war committee of the cabinet, to provide advice on European matters and relations with the US, as well as other issues. See C. P. Stacey, *Canada and the Age of Conflict*, vol. 2: *1921-1948: The Mackenzie King Era* (Toronto: University of Toronto Press, 1981), p. 377.

[92]"Certain Developments in Canada-United States Relations," 18 March 1943, *DCER*, 9: 1138.

[93]N. A. R. Robertson, memo of 22 December 1941, *DCER*, 9: 1125-31.

[94]Excerpts from these reports can be found in *DCER*, 9: 1567-73.

[95]James Eayrs, *In Defence of Canada*, vol. 3: *Peacemaking and Deterrence* (Toronto: University of Toronto Press, 1972), p. 349.

[96]Malcolm MacDonald, "Note on Developments in North-Western Canada," 6 April 1943, *DCER*, 9: 1570.

[97]"On the U.S. side, no responsible official had envisaged a position of special privilege for the United States in Canada as a result of the wartime operations there." Dziuban, *Military Relations*, p. 322.

[98]Willoughby, *Joint Organizations*, p. 122.

[99]"Memorandum from Department of External Affairs to Cabinet War Committee: Alaska Highway — Use of Connecting Roads," 20 February 1943, *DCER*, 9: 1195-96.

[100]"Final Report of Advisory Committee on Post-Hostilities Problems," p. 1571.

[101]Memo, working group of the committee on postwar problems, 27 May 1945; cited in Eayrs, *Peacemaking and Deterrence*, p. 325.

[102]Holmes, *Shaping of Peace*, p. 160.

[103]Perras, *Franklin Roosevelt and the Origins*, p. 121. The source of the quote regarding "conscience" is John Holmes. Fiorello LaGuardia, a confidant of Roosevelt and mayor of New York City, was one of the American members of the PJBD.

[104]"The Board helped to modify, to some degree, the demands of the American armed forces. Through the Board, Ottawa was able to exercise a degree of political influence on the United States government, and thereby make Washington pay more respect to public opinion in Canada than would have been the case without the PJBD." Conliffe, "Permanent Joint Board on Defense," p. 147.

CHAPTER SEVEN

Business as Usual: The Joint Defence of North America, 1945-1958

PLUS ÇA CHANGE?

B oth liberal and conservative historians in Canada tend to paint a rather sombre picture of Canadian-American relations following the Second World War, one that has Canada's leaders driving the country into the arms of the US, either unconsciously or out of necessity. It is an interpretation supportive of the balance-of-power thesis, in that Britain's disappearance as a "counterweight" laid bare the fundamentally unequal relationship between the North American countries. Nor is this depiction undercut by the difficulties Canada encountered in the period 1942-44, which we examined in the previous chapter.

That said, two arguments advanced in that chapter give us reason to pause before embracing the bleak analysis emanating from the counterweight school. Firstly, the situation was not as disastrous as some imagined it to have been during the war: the Canadian government showed itself surprisingly resistant, and as we saw all issues were resolved to the satisfaction of both sides. Secondly, the period has to be taken as part of an evolutionary process. Just as the institutions created during the war flowed directly from the International Joint Commission, so the solutions to the problems arising during the years 1942-44 can be traced back to an earlier time. Seen in this light, the wartime institutions must also be understood as part of the North American liberal order.

In this chapter, I am going to show that the wartime controversies never did re-emerge (even though perceived threat at the height of the Cold War was more acute than that of the post-Pearl Harbor period), and that when bilateral tensions did arise, in a new and different form from those of the early 1940s, they were managed as efficaciously as the previous ones had been. The new problems can be seen as an inevitable consequence of the exponential growth in cooperation during the period, and are therefore associated more with a "crisis of growth" than with any structural problem in the relationship.

John Holmes raised an interesting, albeit misleading, question with respect to the nature of that post-1945 cooperation: "that Canadians and Americans were bound to get more mixed up together in their various activities was taken for granted. Why then was more thought not given to the creation of structures to cope with the inevitable?"[1] In his view, the existence of a European counterweight explains why Ottawa did not seek a formal alliance with Washington. And yet, postwar relations did become increasingly institutionalized. In 1946 the military representatives on the PJBD formed a committee for military cooperation (the Canada-US Military Cooperation Committee, or MCC). The following year, the two countries publicly declared they would continue to cooperate closely on security matters in the postwar era. By 1953 a Joint Military Study Group (MSG) was conducting feasibility studies of proposed shared projects, and facilitating the exchange of technical information.

Perhaps most significantly, in 1958 the North American Air Defence Command (NORAD) was set up, in the same year as yet another body, a joint ministerial committee on defence, was formed. Nor was that all: a network of committees had arisen whose chief concern was with the economics of defence, notably the Joint Industrial Mobilization Planning Committee (JIMPC), dating from 1949. To cap things off, there existed a series of multilateral institutional linkages involving Canadians and Americans, in the context both of the United Nations and of NATO, and some of these had regional (i.e., North American) applicability — though not very much of it.

As a result, Canadian-American bilateral defence cooperation in North America extended to a variety of domains, from joint maritime and air defence to arms production and equipment standardization. These agreements extended the cooperation begun during the war (joint defence planning and construction of infrastructure) and provided guidelines for joint defence operations. It is therefore incorrect to say there was no process of institutionalization in security and defence cooperation.

Holmes's question, nevertheless, remains pertinent to the extent that these institutions did not result in any formal treaty of alliance. They did not provide for specific mutual assistance in the way that the 1949 Washington treaty's article 5 did, at the multilateral level. In truth, Canadian leaders have steered clear, for various reasons including some relating sovereignty-protection, of bilateral accords adjudged to be too restrictive. This accounts to their refusal to establish what Holmes called any "constitutional" linkages with the US.[2]

Realist theories supply some possible explanations of the dynamics of the postwar bilateral. Hegemonic stability theorists would claim that by assuming the so much of the burden of defending the continent, the US in effect made Canadian cooperation obligatory. The so-called "involuntary guarantee" from which Canada is said to benefit can often appear to be a type of "free-riding," or burden shedding. Another approach, often formulated by diplomats, holds that NATO provided Canada with a new European counterweight, thereby enabling it to solve its bilateral problem at the multilateral level. Accordingly, the dynamics of the relationship between a great power seeking the cooperation of its weaker neighbour, and a small power desirous of keeping as much of its sovereign authority as possible without upsetting its more powerful neighbour, explain the form and content of their bilateral institutions. Such a realist interpretation need not be inconsistent with an institutional approach. If, as John Holmes was the first to admit, continentalism necessitated the imposition of discipline shaped by institutions and rules,[3] then institutions themselves can and do constitute an equalizing factor in a relationship between states of unequal power.

Another popular approach to bilateral defence cooperation attributes it to the interaction between individual bureaucratic actors — heads of state and of government, cabinet ministers, armed forces personnel, and the like — in the respective decisionmaking processes.[4] Similarly, other studies emphasize the role of certain individuals and the personalities of the decisionmakers.[5] Such bureaucratic and individualist approaches can be embedded within a transnational perspective that consistently stresses that Canadian-American practices and institutions result from the interplay between transgovernmental coalitions, especially in the military domain.[6] This approach holds institutions and transgovernmental relations to be mutually dependent, since the functioning of the former engenders the creation of the latter, whose participants have a common interest in maintaining and developing the institutions.[7]

These approaches fail to explain why these institutions were created, in such a way as to permit the establishment of an egalitarian relationship. In order to better understand this aspect of Canadian-American relations, it is necessary to examine more closely the sociopolitical and historical context of the creation of these postwar institutions. From a sociopolitical standpoint, the liberal democratic nature of the two states is at the heart of the analysis. On the one hand, it is reasonable to expect that the institutions will reflect the norms and rules used by each of the states in handling their internal problems. On the other, we can posit that the formation of transgovernmental coalitions was in large part possible because the two governments operated on the basis of similar politics. The historical enquiry seeks to determine the extent to which the postwar institutions and practices were indebted to those in place since the beginning of the century, and which contributed to the North American liberal order.

The postwar rhetoric of liberal governments in response to the military and ideological threat they saw emanating from the Soviet Union muddies the analytical waters a bit, given that the Soviet Union had supporters in the West, thanks both to its contribution to the defeat of the Nazis and to the appeal of communist ideology among certain circles. Western leaders, not surprisingly, favoured a discourse highlighting the virtues of democratic liberalism, but we have to be careful not to infer from the rhetoric "proof" that Canadian-American cooperation arose out of the liberal order.

Instead of heeding closely the words, it is better if we examine the actions, of those who shaped Canadian foreign policy. In particular, we look to the practices and content of the institutions in our quest for evidence of a postwar liberal order. The flexibility of the institutions created during and after the war is the most telling sign of the existence of this liberal order.

The institutions were the result of a compromise satisfying the American interest in the continental security and the Canadian interest in national sovereignty. As Shelagh Grant points out, the postwar years featured an ongoing attempt to resolve the contradictions embedded in the sovereignty/security dichotomy conundrum. "The key was to build upon agreements and institutions that offered the optimum of flexibility."[8] Canadian nationalists might regard bilateral accords as constraints, but they were obviously entirely different from the kinds of agreements entered into between the USSR and its satellite countries — or even those between the US and the authoritarian states of Latin America! They resembled nothing so much as the ties that bound together allies within NATO — a democratic alliance *par excellence* — even though, as we shall see below, a firewall separated the Atlantic and the North American institutions.

INTERNATIONALISM AND CONTINENTAL DEFENCE

Post-1945 Canadian security policy differed greatly from that of the inter-war period. A resolutely internationalist approach centred around the UN replaced the earlier isolationism. More generally, the principles based on a narrow conception of the national interest that guided Mackenzie King's foreign policy during the 1930s[9] were discarded in favour a body of more diffuse ideals, which reflected the leaders' preoccupation with international stability after the war. A new foreign policy took shape, based on the following imperatives: that it not damage national unity; that it be dedicated to the pursuit of freedom; that it demonstrate a respect for the supremacy of law; that it draw inspiration from a certain conception of human values; and that it reflect a willingness to assume international responsibilities. Three of the imperatives were projections onto the international level of domestic liberal-democratic ideals. As St-Laurent remarked in his Gray Foundation lecture of 1947, "a policy of world affairs, to be truly effective, must have its foundations laid upon general principles which have been tested in the life of the nation and which have secured the broad support of large groups of the population."[10]

The same tendency is perceptible in the US, where liberal ideas inspired the drafting of a framework for an eventual international political and economic order.[11] Canadian researchers have rarely noted this convergence of ideals, tending rather to stress the differences between the two countries. Yet this convergence was evident on several levels. To begin with, the two North American states shared a similar view of the United Nations — and not only in comparison with the positions of the Western European democracies, including Britain. The Wilsonian internationalism that coloured American foreign policy during the period 1945-47 was very close to the middle-power internationalism guiding Canadian policy at the time. Both governments drew a link between peace and prosperity in the context of participation in UN committees dealing with economic and social questions.

Nor was the convergence a new phenomenon; as the following citation shows, during the 1920s and 1930s, Canadian representatives at the

League of Nations took positions similar to those defended by the US elsewhere:

> It is probably correct to say that on nearly every important political question that has come before the League, Canada has adopted a point of view which may be described as North American, one that would probably have been adopted by the United States herself if she had become a member of the Geneva organization.[12]

The same convergence of ideas was evident at the level of the perception of threats, especially concerning the intentions attributed to Soviet leaders. Once again, Canadian researchers have tended to dwell upon the two governments' differences in this area and explain it as flowing from the power differential.[13] Although one can discern clear differences between Canadian political leaders and American *military* leaders, a comparison of the political élites of the two countries shows less division. Apart from tactical considerations, analyses by Canadian leaders during the early years of the Cold War were often similar to those of their American counterparts. Note two students of the bilateral relationship, "[a]lthough Canada was less inclined to confront the USSR, preferring negotiation and accommodation, Canadian and American officials shared fundamental assumptions about the Soviet Union and the threat it posed to the West and acted accordingly in the establishment of a military alliance."[14]

The Gouzenko affair of September 1945, which unmasked the operation of a Soviet spy network in Canada, reinforced this tendency, among even the most pusillanimous politicians, such as Mackenzie King.[15] The congruence represented more than just a consequence of Canadian dependence upon British and American intelligence; it also bore witness to a shared mistrust of the Soviet Union and its values. Louis St-Laurent ascribed the similarity in the Canadian and American reactions to the threat to their convergent ideas and values. He observed in the House of Commons in late April 1949 that in a world racked with tension and danger, Canadian-American "friendship" and "solidarity" constituted a rare exception, and went on to explain that the reason the two countries so often seemed to adopt similar policies bore witness to the fact that "our two peoples have the same ideas, the same way of life."[16]

Canadian leaders and diplomats thought that the UN, the cornerstone of Canadian security policy during the first two postwar years, should play a role in the management of relations with the US. Giving the international organization more functions would better enable it to balance and to limit the influence of the great powers; further, by reinforcing the power of the UN in security matters, Canadians hope to avert an American isolationist current. This "global" security approach did not, however, entail any Canadian avoidance of regional military commitments, especially in North America. John Holmes writes:

> In defence as in economics, it was better to have extracontinental ballast, but with or without it the continent could not be ignored. The defence of North America and the swelling volume of Canada-United States commerce and investment had to be organized and controlled whether or not world security and a world economy came to pass. It would be best, essential perhaps, that they be fitted into wider schemes, but they had to be coped with in any case.[17]

Nor did the end of the Second World War imply any change in the established US-Canadian rapports on continental defence. Although cooperation between the two states had, as we saw in the previous chapter, resulted in some Canadian discomfiture, Ottawa decided to maintain the commitments in force since 1940. Strategic considerations lay behind this decision. The development of long-range bombers and nuclear weapons made it easy to imagine that North America itself could be vulnerable to direct attack.[18] The conviction that the USSR would be the next adversary were a new war to break out in Europe both heightened the strategic importance of Canadian territory and encouraged the pursuit of US-Canadian cooperation.

Leaders of both countries realized the security of their countries to be inextricably interconnected. Thus one American official could write in 1943: "It is improbable that future events might occur which would see the US at war and Canada strictly neutral."[19] This meant that Canada would rebuff any British attempts to create an alliance between former members of the empire, something MacKenzie King did not hesitate to do, partly because of his abhorrence of the colonial overtones of such a proposition, but also because it might interfere with Canadian-American cooperation.[20] Despite its historic and political ties with Britain, Canada opted for a continental rather than an imperial defence strategy; Canada's geostrategic realignment, begun at the end of the 1930s, was completed in the early postwar period. Interestingly, the mood in the two capitals differed. In Washington, State Department officials were fairly glowing in their assessment of Canada and of Canada-US defence cooperation.[21] Helping Canada was argued to make good sense, for in doing so the US was helping itself, and also showing the rest of the world that democracies could cooperate in pursuit of peace and prosperity. Over at the new Pentagon, the atmosphere was less effusive, as American military officials, preoccupied with the needs of operational effectiveness and spurred on by interservice rivalries, sometimes suggested policies that could be counted upon, however inadvertently, to offend Canadian sensitivities on sovereignty issues.

The climate in Ottawa was frostier. King nursed unpleasant memories of the "occupation" army, and he was distressed by the death of President Roosevelt, with whom he had close ties. In some ways, American requests for military commitments had upon him a similar effect to prewar British proposals for an imperial defence system. The aging prime minister became more mistrustful and unpredictable after the war, to the point that he seemed to some to be reverting to his prewar isolationism. On the other hand, such rising stars of Canadian diplomacy as Louis St-Laurent, Lester Pearson, and Hume Wrong, more aware of the new postwar geopolitical reality and less marked by the incidents of 1942-43, were more open to cooperating with the US. Pearson displayed a great confidence in the ability of democratic states to learn from their errors and to cooperate with each other in creating institutions capable of guiding and framing their future collaboration.[22] But Pearson was simply echoing a widely held Canadian view at the time, exemplified by one commentator, writing in 1950:

> [T]he military dispositions fencing us in on both east and west are acceptable on two assumptions: the continuing political sanity of the United States, a postulate to which Canada is inescapably committed, and the uncertain strategic behaviour of the USSR. Our existence depends on the first even more intimately perhaps than it does on the second. A viable, adaptive and humane democracy in the United States, whose expansive internationalism is kept compatible with the prejudices as well as the needs of others will not forfeit the confidence of her allies.[23]

THE JOINT DECLARATION OF 1947

The end of the war had done little to attenuate American pressure for a strengthening of cooperation with respect to the joint defense of the continent. The question was raised in an early meeting between King and the new US president, Harry S Truman, but it did not seem to have dominated their discussions, which were instead mostly concerned with the use of the airbase at Goose Bay, Labrador — which King pointed out was not a Canadian affair, given that Labrador was not part of Canadian territory. King did take the opportunity, however, to point out to Truman that Canadians were touchy on matters of sovereignty.

King was not understating the matter, for although the Canadians would agree to continue defence cooperation with the Americans, their attitude was one of prudence. The report of the advisory committee on post-hostilities problems, on which future Canadian policies would be based, recommended maintaining the cooperative ties, but at the same time cautioned that the "possibility ... of the United States being moved to exert undue pressure on Canada, particularly as respects matters of defence, should not be overlooked." It consequently urged that Ottawa retain full responsibility for defence measures taken on Canadian territory. Cooperation with the US should not call into question Canadian control over the country's armed forces, allow the presence of American troops or installations exclusively under the control of Washington, or otherwise threaten Canada's territorial integrity.[24]

The cooling of relations with the Soviet Union triggered a fear in Ottawa that harked back to the crisis mood prior to Pearl Harbor — the fear that Washington might act unilaterally if it judged that American security required the implementation of certain measures on Canadian soil. This possibility, although dismissed in the final report of the advisory committee, continued to bother some officials, who preferred to negotiate with Washington, prior to any crises arising, clauses enshrining Canadian sovereignty in whatever accords would be struck. The following quotation from a 1946 US Air Force document indicates that Canadian sovereignty fears were not baseless:

> If the American Government had good reason to believe that invasion or occupation of the Canadian Arctic by [a] foreign nation were imminent, it would be justified in taking suitable counter measures, *with or without Dominion consent*, on the ground that the security of the United States was directly threatened.[25]

The wartime establishment of transpolar and circumpolar air routes had clearly heightened the strategic value of the Arctic archipelago separating the USSR from North America, much of which Canada claimed as its own territory. The foundations for that Canadian claim, however, were fragile, given that most of the islands were uninhabited and that certain areas had not even been explored. Although the Americans had not seriously questioned the Canadian claim, their refusal explicitly to recognize it did reinforce Ottawa's mistrust. Washington, conscious of these apprehensions, chose not to challenge Canada on the matter so as not to damage other aspects of the bilateral relationship; but it held in reserve, should the need arise, the option of claiming certain uninhabited islands.

American interest in the area remained, so much so that Mackenzie King declared in early 1946 that the "long range policy of the United States is to absorb Canada. They would seek to get this hemisphere as completely as possible."[26] To forestall this, certain high-level officials in Ottawa suggested using the same approach as in 1943-44: Canada should insist that any military projects in the far north be jointly financed and managed, and remain explicitly under Canadian control.[27] A Canadian refusal to cooperate, it was felt, would only lead to a hardening in the American position, with grave implications for Canadian sovereignty. So as to avoid any misapprehensions, Pearson, at the time ambassador to Washington, published an article in *Foreign Affairs* in which he diplomatically noted that

> [t]here is no question now as to ownership and control of bases and such things, which might give rise to misunderstandings between the two countries. On the contrary, there is a clear understanding by the United States *that Canada has complete responsibility for everything within her borders*, while ready and anxious to cooperate with the United States to the fullest extent in everything that pertains to the development and security of the Arctic regions.[28]

On 23 May 1946, the MCC had approved two documents, the first setting out the need for a joint defence plan, and the second establishing the contours of such a plan (outlining, for instance, a series of such defensive measures as radar systems, air bases, and antiaircraft installations); these were, respectively, titled, "An Appreciation of the Requirements for Canadian-US Security," and "Joint Canadian-United States Basic Security Plan."[29] The American members of the committee had not been given precise instructions from Washington, in part because a clear global strategic vision had yet to emerge in 1945 and 1946. Even so, American leaders did want assurance of Canada's "signing on" to continental defence.[30] At the same time, they were sensitive to Ottawa's stated concerns about sovereignty. The secretary of state, Dean Acheson, had remarked in October

1946 that at times American military planners could give the impression that the US government was on the verge of unveiling ambitious, and even unnecessary, initiatives; it was the duty of State Department officials, he said, to "assure Mr. King that our non-military authorities are convinced that the program is necessary and also that you and they are watching to prevent any over-extension of military plans."[31]

Although the plans drawn up by the MCC in 1946 had little relation to America's real strategic needs and capabilities at the time, Ottawa's acceptance of them would assure the US of Canadian collaboration. The Canadian government had no way of knowing what the America's real intentions were, or of contesting the veracity of the strategic analysis upon which the plans were based. Certain cabinet members, including Brooke Claxton, minister of national defence, were dubious of USSR's capability of launching attacks against North America. This skepticism created uneasiness in Ottawa, where awareness was acute of the problems that could ensue from differential threat perceptions as between Canadians and Americans. One official in the Department of External Affairs spelled out the nature of the problem:

> There is no doubt that, from several points of view, these developments will constitute one of the most difficult and serious problems with which the government will have to deal, within the next few years.... It is, I think, likely that the importance which the US government attach to acceptance and implementing of joint plans will be emphasized by an approach on the highest level. In these circumstances, the government will probably have to accept the US thesis in general terms, though we may be able to moderate the pace at which plans are to be implemented and to some extent the nature of the projects which are to be undertaken.[32]

In November, discussions on continental defense planning were indeed moved to higher diplomatic levels, resulting the following month in a distinction being drawn between "planning" and "execution," with the latter requiring prior approval from each government.[33] This cleared the way to the issuance, on 12 February 1947, of the "Joint Canada-United States Defence Public Statement." This document did not amount to a treaty of alliance, any more than had that issued at Ogdensburg, back in August 1940. King took care to remind everyone that no legal commitments bound either of the two parties; each was free to decide upon the nature and scope of the defence collaboration. General Andrew McNaughton, chairman of the Canadian section of the PJBD, agreed, and lauded what he termed a "permanent and sensible arrangement," but not an alliance.[34]

Interestingly, the statement did not entail the creation of any new institutions or mechanisms; existing ones were judged adequate to the tasks at hand. It did, however, enunciate a set of guidelines for Canadian-American military cooperation, providing *inter alia* for: limited exchanges of military personnel; exchanges of observers during exercises and trials of new systems; reciprocal furnishing of military installations; standardization of military equipment and procedures; and supervision by the host country of all joint military projects or activities. Neither country was to obtain permanent rights in the other as a result of these undertakings.[35]

These guidelines reflected a compromise: the US obtained a clear commitment from Canada in favour of the common defence; Canada obtained a guarantee of its territorial sovereignty. More generally, the nonconstraining nature of the guidelines testifies to the egalitarian nature of the North American liberal order. The US could be satisfied with the relatively vague wording contained therein because the norm of reciprocity, well established in its dealings with Canada, would oblige both to give up some autonomy in defence matters. Reciprocity thus nullified the option of American unilateral imposition, because it made the latter redundant. Moreover, the ambiguous and conditional nature of the obligations, coupled with the safeguards for Canadian sovereignty, argue for the existence of a regional order modulating the balance of power.

A MULTILATERAL SOLUTION TO A BILATERAL PROBLEM?

In August 1947, a draft memorandum written by Escott Reid, a high-ranking member of the Department of External Affairs, made the rounds in Ottawa policy circles. Commentary by the readership of Reid's document provides insight into élite thinking concerning Canada's place in the bipolar world and, in particular, its relations with the US.[36] Reid's paper foresaw only a slight risk of war in the coming decade; nevertheless, it proposed a set of measures aimed at lessening that risk, including the creation of a new regional security organization whose member states would commit themselves to pooling their economic and military assets to halt aggression launched against any member. It also recommended strengthening

North American defence measures and evaluated the kind of relationship that Canada might be able to establish with the US.

> Canada is being brought into still greater dependence upon the United States.... In the event of war we shall have no freedom of action in any matter which the United States Government considers essential.... In peacetime our freedom of action will be limited but it will not be non-existent. It will still be open to us to oppose the United States on certain issues in United States-Soviet relations.

> The weight of the influence the Canadian Government can bring to bear on Washington is considerable. If we play our cards well we can exert an influence at Washington out of all proportion to the relative importance of our strength in war compared with that of the United States.[37]

Most of Reid's readers agreed with the above, though some differed. One who differed was Maurice Pope, chief of the military mission to the allied commission controlling Germany, who was skeptical of Canada's ability to "oppose" the US on issues relating to the Soviet Union. "If I know anything" of the US, said Pope, "it is that when they rightly, or wrongly, feel that their security is threatened or that their interests may suffer, they brook no opposition."[38]

Pope represented the position of those policymakers who were most cynical and fatalistic concerning the US, believed Canadian-American cooperation to be inevitable, and feared unilateral American actions in defence of the continent that did not respect Canadian sovereignty. He had expressed his views on this subject as early as 1944, when he observed that "what we have to fear is more a lack of confidence in the United States as to our security, rather than enemy action. I can put this in another way. If we do enough to assure the United States, we shall have done a good deal more than a cold assessment of the risk would indicate to be necessary."[39]

Others considered unacceptable the idea that the US should undertake part of the defence of Canada. Commented Canada's ambassador to Argentina:

> A Canada that accepted the main implications of Part VI [of the memorandum] would be going back to a new colonialism and a position not much better than that of some Latin-American states.... I would think that a policy that could lead to such a consequence was an unsound policy for us and for our world, and much too costly a price to pay for protection against aggression. And I see

no need to be hypnotized into such a position if we properly assert the importance of the rest of the Western World and the real principles that should join us all together.[40]

Certain commentators thought Reid underestimated the impact other Western powers might have on the Canadian-American relationship. Should the European states recover economically and militarily, they would be able to counterbalance American influence, and in so doing reduce Canada's dependence upon its powerful neighbour.[41] Between this suggestion and the proposal to create a new regional security organization it was but a small step, one that Reid, St-Laurent and Pearson would soon take in promoting the creation of an Atlantic alliance.

The absence of an immediate threat to the continent during the years 1944-47 led Ottawa to focus more on sovereignty in its dealings with the US than on the construction of impenetrable system of North American defence. The onset of the Cold War reversed this order of priorities. The 1948 Prague coup and the Berlin blockade resulted in the 1949 signing of the treaty of Washington, which gave birth to the Atlantic alliance. Although the perception of a Soviet threat was a major factor motivating its active role in creating the alliance, Canada also hoped that the formation of an "Atlantic community" might furnish it with a counterweight to American power, thereby attenuating the negative effect of its unequal relationship with the US.

Thomas Risse-Kappen has argued that the norms and rules of the Atlantic alliance stemmed from the liberal order.[42] Canadian diplomats made a substantial contribution to this democratic character by their drafting of article 2 and by their commitment to the norms of consultation and reciprocity.[43] Furthermore, the failed attempt by Reid and Pearson to transform the alliance into an Atlantic "community" — i.e., into a supranational institution endowed with real powers — has interesting parallels with the "republican union" proposed 150 years earlier by Kant.[44]

Canadian diplomats thus believed that the Atlantic alliance, whether by providing Canada the opportunity to establish ties with other states or by enshrining liberal norms, or both, would operate as a counterweight to American influence. As discussed earlier, the counterweight is one of the most cherished metaphors of Canadian foreign policy lore. John Holmes recalled:

There was the important consideration of counter-weight. This was not excessively stressed in public pronouncements as it could be construed in Congress as anti-American, but politicians and officials saw in the Atlantic link a balancing of the commitment which they had just made, after heart-searching, for joint continental defence.[45]

Some used more vivid language to express the idea, and one former minister of national defence is reported to have said, apropos the virtues of a multilateral as opposed to a bilateral alliance, "with fifteen people in the bed you are less likely to get raped."[46] Pearson, ever the diplomat, put the same thought more gently: "In one form or another, for Canada there was always security in numbers. We did not want to be alone with our close friend and neighbour. As a debutante on the world stage we were worried, not about rape, but seduction."[47]

The alleged existence of this counterweight is often taken as decisive proof that the best way to contain American ambitions and to influence Washington was through transatlantic multilateralism. The utility of the metaphor, and by extension the Atlantic alliance, for these purposes has to be questioned, however, for the good reason that bilateral Canadian-American agreements reflected precisely the same set of egalitarian values and norms as those presumably associated with the multilateral Atlantic alliance.

One way to test the hypothesis of the multilateral counterweight would be for us to gauge the effect the creation of NATO had upon the Canadian-American bilateral relationship. In particular, did the existence of the alliance permit the transfer of matters hitherto dealt with only at the bilateral level to this new multilateral level, thereby affecting Canada's earlier exclusive dialogue with the US?

An examination of the available documents reveals the answer to be a clear "No." Bilateral and multilateral activities were and remained separate, reflecting not only Washington's desire to prevent the European allies from meddling in the management of American territorial defence (or later in the control of the US nuclear deterrent) but also, more curiously, *Canada's* desire to compartmentalize security. Significantly, Canadian diplomats involved in the 1948-49 negotiations leading to the creation of NATO rarely referred to North American defence or to cooperation with the US as being within the writ of the new organization.

Some North American considerations did, however, play a role in the alliance's formation. Indeed, one of the reasons why a new entity was created in the first place, instead of merely enlarging the Brussels treaty membership, was the incompatibility of the latter with Canadian-American agreements.[48] And it is true that Reid and other officials continued to entertain high hopes for the therapeutic virtues of the counterweight metaphor, in the North American setting. But what is striking is the scant impact such sentimentality had upon concrete developments: very little of the planning of North America's defence took place in NATO precincts.

Bilateral defence matters might have been brought within the alliance's ambit. After all, in 1949 five strategic regional planning groups had been created, each charged with planning operations in the NATO zones — including one for the Canada-US region (the CUSRPG). As early as August 1949, when talks began on the future military structure of the alliance, Pearson considered it unnecessary to create a chiefs of staff committee for the North American region, even though such committees were set up for the four other regions, in large part because he thought the existing mechanisms (in particular the MCC) were working well.[49]

Nevertheless, at the beginning of 1950, Canadian diplomats did begin to envisage transferring some attributes of the PJBD (and therefore of the MCC) to the CUSRPG. American military personnel resisted this suggestion, fearing that it would give Europeans a voice in North American continental defence matters and, as a result, in the control of those elements of the country's nuclear deterrent on American soil. They also feared that the Europeans might demand a system of air defence similar to that about to be put in place in North America, and that since the CUSRPG reported to NATO's Military Committee, sensitive information concerning the defence of North America might be transmitted to the European allies.

The chief of Canada's defence staff, General Foulkes, accepted these arguments, and his adoption of the US position ending the project, rendering futile Pearson's pleas for coordinated defence of the two continents.[50] But even though different institutions might have been planning the defence of separate continents, there were links between North America and European regional planners, given that the members of the CUSRPG were the same as those of the MCC. In practice, the only real function of the CUSRPG was to enable the Canadian military to obtain American matériel under the Mutual Defence Assistance Act (MDAA), without thereby creating a precedent that could be invoked by other states, in particular by those of Latin America.

Another occasion presented itself in 1952, when NATO members decided to transform the regional planning groups into regional commands. Despite Canadian suggestions to the contrary, the CUSRPG was the only group not to be so transformed. Aside from the usual American opposition, the Europeans did not support the proposal, since they had no wish to take on responsibilities with respect to the defence of North America.[51] With hindsight, certain commentators have observed that the maintenance of this distinction concerning the defence of North America actually worked in favour of Canadian interests.[52] This is because the setting up of a regional command position such as NATO's Supreme Allied Commander Europe (SACEUR) would have meant, for all intents and purposes, that Canadian Forces *at home* might have been under the command of an American general (as they were in Europe under SACEUR), thereby contravening a hallowed principle of Canadian defence policy. Furthermore, such a structure might have led to an increase in the American military presence in Canada.

The European counterweight — to the extent one actually existed — was not about to alleviate any potential hazards Canada might encounter in its bilateral dealings with the US. Its postulated beneficial effect may better be sought at the level of European security problems and, more generally, of East-West problems, although even here the impact of multilateralism is not at all clear. During the Korean War, for example, Canadians had only a very limited influence on American decisions that, in so many ways, might have affected Europe's security as much as Canada's.[53] Cold War cases in which the Canadian government made common cause with the European allies in a bid to influence the US were rare, if not nonexistent. To the contrary, on most significant matters, the Canadians seem to have defended positions closer to the those of the Americans than of the Europeans.

Given the importance attached by Canadians to the notion of a counterweight, what explains the lack of ardour with which they actually pressed for closer ties between the defence of the two continents? John Holmes, one of the most fervent opponents of the idea of a "two-pillared" alliance that would enshrine the distinction between the security of the two continents,[54] has suggested a possible answer to this question.

> The principal reason for keeping continental relations in a separate compartment was probably Canadians' confidence in their ability to deal with the Americans. They did not entirely swallow the American assumption of being more virtuous than other countries, but there nevertheless was a belief in Canada that North American relations were conducted on a higher moral plane than

those of other continents.... Although they would never admit for a moment that Canadian-American relations were other than those between two sovereign countries, there was a tendency in Canada to think of these relations as their own private business in which outsiders, even an international organization, should not interfere.[55]

Although the above comment was in the context of the United Nations, it also applies to the Atlantic alliance. Holmes implicitly evoked the existence of a distinct North American international order whose efficiency did not depend on the kind of dynamic or balancing inherent in multilateralism. An examination only of the immediate postwar period in Canadian-American relations might not warrant this order's being labelled a liberal one, but to the extent that it is directly descended from the practices and institutions developed since the end of the nineteenth century, what else should we call it?

The manner in which plans to transfer the functions of the PJBD or the MCC, or both, were dismissed by the Canadian government is revealing on yet another level. The decisive factor was not so much the *opposition* of the American military to the plans, but rather the favourable reception of these arguments by their Canadian counterparts. Thus the intermilitary transgovernmental coalitions that appeared during the war (and whose effect was manifest in the workings of the PJBD in those years) continued to play a significant role in decisionmaking during the 1950s.

LINES OF DEFENCE, TRANSGOVERNMENTAL COALITIONS, AND REGIONAL ORDER

The position of the different actors in various parts of the Canadian governmental apparatus at the beginning of the 1950s is sufficiently clear as to allow the drawing of certain distinctions with respect to relations with the US. As noted earlier, the political leaders, in particular St-Laurent, Claxton, and Pearson, had confidence in their southern neighbours, in part because (unlike Mackenzie King or the proponents of stronger imperial ties) they did not see these relations in terms of conflict or domination. Their discourse, formed by the experience of the war against fascism and the emergence of the Cold War, was based on Canada and the US being partners in the "free world," whose relations were based upon a common

Western liberal political heritage. The political leaders also seemed to believe that Canada had certain protective measures available to it that might limit any excessive American zeal, and serve as ultimate ramparts for the defence of Canadian interests. That they might also have considered international organizations, especially the UN and NATO, as potential counterweights indicates that their fundamental confidence in the US did not exclude a circumspect attitude in individual cases.

Given the close links established between certain influential cabinet members and the Ministry of External Affairs, it is not surprising that officials of the latter should think so much like the political leaders. St-Laurent had been minister of external affairs between 1946 and 1948, before becoming prime minister (until 1957); and Pearson had had a long career in external affairs prior to succeeding St-Laurent as minister, which position he held from 1948 until he became leader of the Liberal party in 1957. The ministry had undergone a period of profound change since the end of the 1930s, thanks to the emergence of a new generation of diplomats.[56] The new team, made up of such notable figures as Norman Robertson, Escott Reid, Hume Wrong, Dana Wilgress, and John Holmes, took an activist approach to policy, in line with Canada's postwar status as a "middle power," which would enable it to contribute to the reshaping of international order.

Unlike their predecessors, who had of necessity been preoccupied with efforts to redefine relations between the dominion and the empire, the diplomats of this rising generation were able to concentrate on Canada's place in the wider postwar world. Like the political leaders, they viewed relations with the US in a mixed way. Having witnessed at first-hand the wartime difficulties, they began to champion an "independent" foreign policy devoted to Canada's national interests. Some — the "realists" as Holmes saw them — considered American leadership of the "free world" as inevitable, meaning that Canada must manage as best it could the difficulties attendant on this reality; there ranks included Hume Wrong (ambassador to the US), Dana Wilgress (ambassador to the Soviet Union and later member of the PJBD), and Norman Robertson (high commissioner in London). Others, notably Escott Reid, were more mistrustful of American intentions and also more idealistic, and openly looked to multilateral institutions for a solution to the problems of cohabitation with the US.

Contrasted with the ambivalence of these officials were the experiences and preoccupations of Canadian military personnel and others responsible for the defence of North America. These officials had learned to work closely with their American colleagues during the war, and the tendency was reinforced afterwards, especially subsequent to the 1947 joint declaration, formalizing processes of standardization of procedures and equipment. It was particularly evident in the air forces, where personnel from both the Royal Canadian Air Force (RCAF) and the US Air Force (USAF) seem to have rapidly discovered that they shared some powerful interests. These officials worked together, often at an informal level. They tended to have the same perception of the threat, which meant that often Canadian air force thinking more closely resembled US air force thinking than it did thinking in the Ministry of External Affairs.

Air forces on both sides of the border saw political constraints as obstacles in the path of the realization of their assigned objectives. As a result, RCAF personnel minimized political (including sovereignty) considerations and tended to be preoccupied with the purely technical aspects of the projects they proposed.[57] Here, therefore, was to be found a channel of transgovernmental exchange that looked to be autonomous and could, on occasion, even short-circuit regular decisionmaking processes. Such transgovernmental solidarity began to affect those processes at the beginning of the 1950s, when the Canadian military increasingly supported American requests in negotiations concerning interception procedures and the installation of radar networks.[58] It would play a capital role in the final stage of the integration of continental air defence, leading to the formation of a unified air defence command.

Fears about an air attack on North America had begun to develop and intensify in the months following the joint declaration of February 1947. The Soviets deployed their first long-range bomber in 1947, and were thought to be well on the road to developing a nuclear weapon (which they would do in July 1949); accordingly, US defence planning began to focus on air defence systems for American territory. In Canada, Claxton only slowly convinced himself of the possibility of a massive air offensive against North America (though he had thought conceivable a simple diversionary attack); thus it was not until December 1948 that the first two Canadian fighter squadrons were activated. These would fly US F-86 interceptors until such time as they could be equipped with the CF-100 "Canuck," the first (and last) fighter jet entirely conceived in Canada and used in active service.

Heightened international tensions also revealed themselves in the Arctic, where American military action had steadily been increasing since 1946.

A November 1947 report to the cabinet secretary, A. D. P. Heeney, indicated that the Americans seemed to be taking control of certain airfields in the far north.[59] Not until the 1948 creation of an advisory committee on northern development, however, would Ottawa become seized of the problem. Although the first reports presented to the committee turned out to be exaggerated, members were troubled to learn that it was impossible to know the number of American soldiers stationed in the region. Moreover, they were told that these soldiers showed little respect for the procedures in place to govern their activities on Canadian territory.[60]

But just as in 1940-42, the perceived Soviet threat to Canada had the effect of diminishing the significance of sovereignty considerations, and discussions of American "military infiltration" took up less and less of the committee's time during 1949. Ottawa adopted a series of measures aimed at controlling American activities, notably the increase of a Canadian military presence in the region, and the situation appeared less worrisome by the beginning of the 1950s. The relative facility with which the two governments found mutually acceptable solutions, despite some dissatisfaction here and there, indicates that their Second World War experience bore fruit: the norms and practices worked out with such great difficulty then, seemed now to have been sufficiently assimilated by the actors as to have become durable.

Starting in 1950, Canadian-American continental defence discussions would centre around three questions: 1) interception of unidentified aircraft nearing the continent; 2) American military basing in Newfoundland; and 3) radar coverage of the continent. In August 1950, Washington asked Ottawa to authorize USAF planes controlled from the US to intercept unidentified aircraft over Canadian territory. Ottawa deemed the request excessive, but agreed to open discussions on the matter. This led to an August 1951 PJBD recommendation to authorize either country to send fighter jets into the other's air space in order to track unidentified aircraft flying towards their territory, if the other country was not able to do so itself; the intercepting jet must, however, be placed under the operational control of the "host" country. An additional PJBD recommendation called for the emergency deployment of the air force of each country in the territory of the other, but again under the operational control of the host.

USAF officials saw the recommendations more as hindrances than as help, and demanded further discussions with the hope of getting Ottawa's approval to carry out interceptions over Canadian territory as expeditiously as possible — in effect, through some form of "pre-clearing" procedure. The PJBD suggested, in January 1953, that measures be adopted authorizing the peacetime interception of enemy aircraft over the territory of either country in the event one country were unable to do so itself; this recommendation was accepted by Canada in November, after the detonation of a Soviet thermonuclear device increased the salience of air defence.[61] Although Canadian prerogatives seemed secure enough on paper, in practice the holes in the Canadian defence system, in the Prairies and in Newfoundland, meant that the USAF would immediately assume operational control of any interceptions in those areas. More generally, the Americans expected the RCAF to delegate its authority in the event of an emergency.

The provisions concerning operational control were important to the Canadians. In theory, they conformed to the principle that Canadian authorities would maintain control over any US forces stationed on, or operational in, Canada. In practice, things were otherwise. The principle of Canadian control over US forces was thrown into question in three stages.

Unlike so many of America's allies, Canada had not been obliged to accept American bases on its territory after 1945, apart from the exceptional circumstances relating to the base at Goose Bay, Labrador, which only became Canadian territory in 1949. The Americans had leased Goose Bay from Britain in 1941, as a consequence of "destroyers for bases" exchange of September 1940. America disposed of vast powers at Goose Bay, ranging from the application of its criminal law to the exemption from taxes for both its soldiers and Newfoundland residents working there. Starting in 1947, bombers from the Strategic Air Command (SAC) were stationed at the base, which had become integrated into America's strategic infrastructure. Newfoundland's admission into Canada in 1949 posed problems, since Canada was not prepared to give the American tenants such generous rights as had been accorded by the British. A compromise was reached by which Washington agreed to modify the extraterritorial provisions adopted in 1941 in exchange for Ottawa's concession to SAC of special rights. Although the agreement bestowed Canadian sovereign control over certain aspects of the base's functioning, it was and would remain an important exception to the principle of Canadian control over foreign forces stationed on Canadian territory.[62]

The second breach of the principle came via the gradual installation of a series of radar and other alert systems during the 1950s. Washington's fear of a Soviet bomber attack from the over the North Pole pushed it to devise a network for the detection and early elimination of such a threat. Logically, part of the job had to involve Canada. For geographic, logistical, and financial reasons, Washington and Ottawa agreed to make the task a joint rather than a national undertaking.

Important to the resolution of the challenge was a PJBD recommendation, approved in 1951 but not made public until two years later, calling for the construction of what became known as the Pinetree network, a series of thirty-one radar stations arrayed along the 50th parallel; this would extend into Canadian territory a system already in place in Alaska. In 1953 and 1954, spurred on by the Soviet development of an H-bomb, Washington planned the more ambitious Distant Early Warning system, or DEW Line, which would entail radar far to the north of the Pinetree Line, along the 70th parallel. Lastly, Canada agreed to be solely responsible for the erection of a third detection system, the Mid-Canada Line (or McGill Fence), to run between the other two radar lines, along the 55th parallel. Canada agreed to contribute to the financing of two and the management of three of the systems, assuming the entire $210-million cost of the Mid-Canada Line and a third of the $160-million cost of the Pinetree Line; the US would pay all the costs of the DEW Line.[63]

It is important to note that Canadian military authorities participated willingly in breaching the principle. In 1953, before going ahead with negotiations on the DEW Line, Brooke Claxton insisted on the creation of a new entity, the Canadian-US Joint Military Study Group, which would enable the Canadian military to obtain from their American colleagues the technical information required in order to make an independent assessment of the project. This turned out to be a double-edged sword, for as David Cox recounted, Claxton and his successors were "wrong to think that Canadian Air Force officers would cast a skeptical eye on the proposals of their American conferees [in the MSG]. The first head of the Canadian section of the [group] was Air Vice-Marshall Frank Miller, one of the most aggressive advocates of Canadian-American cooperation."[64]

CREATION OF NORAD, 1956-58

The third stage of the breach came with the formation of the NORAD. Interest in an integrated air command covering the whole northern portion of North American emerged gradually. In the US, it was not until 1954 that a single air defence command took over responsibility for what had previously been divided among three forces. The two countries did not see any need for a binational air defence command until the mid 1950s.

Personnel of the RCAF and the USAF, however, convinced of the need for a joint command they believed would improve their ability to carry out their missions, brought their case to the MSG in February 1955. The latter body, in turn, sought to convince the respective countries' general staffs. But Canadian and American political leaders were circumspect, however, and refused to consider the establishment of any NATO-type command. The final proposal submitted by the general staffs for government approval, therefore, avoided all reference to the term "command," even though it was envisioned that the new entity be directed by a "commander," namely the Commander-in-Chief, Air Defense, Canada-United States (CINCADCANUS). It further limited the future headquarters to purely operational functions, and provided that the second in command to the American commander would be a Canadian.[65]

The conclusion of this agreement led in fact to the complete collapse of the principles defended by the Canadian government since the Second World War. In 1957, General Charles Foulkes, Canadian chief of staff, did not foresee any obstacle in the path of government approval of the project. He misjudged, for the general election of 10 June 1957 brought to power a Conservative government headed by John Diefenbaker. The Conservatives, out of office for twenty-two years and therefore out of touch with foreign and defence policy, were unsure how to react to the proposal. At the urging of Foulkes and George Pearkes, the new minister of defence, who presented the agreement as merely a minor accord, Diefenbaker gave his assent. An official joint announcement of the creation of the CINCADCADUS was made on 1 August 1957, with diplomatic notes being exchanged in May 1958. Several weeks after the official announcement, the new commander-in-chief requested that the organization, which was in fact a command, be called the North American Air Defence Command (NORAD).

The agreement to create NORAD resulted in the Conservative government's first crisis. Far from being simply the minor accord it was made out to be, the arrangement signalled the end of the road for the principle that Ottawa would control Canadian forces stationed in Canada. For NORAD's creation meant that a significant portion of the RCAF would henceforth be placed under the orders of an American commander. Although this last step flowed logically from the process of military integration begun nearly twenty years earlier, it was nonetheless an extremely important political event — as the Conservative government was reminded time and time again, during House of Commons debates in the fall of 1957 and the winter of 1958.

Those debates put paid to attempts to link continental air defence with NATO. General Foulkes, in a memorandum aimed at convincing the members of the new government to sign the accord, drew a close — if tortuous and exaggerated — link between NORAD and NATO, and Diefenbaker presented the agreement in this light to the House, in an attempt to calm the apprehensions surrounding it.[66] The prime minister claimed that NORAD was no more than an extension of the activities of the CUSRPG, and should be considered similar to the other regional commands of the Atlantic alliance. The categorical rebuttals of these claims by both the US and the secretary general of NATO definitively settled the matter.[67]

Most commentators agree that military advice was decisive in this affair. The role of civilian bureaucrats was limited, and restricted to raising the alarm about the potential risk for the norm of consultation. Though the Department of External Affairs had but a limited role, officials there did come up with a suggestion regarding the safeguarding of consultative procedures that, had it been accepted as policy, would have preserved the core of the commitments undertaken eighteen years earlier at Ogdensburg. But in matters related to air defence, the consultation norm was honoured more in the breach than in the observance.[68] There were reasons why consultation would be difficult, and the Cuban missile crisis four years later would lay these bare: it is impossible to follow "normal" politico-military consultative procedure during a crisis, while at the same time respecting operational realities.

The governments did, however, seek to increase the level of peacetime *political* consultation. The most serious effort in this direction was the creation of a Canadian-American joint ministerial committee on defence, in August 1958. The committee's mandate was vague, described thusly in a Canadian note:

1. To consult periodically on any matters affecting the joint defense of Canada and the United States;

2. In particular, to exchange information and views at the Ministerial level on problems that may arise, with a view to strengthening further the close and intimate cooperation between the two Governments on joint defense matters;

3. To report to the respective Governments on such discussions in order that consideration may be given to measures deemed appropriate and necessary to improve defense cooperation.[69]

The committee was to be an annual forum of Canadian and American ministers of external affairs, defence, and finance; it met only four times — in 1958, 1959, 1960, and 1964 — before falling into oblivion. While the personal animosity between Diefenbaker and key figures in the Kennedy administration may explain the absence of meetings between 1960 and 1964, the committee was primarily done in by a lack of subjects for discussion sufficiently important to justify the attendance of its high-level membership. There was one exception: the issue of nuclear arms for the Canadian Forces. Day to day management of most other defence affairs was adequately handled by such entities as the PJBD and the MCC, to say nothing of diplomatic channels and informal intergovernmental contacts.

NORAD, despite the support it regularly attracts in Canadian public opinion surveys, has been one of the arrangements that provoked, and continue to provoke, virulent criticism by commentators and historians, in part due to the questionable role played by the military in its creation, but also because it contributed, more than any other international agreement, to a reduction of Canada's autonomous decisionmaking authority, with all that this implies for Canadian sovereignty. As Desmond Morton put it: the NORAD agreement "conceded to Washington a control over Canadian autonomy that Whitehall had not claimed in generations."[70] The rules of engagement, combined with the existence of an integrated command led by an American officer, meant that Canadian air power could be sent into battle without Ottawa having any say in the matter — in other words, that Canada could be at war without having had the opportunity to make that decision. Furthermore, this integrated command signified that Canada was henceforth going to be tied not only to the American military's territorial defensive structures, but also to their *offensive* ones. For NORAD was charged with sounding the alert that could ultimately lead to an American launch of nuclear weapons. The creation of NORAD was to fuel and complicate the debate over the acquisition of defensive nuclear arms by the Canadian Forces.

Apart from the political problems engendered by its creation, NORAD stands out in having been merely the logical conclusion of a dynamic of military integration begun in 1947, if not in 1940. From a strictly military standpoint, it was and remains a valuable entity, one that does not reflect the real differential in power between the two partners. As Serge Bernier has pointed out, despite the expectation that an arrangement between two such disparate powers should have led to frequent disagreements, especially triggered by the "smaller" ally, the reality has been otherwise: "very few traces of daily problems ... remain."[71]

Although the principle of political consultation in times of crisis proved impracticable, and regular high-level consultation unnecessary — at least in the limited context of this accord — it is nonetheless true that military consultation on a daily basis has worked relatively well. NORAD does permit a form of reciprocity. The Canadian military, sensitive to the frequent criticism of the unified command structure, have been quick to point out that the second in command is always a Canadian, and that given the frequent absence of the American commander, it can be argued that a Canadian is often responsible for *American* as well as *North American* air defence. Such was the case on the morning of 11 September 2001.

NORTH AMERICA'S LIBERAL ORDER AND CONTINENTAL DEFENCE

The general view of the decade 1947-57 is that the Canadian government had no choice: American pressure on it was too strong, given that the Cold War was at its apogee and that the USSR had made rapid progress in developing nuclear arms and long-range bombers. The so-called "bomber gap," publicized in 1956, testifies to the then climate of insecurity in the US, even though we now know the perceived threat had little relation to objective reality. The Canadians had little ability to evaluate the situation themselves, and even less to oppose American projects. Faced with a unilateral definition of the threat and proposed American countermeasures, the best Ottawa could hope for was to limit the damage to its sovereignty.

The scale of these American countermeasures was such as to prevent Canada from maintaining the wartime and early postwar principle that it had sole responsibility for military activities conducted on its territory. It was clearly beyond Canada's reach at the beginning of the 1950s to put in place a purely Canadian system that would suffice to calm American security fears.

Canadians indeed had reason to worry and protest. Pearson's expressed regret about Canada's not being consulted, in 1953, about certain American continental defence decisions drew a scathing response from Acheson and, later, from Dulles.[72] The creation of close security relations with the US did not provide Canada with a "special relationship" capable of giving it a measure of influence over the shaping of American policy. The Canadian government did not attain a singular status allowing it entrée to the mysteries of American security policy, nor did Ottawa even get the privilege of being consulted on a priority basis, even when American decisions would affect Canadian security.

This negative assessment begs to be qualified. For generally speaking, Canadian-American relations during the period 1948 to 1956 (the Eisenhower-St-Laurent years) were harmonious, even cordial. Official American documents of the time reveal a different situation, of American political authorities being conscious of the sensitivities of a Canadian government bent on defending the country's sovereignty and its prerogatives, and of treating Canada with a certain regard. The documents that set out the framework for continental defence and stressed the necessity of strengthened cooperation with Canada had a relatively conciliatory tone. Thus the modified National Security Document 159, of 16 September 1953, affirmed that

> Canadian agreement and participation on an adequate scale is essential to any effective continental defense system ... [T]he Canadian government should at once be approached at the highest levels *to establish a common appreciation of the urgency... [T]he United States should be prepared to agree that Canada take leadership in developing parts of the system and contribute to its expense.*[73]

In contrast with Claxton's fatalism or Pearson's impatience, St-Laurent was prepared to recognize the positive nature of Canada's relationship with the US:

> We have been negotiating many times with our American neighbours. We have been agreeing to a great many things and they have been agreeing to do a great many things. But never have we been made to feel that we obliged to agree to something because they were bigger and stronger than we were.[74]

The tension between the American attitude, both cavalier and respectful, and the prickly yet ultimately conciliatory Canadian reaction makes sense when it is seen not as the result of the conflict dimension of a relationship between two sovereign entities united by a common threat (as the realists would have it), but rather as the product of the relations between two societies so closely bound together that they seem to engender the formation of a political community. St-Laurent diplomatically presented the problematique of the bilateral relationship when he told the House of Commons, in April 1948, that occasionally problems could arise as a result of an American tendency, "at times a trifle embarrassing," to want to flatter Canadians, and to treat them as being basically indistinguishable from them. Thus, even though they possessed no malice whatsoever to Canada, Americans could sometimes forget that "we are as sensitive as any other nation about having control over our own affairs; if any country can be said to have control of its own affairs these days."[75]

Bilateral institutions, despite their questionable value in the eyes of Canadian nationalists, have given Canada a margin of maneuverability that it would not otherwise have possessed. Through them, Canadian leaders have been able to define the terms of an American military presence that, in a crisis, might have been much more onerous than they turned out to be. Ottawa was thus able to conserve a minimum of control over activities carried out on its territory and, above all, to ensure that such activities did not call into question the integrity of that territory. John Holmes, in summing up the impact of those bilateral institutions between 1940 and 1957, concludes:

> Those few [continental] institutions that were continued or set up new, whether they were formal bodies or agreed principles, were designed to stake out and protect the Canadian interest against the uninhibited power of American society. The protective role of the IJC and the PJBD is obvious. The 1947 Joint Statement on Defence and the 1950 Statement of Principles for Economic Cooperation enunciate guidelines to which not only the Canadian government can appeal but also the United States administration when Congress feels unrestrained. They will not always work, but they are better than no code at all. Likewise, of course, the United States can thereby expect the Canadian government to play fair. NORAD, which seems a step in the continentalization of North American defence, can be regarded from another angle as a means of preserving a Canadian role and an appropriate degree of sovereignty in a situation in which, if there were no rules, the Americans would simply take over the defence of the continent.[76]

Furthermore, the transnationalist approach also seems to explain outcomes better than does realist alliance theory. As stated earlier, the most convincing factor in accounting for the dynamic of bilateral military cooperation during the 1950s was the formation of increasingly close *transgovernmental* coalitions —in this case, between the two countries' air forces. These officers were able to formulate their own conception of the respective national interests, and consequently, their own list of priorities, because of their professional nature, their isolation from the hurly-burly of politics, and the absence of close relations between the ministries of defence and of foreign relations. In the context of an alliance with a great power, the Canadian military became subject to the influence of their American colleagues.[77]

What sociopolitical factors permitted the formation, after the Ogdensburg declaration, of these powerful transgovernmental coalitions? Even more to the point, can we really cite military transgovernmentalism as an element of a "liberal order"? So long as the military is ultimately subject to civilian control, the answer would have to be, "Yes." Moreover, by the very nature of things, transgovernmental coalitions between militaries in liberal democracies tend to evince greater solidarity and cohesiveness than purely civilian transgovernmental groupings. Their being subject to the same kind of constraints — legislative control of the budget, sensitivity to public opinion, regular changing of political figures, constitutional subordination and marginalization in political life, missions largely if not exclusively oriented towards external threats — results in fostering of in-group solidarity. The support the Canadian and American militaries offered each other to convince the respective political authorities to endorse their large-scale defence proposals substantiates this.

The creation of transgovernmental solidarities can be associated with the more general phenomenon of regional integration, which can also be studied from the standpoint of the impact of norms and political values. All the bilateral institutions created since the Second World War, including those directed at security challenges, reflect the workings of the domestic institutions found in the two states, and this irrespective of whether they issued from military or civilian sources. More generally, Shelagh Grant correctly sees the bilateral agreements concluded since the war as extending the practices already in widespread use:

> The procedures and tensions involved in the negotiations for the Auto Pact, the Distant Early Warning System, the Columbia River Treaty, or, more recently,

the free trade agreement and attempts to resolve sovereign claims to the North-west Passage were vaguely similar to those involved in Canada's federal-provincial relations.... The question which should concern Canadians is whether the country is moving from *de facto* North American binational confederation, less formalized that the European Economic Community, to-wards an unofficial co-operative federal-style association.[78]

Similarly, the process leading to the creation of NORAD is not funda-mentally different from that relating to the reorganization of internal national military structures. Had it not been for the circumstances surrounding its conclusion, the NORAD agreement would probably have gone unnoticed, at least for a time. It represents not only the logical extension of the strat-egy embarked upon by the two countries since the end of the 1930s, but also that of the two liberal states' domestic political practices.

Notes

[1]John W. Holmes, *The Shaping of Peace: Canada and the Search for World Order, 1943-1957*, vol. 1 (Toronto: University of Toronto Press, 1979), p. 160.

[2]Ibid., p. 160.

[3]As he remarked before the standing committee on external affairs and na-tional defence of the House of Commons, on 10 October 1985.

[4]For example, see Joseph T. Jockel, "The Canada-United States Military Co-operation Committee and Continental Air Defence, 1946," *Canadian Historical Review* 64 (September 1983): 352-77; Idem, "The Military Establishments and the Creation of NORAD," *American Review of Canadian Studies* 12 (Autumn 1982): 1-16; and Idem, *No Boundaries Upstairs: Canada, the United States, and the Origins of North American Air Defence, 1945-1958* (Vancouver: University of British Columbia Press, 1987).

[5]For example, Christopher Conliffe, "The Permanent Joint Board on Defense, 1940-1988," in *The U.S.-Canada Security Relationship: The Politics, Strategy, and Technology of Defense*, ed. David G. Haglund and Joel J. Sokolsky (Boulder: Westview, 1989), pp. 145-65.

[6]Robert O. Keohane and Joseph S. Nye, *Power and Interdependence: World Politics in Transition* (Boston: Little, Brown, 1977); Roger Frank Swanson, "An Analytical Assessment of the United States-Canadian Defense Issue Area," in *Canada and the United States: Transnational and Transgovernmental Relations*, ed. Annette Baker Fox, Alfred Hero, and Joseph S. Nye (New York: Columbia University Press, 1976), pp. 188-209. The transgovernmental approach is also employed by Ann Denholm Crosby, "A Middle-Power Military in Alliance: Canada

and NORAD," *Journal of Peace Research* 34 (February 1997): 37-52. It is implicit in the work of David Cox, "Canada and NORAD, 1958-1978: A Cautionary Retrospective," *Aurora Papers* no. 1 (Ottawa: Canadian Centre for Arms Control and Disarmament, 1985); and in that of J. L. Granatstein, "The American Influence on the Canadian Military, 1939-1963," in *Canada's Defence: Perspective on Policy in the Twentieth Century*, ed. Barry D. Hunt and Ronald G. Haycock (Toronto: Copp Clark Pitman, 1993), pp. 129-39.

[7]For this dynamic, see John S. Duffield, "International Regimes and Alliance Behavior: Explaining NATO Conventional Force Levels," *International Organization* 46 (Autumn 1992): 819-55; see pp. 839, 845.

[8]Shelagh D. Grant, *Sovereignty or Security? Government Policy in the Canadian North, 1936-1950* (Vancouver: University of British Columbia Press, 1988), p. 242.

[9]These principles were enunciated in Escott Reid's 1937 analysis, "Canada and the Threat of War," reproduced in *Canadian Foreign Policy: Historical Readings*, ed. J. L. Granatstein (Toronto: Copp Clark Pitman, 1986), pp. 118-24.

[10]Louis St-Laurent, "The Foundation of Canadian Policy in World Affairs," Toronto, 13 January 1947 (commonly known as the Gray Lecture); published in Government of Canada, *Statements and Speeches*, no. 47/2 (Ottawa: Information Division, Department of External Affairs, 1947); Donald M. Page, "Introduction," *Documents on Canadian External Relations* (Ottawa: Supply and Services Canada, 1977). (Hereafter cited as *DCER*.)

[11]Anne-Marie Burley, "Regulating the World: Multilateralism, International Law, and the Projection of the New Deal Regulatory State," in *Multilateralism Matters*, ed. John G. Ruggie (New York: Columbia University Press, 1993), pp. 125-56; Lawrence Aronsen, "From World War to Cold War: Cooperation and Competition in the North Atlantic Triangle, 1945-1949," in *The North Atlantic Triangle in a Changing World: Anglo-American-Canadian Relations, 1902-1956*, ed. Brian J. C. McKercher and Aronsen (Toronto: University of Toronto Press, 1996), pp. 184-85.

[12]R (anon.), "Neighbors: A Canadian View," *Foreign Affairs* 10 (April 1932): 423. On this policy convergence during the interwar years, see David G. Haglund, "'Are *We* the Isolationists?' North American Isolationism in a Comparative Context," *International Journal* 58 (Winter 2002-3): 1-23.

[13]For example, see C. P. Stacey, *Canada and the Age of Conflict: A History of Canadian External Policies*, vol. 2: *1921-1948: The Mackenzie King Era* (Toronto: University of Toronto Press, 1981).

[14]John Herd Thompson and Stephen J. Randall, *Canada and the United States: Ambivalent Allies* (Montreal and Kingston: McGill-Queen's University Press, 1994), p. 180. Also see Robert Bothwell, *The Big Chill: Canada and the Cold War*, Contemporary Affairs no. 1 (Toronto: CIIA/Irwin, 1998).

[15]James Eayrs, *In Defence of Canada*, vol. 3: *Peacemaking and Deterrence* (Toronto: University of Toronto Press, 1972), pp. 331-32.

[16]Louis St-Laurent, *Hansard*, 29 April 1948, 4: 3443.

[17]Holmes, *Shaping of Peace*, vol. 2, pp. 76-77.

[18]"Final Report of Advisory Committee on Post-Hostilities Problems," January-February 1945; in *DCER*, 11: 1567-73. The strategic significance of polar air routes had already been prefigured during the war itself; see Walter Lippmann, *U.S. Foreign Policy: Shield of the Republic* (Boston: Little, Brown, 1943), pp. 119-20.

[19]J. H. Jenkins, 16 March 1943, in *DCER*, 9: 1197.

[20]See a telegram King sent on 3 October 1946; in *DCER*, 12: 1334-35.

[21]Lawrence Martin, *The Presidents and the Prime Ministers* (Toronto: Doubleday, 1982), pp. 147-48.

[22]Lester B. Pearson, *Politique mondiale et démocratie* (Paris: La Colombe, 1958), p. 147.

[23]W. Eric C. Harrison, "Canadian-American Defence," *International Journal* 5 (Summer 1950): 190-91.

[24]"Final Report of Advisory Committee on Post-Hostilities Problems," *DCER*, 11: 1568. On the report itself, see Eayrs, *In Defence of Canada*, 3: 331.

[25]"Problems of Canadian-United States Cooperation in the Arctic," 29 October 1946; cited in Grant, *Sovereignty or Security?*, p. 308 (emphasis added).

[26]Quoted in Martin, *Presidents and Prime Ministers*, p. 148.

[27]*DCER*, 12: 1555-66.

[28]Lester B. Pearson, "Canada Looks 'Down North'," *Foreign Affairs* 24 (July 1946): 643 (emphasis added).

[29]*DCER*, 12: 1615-27.

[30]Jockel, *No Boundaries Upstairs*, pp. 20-21.

[31]Dean Acheson, "Joint Defense Measures with Canada," memo of 26 October 1946; cited in Grant, *Sovereignty or Security?*, p. 290.

[32]A. D. P. Heeney, "Defence of North America: Canada-U.S. Joint Planning," 12 June 1946, in *DCER*, 12: 1628.

[33]See Jockel, *No Boundaries Upstairs*, pp. 27-28.

[34]Cited in Holmes, *Shaping of the Peace*, 2: 87.

[35]*DCER*, 12: 1650-53.

[36]On the memorandum and the reactions it elicited, see Denis Smith, *Diplomacy of Fear: Canada and the Cold War, 1941-1948* (Toronto: University of Toronto Press, 1988), pp. 198-212.

[37]Escott Reid, "The United States and the Soviet Union: A Study of the Possibility of War and Some of the Implications for Canadian Policy," 30 August 1947, in *DCER*, 13: 367-82, quotes at pp. 380-81.

[38]Maurice Pope, "Comments on Escott Reid's Paper...," 29 September 1947; in *DCER*, 13: 393

[39]Quoted in Eayrs, *In Defence of Canada*, 3: 321.

[40]Warwick Chipman, "Ambassador in Argentina to Under-Secretary of State for External Affairs," 7 November 1947; in *DCER*, 13: 422.

[41]See C. S. A. Ritchie, "Memorandum by Counsellor, Embassy in France," 6 November 1947; in ibid., p. 415.

[42]See Thomas Risse-Kappen, *Cooperation Among Democracies: The European Influence on U.S. Foreign Policy* (Princeton, NJ: Princeton University Press, 1995).

[43]Roger Epp, "On Justifying the Alliance: Canada, NATO and World Order," in *North American Perspectives on European Security*, ed. Michael K. Hawes and Joel J. Sokolsky (Lewiston, NY: Edwin Mellen, 1990), pp. 89-121; Robert Wolfe, "Atlanticism Without the Wall: Transatlantic Co-operation and the Transformation of Europe," *International Journal* 46 (Winter 1990-91): 137-63; Idem, "Article 2 Revisited: Canada, Security, and Transatlantic Economic Cooperation," in *North American Perspectives*, pp. 305-35.

[44]Stéphane Roussel, "L'instant kantien: la contribution canadienne à la création de la 'communauté nord-atlantique' (1947-1949)," in *Le Canada et la guerre froide, 1943-1957*, ed. Greg Donahy (Ottawa: Ministère des Affaires étrangères et du Commerce international, 1999), pp. 119-56.

[45]Holmes, *Shaping of the Peace*, 2: 106.

[46]Quoted in John Sutherland, "Canada's Long Term Strategic Situation," *International Journal* 27 (Summer 1962): 207.

[47]Lester B. Pearson, *Memoirs*, vol. 2: *1948-57: The International Years* (Toronto: University of Toronto Press, 1973), pp. 32-33.

[48]Memo written by T. A. Stone, 28 July 1948; in *DCER*, 14: 546.

[49]Pearson, in a telegram of 24 August 1949; in *DCER*, 15: 652.

[50]See Jockel, *No Boundaries Upstairs*, pp. 96-97.

[51]William R. Willoughby, *The Joint Organizations of Canada and the United States* (Toronto: University of Toronto Press, 1979), p. 133.

[52]Joel J. Sokolsky, "A Seat at the Table: Canada and Its Alliances," in *Canada's Defence*, p. 152.

[53]Martin Kitchen, "From Korean War to Suez: Anglo-American-Canadian Relations, 1950-1956," in *North Atlantic Triangle in a Changing World*, pp. 220-55.

[54]John W. Holmes, "The Dumbbell Won't Do," *Foreign policy*, no. 50 (Spring 1983), pp. 3-22.

[55]Holmes, *Shaping of the Peace*, 2: 252-53.

[56]J. L. Granatstein, *The Ottawa Men: The Civil Service Mandarins, 1935-1957* (Toronto: Oxford University Press, 1982).

[57]See Crosby, "Middle-Power Military."

[58]Jockel, *No Boundaries Upstairs*, pp. 44-45, 51.

[59]W. W. Bean, "Control of Arctic Projects," 13 November 1947, *DCER*, 13: 1516-19.

[60]See Grant, *Sovereignty or Security?*, pp. 223-26.

[61]Cox, "Canada and NORAD," p. 8.

[62]See David J. Bercuson, "SAC vs. Sovereignty: The Origins of the Goose Bay Lease, 1946-52," *Canadian Historical Review* 70 (June 1989): 206-22; and

Raymond B. Blake, "An Old Problem in a New Province: Canadian Sovereignty and the American Bases in Newfoundland, 1948-1952," *American Review of Canadian Studies* 23 (Summer 1993): 183-201.

[63]Michel Fortmann, "La politique de défense canadienne," in *De Mackenzie King à Pierre Trudeau: Quarante ans de diplomatie canadienne, 1945-1985*, ed. Paul Painchaud (Québec: Presses de l'Université Laval, 1988), pp. 479-81.

[64]Cox, "Canada and NORAD," p. 14.

[65]Jockel, "Military Establishments."

[66]*Hansard*, 13 November 1957, 2: 1059-62; 21 December 1957, 3: 2719-24.

[67]Fortmann, "La politique de défense," p. 489.

[68]Serge Bernier, "La perception du NORAD par divers commentateurs du Canada," *Revue internationale d'histoire militaire*, no. 54 (1982), pp. 256-57.

[69]Cited in Willoughby, *Joint Organizations*, p. 144.

[70]Desmond Morton, "Defending the Indefensible: Some Historical Perspectives on Canadian Defence, 1867-1967," *International Journal* 42 (Autumn 1987): 640.

[71]Bernier, "La perception du NORAD," p. 249.

[72]Martin, *President and Prime Ministers*, pp. 171-72.

[73]Quoted in Cox, "Canada and NORAD," p. 10 (emphasis added).

[74]Quoted in Martin, *Presidents and Prime Ministers*, p. 164.

[75]Louis St-Laurent, *Hansard*, 29 April 1948, 4: 3443.

[76]Holmes, *Shaping of the Peace*, 2: 291.

[77]Crosby, "Middle-Power Military," pp. 40-41.

[78]Grant, *Sovereignty or Security?*, p. 241.

PART THREE

CONCLUSION

CHAPTER EIGHT

Conclusion

THE NORTH AMERICAN LIBERAL ORDER

Politicians and commentators during the first quarter of the twentieth century liked to stress that relations between the two North American neighbours were different from those between European states. Nevertheless, "North Americanism" lost its exceptional quality with the advent of the Western European security community. Today, as has been the case for several decades, we can say that the chief characteristic of the North American international order derives not from something unique to the Canadian-American relationship, but rather from a quality equally on display in Western Europe in the postwar era, something broadly known as an international "liberal order."

The particular North American aspect of this order has often been overlooked because, unlike various European international systems created after major conflicts,[1] its elements are defined more by practices than by formal enunciations. This absence of stated formal principles reflects the parties' desire to preserve a maximum of latitude in the conduct of their security policy. This order has, however, well and truly existed; it is apparent in the patterns of cooperation between the two states and comes most into focus when these patterns are viewed through the prism of their shared liberal values. In other words, this convergence of values helps to explain the dynamic of Canadian-American security relations, and does so throughout the period studied in this monograph. A brief summary of the terms underlying this book's thesis, and their application to the two main areas of military cooperation — conflict resolution and common defence — illustrates this causal link.

The process that enabled the two governments peacefully to resolve their differences during the last quarter of the nineteenth century is part of a broader trend that has militated against interstate war in North America ever since 1814. Even though good arguments can be mustered to support explanations for this trend that differ from the one I offer here (for instance, the claim that the Anglo-American balance of power has kept the continental peace), certain elements work in favour of the "democratic peace" thesis that I have relied upon in this book. The principal argument in favour of this thesis depends less upon the political élites of the two states sharing certain liberal-democratic values and norms than it does upon these latter having at least in part determined the way in which Canadians and Americans perceived each others' intentions. Admittedly, to the extent that what really interested the Americans during much of this period were *British* intentions, the phenomenon is less evident on the American side. Nevertheless, after the Civil War the only project developed for the annexation of Canada was one in keeping with liberal political ideas; for it was assumed by its promoters that annexation could only be worth accomplishing if done with the consent of the Canadian population.

On the Canadian side, the phenomenon is clearly evident. What divided the political élite of the era when it came to divining the American government's intentions was the degree to which they understood the American political system to be a liberal-democratic one. Those who thought the US a weak or corrupt democracy — typically the Conservatives and the Imperialists — distrusted America's leaders, and readily attributed to them hostile intentions; thus they could and did take the annexationist discourse seriously. By contrast, those who held the American political system to be a working democratic regime in conformity with liberal values — most typically they were associated with the Liberal and Reform parties — were likely to interpret American intentions in a friendlier manner, posing no political or military threat to Canada.

This observation, although most clearly applicable between 1867 and the end of the 1920s, in fact applies for the entire period studied in these pages. After the 1920s, the perceptions of Canada's Liberal and Conservative leaders tended to converge, with few in any doubt about the liberal-democratic character of the American political system. And to the extent the Conservatives continued to promote an anti-American discourse, it was sustained more by economic and cultural nationalism than by mistrust of the US political regime; indeed, many Conservative initiatives, both in the economic and the military (e.g., NORAD) dimensions, worked in favour of rapprochement between the two countries.

Contrary to what realist theory would predict, these attitudes did not vary according to the level of geopolitical upheaval in North America during the 1860s and subsequent decades. Although periods of tension and calm could alternate rapidly during these years as a result of one crisis or another capable of leading to armed conflict (e.g., in 1862, 1866, 1896, and 1903), Canadian élites' reading of American intentions remained relatively stable. Liberal and Reformist confidence in Washington was not seriously affected by the crises, whereas the Conservatives maintained their latent mistrust, notwithstanding signs of a marked improvement in the relations with the US. And even the most noteworthy Liberal exception to the rule, namely Mackenzie King's wartime misgivings, which grew after the death of FDR in April 1945, did not lead him to question the 1946-47 renewal of military cooperation with Washington.

The convergence of liberal values may not have been the only cause of the "long peace" between the countries, but it certainly was not a bit player in the evolution of bilateral security and defence cooperation, *pace* the legions of analysts who prefer to see cooperation as the byproduct of the Anglo-American balance of power. That balance was obviously important, but so too were the "subjective" elements bound up in the way the actors perceived each others' intentions.[2]

The process of peaceful conflict resolution, more than the actual absence of war, provides perhaps the best evidence of the existence of an international liberal order. To the extent that the resolution of conflicts results in an internationalization of these norms, the convergence of liberal values and norms manifests itself most clearly at this level. The ad hoc committees of equal representation created for the resolution of territorial quarrels incarnated, almost from the outset, those international norms that seem directly inspired by the hard-core liberal values of equality, peaceful resolution of differences, depoliticization of conflicts, and respect for the law. At the turn of the century these practices, and the norms on which they were based, became institutionalized through the International Boundary Commission, the International Fisheries Commission and, above all, the International Joint Commission. As several commentators have noted, these international procedures aimed at levelling power differences reflected the two states' internal methods of dealing with conflicts, and thus testified both to the shared internal norms and the confidence each government had in the judicial system of the other state. This is yet another indication that the North American order results in large part from the internationalization of liberal norms.

The institutions set up initially to resolve conflicts appear to have strongly influenced those created after 1940 to coordinate common defence efforts. The Permanent Joint Board of Defence best displays this heritage, both in its workings and its composition. The same influence is perceptible, albeit to a lesser degree, in the institutions created subsequently, notably the MCC, the MSG and NORAD. Their exclusively military and technical nature, coupled with the virtual absence of civilians, accounts in large part for the less-visible impact of liberal norms upon their functioning. Still, influence derived from converging political values comes through clearly when we regard the emergence and multiplication of transgovernmental links, in the military domain no less than elsewhere.

Canadian-American relations in the common defence conform in many ways to Risse-Kappen's model of "cooperation between democracies." Relations are founded upon such norms as the obligation to consult, the search for compromise and consensus, and the respect of equality; for this reason certain negative effects typical of a power imbalance, such as recourse to force, threat, and coercion, are absent.

It is further arguable that the recognition of the existence of this liberal North American order, which minimizes the negative effects of the continental power imbalance, calls into question the idea that such a liberal international order must, a priori, be a *multilateral* one. The conflict-resolution procedures adopted in North America are interesting in that they stem from a *bilateral* relationship, firstly Anglo-American, and then Canadian-American. It is not surprising that the UK and the US should have set up such procedures on an ad hoc basis, once they had achieved military parity during the late nineteenth century. What *is* surprising, however, is that the Americans agreed to extend this approach to the Canadians. It is thus tempting to conclude that the emergence and strengthening of the North American order had more to do with the convergence of values and norms than with the number of players (as the institutionalists argue) or the balance of power (as the realists argue). The evolution of continental defence cooperation tends to reinforce this conclusion: the formation of multilateral institutions (UN and NATO) had only a small impact on the Canadian-American bilateral security relationship, despite the hopes of certain Canadian diplomats to the contrary.

The above conclusions differ in one respect from those of Risse-Kappen, who argues that the democratic nature of transatlantic relations enabled European governments to influence decisionmaking in Washington during such major international crises as those arising over the Korean war, Suez, Berlin, and Cuba. Despite the expressed desire of Canadian leaders and diplomats, Ottawa has never been able to lay claim to a "special relationship" with the US giving it influence over the broad contours of American security policy. Although the liberal order certainly enables Canada to resist American projects directly affecting it, it does not confer any ability to affect *American* decisions beyond the North American defence arena. The difference between multilateralism and bilateralism can no doubt be found on this level.

It should, however, be noted that my examination of conflict resolution and common defence procedures only concerns cases in which the territorial security of the two states was directly in question, rather than peripheral crises. In only rare cases (the 1940 surrender of France, and the Cuban missile crisis) did extra-continental incidents have such a direct impact on North American defence as to necessitate intensive Canadian-American consultations, and in the latter case they were carried out at the multilateral level, both in the UN and in NATO. The cases I have chosen to examine here do not, therefore, allow an in-depth comparison with Risse-Kappen's conclusions.

THE NORTH AMERICAN TANGO: CYCLICAL OR EVOLUTIONARY?

This study of the impact of values and norms on the Canadian-American relationship has sought to formulate an alternative to the counterweight theory that has largely dominated the historiography of Canadian foreign relations and security policy. As with most realist-inspired proposals, that theory rests on a cyclical view of history, and sees the dynamic of the relationship as alternating phases in the balance of power. The defining characteristic of Canadian-American relations is power imbalance, and the disparity is such that it affects all interactions between the two countries. According to the theory of regional balance of power, Canada was able effectively to manage its asymmetrical security relationship with the US only because a counterweight existed, first in the British Empire, subsequently in NATO, and this allowed for a rebalancing of the power differential. The theory is said to explain not only the egalitarian nature of the Canadian-American relationship throughout most of its history, but also the difficulties in cooperation experienced during the years 1940-49. Britain, weakened by the First World War and then confronting Hitler, was no long able to play the role of counterweight during those years; it was only upon the formation of the Atlantic alliance that a new equilibrium could be reached.

This theory has some weaknesses, discussed in earlier chapters. The increasing power differential between the UK and the US over the period 1867 to 1936, when Britain was in relative decline and America was waxing, does not seem significantly to have affected the relationship — and the "counterweight" was purely theoretical after 1871. From the standpoint of the realists, it is anomalous that peace could have been maintained between the two countries throughout this period when war was still an option, and any number of disputes could have led to it. A second anomaly from their standpoint is the cooperative nature of the Canadian-American relationship: from the end of the nineteenth century, the most important issues tended to be dealt with bilaterally, with informal, ad hoc cooperative relations established on an egalitarian basis. In addition, the relationship improved when the British withdrew from the scene.

By the start of the 1940s, the two countries were well along on a formal process of cooperation, one that meant war simply no longer could be taken seriously as a possible means of conflict resolution between them; strangely, the power imbalance was most evident precisely when the countries were establishing formal relations for security cooperation. Although Canada experienced, during the brief period 1940-46, certain problems related to this unequal balance of power, wartime documents show that it managed the situation well. During the period 1947-58, the cooperative relationship deepened and the major wartime problems faded away. Canadian-American relations, although characterized by fundamental differences in power, were based on the principle of equality — even though the hoped-for European counterweight turned out to be as ethereal as the British one had become, at least insofar as concerned issues related to the common defence of North America.

These anomalies show that a simple analysis based on the distribution of power cannot adequately explain the Canadian-American relationship. The US does not completely dominate Canada, as such a theory would predict. Accordingly, an intersubjective dimension must be added to a strictly rationalist approach if we seek to account for the anomalies. The introduction of liberal values and norms and the mutual perceptions of the actors changes the equation and transforms the history of the security relationship between the two countries from a cycle to an evolutionary process, an integral part of a progressivist view of history. The thesis of the North American liberal order is better able to account for this pattern than any alternative construes. From this standpoint, the Canadian-American relationship evolved from one sometimes marked by armed conflict, to peaceful coexistence with sometime hostile but nonviolent undertones, to improvised forms of cooperation dictated by the urgency of the moment, and ultimately to cooperation structured by norms and formal institutions.

The evolution corresponded to a process whereby the actors learned and integrated the norms. The process had its origins in an internationalization of norms dating back to the British- American dispute-settlement negotiations at the end of the eighteenth century and during the first half of the nineteenth century. Both sides seemed satisfied by the experience, because they increasingly resorted to ad hoc commissions to solve subsequent disputes. Each of the commissions that followed during the course of the nineteenth century (especially the Porter-Ogilvy Commission of 1817-22 and the High Commission of 1871), although modeled on the Jay treaty, contributed in its own way to elaborating the procedures and to forming the bases of a habit of cooperation. This recurrent method of conflict resolution and its evolution reveal the existence of a process whereby the actors recognized and integrated certain norms similar to those guiding the internal judicial and political workings of the two states, including equal representation, non-recourse to violence, depoliticization of problems, and the search for compromise. The agreement by Washington and Ottawa at the beginning of the twentieth century to form permanent commissions that, in turn, would adopt, elaborate, and formalize the practices of the preceding century marked the most important stage of this process.

In hindsight, it is clear that the movement from a bilateral security relationship aimed at the resolution of conflicts to a relationship based on cooperation with a view to common defence was the most difficult step, in part because urgent external events meant the omission of certain normal procedures and in part because the undertaking was such a novel one. Although the PJBD inherited the procedures and norms of the International Joint Commission, the members of the new body had the implicit task of formulating new procedures and norms suited to the activities necessary for the defence of North America. The smoothing over of difficulties experienced in 1942-43, and the fact that these never reappeared during the first decade of the Cold War, is also evidence of the evolutionary rather than cyclic nature of Canadian-American relations. The post-1945 military institutions, although sometimes the object of polemical criticism in Canada, reflected the legacy of their predecessors. They represented the end product of an evolution dictated not only by strategic considerations but also by the actors' assimilation and formalization of a set of norms.

LIBERAL ORDER OR REPUBLICAN ORDER, POST-9/11?

In the new millennium, Canadian-American relations have entered a turbulent period, one that began several months before the attacks on New York and Washington of 11 September 2001. The cordiality apparent in the bilateral relationship during the Clinton years started to dissipate, gradually but inexorably, after the George W. Bush Republicans took over in early 2001, particularly in matters of international and continental security.[3] For starters, there were disagreements over such multilateral accords as Kyoto and the International Criminal Court. But what most set things agley was the aftermath of 11 September, particularly the way it seemed to have led ineluctably to the Iraq war of 2003. Canadians became increasingly worried that the US had abandoned multilateralism and was launched upon a security-driven program of seeking unilateral solutions to problems.

Canadians were especially preoccupied by what was happening in the North American *homeland*. Even before the events of 11 September, relations between the two countries concerning the joint defence of the continent were changing to such an extent that it became possible to detect a fourth phase of cooperation. As we have seen, the first phase (1867-1914) involved the transition from peaceful coexistence to the resolution of conflicts. The second phase (1914-45) witnessed the passage from conflict resolution to the common defence. The third (1945-58) concerned the Cold War-inspired need to extend and deepen continental defence. During the four decades that followed the creation of NORAD in the late 1950s, the continental arrangements functioned reasonably "normally," and very few changes took place in the institutional landscape of North American defence.

The current, fourth phase could well result in another transition, from joint defence to security perimeter.

To be sure, institutional renovation was being discussed in the years preceding 9/11; starting in the mid 1990s, there had been much talk of reforming the common frontier, growing more and more congested as a result of the economic integration attending Canada-US free trade.[4] Already, in October 2000, borders in North America were being re-conceptualized, with the US ambassador to Canada, Gordon Giffin, apparently being the first official to speak publicly of a "security perimeter."[5] But it would require the historic events of September 2001 to invigorate the refashioning of the border. Between December 2001 and July 2002, three important accords would be signed by the two countries, in a bid to strengthen border controls and to fight terrorism: 1) the Joint Statement of Cooperation on Border Security and Regional Migration Issues; 2) the U.S.-Canada Smart Border Declaration; and 3) the Safe Third Country Agreement.

This new phase in the integration of continental defence and security proved worrisome to many in Canada, who thought the country was on the verge of losing whatever sovereignty remained to it in matters of security and defence; there was a worry that Canada's own anti-terrorist laws would be but a mere reflection of legislation enacted in the US.[6] Some went so far as to reawaken the slumbering spectre of the 1960s, so famously evoked at the time by George Grant, namely of the Americanization of Canadian life, and the effective death of Canada.[7]

Also contributing to the sense of foreboding was a growing fear of American unilateralism, which to Canadians (and other allies) looked like requiring that they either toe the administration's line or cease to be regarded as good allies, with all that this could imply for their interests and their autonomy; disagreement would henceforth seem to be an act of insubordination if not treason, and could no longer simply represent a fairly normal aspect of cooperation and consultation among allies. For Canadians in particular, the North American content of unilateralism was a concern. Attention focused upon two main initiatives Washington has taken to counter the new threats to its security: the Department of Homeland Security, and Northern Command (Northcom). Both are, in effect, purely national initiatives, even if they each have direct impact upon US relations with Canada (and Mexico, as well). Although Ottawa managed to overcome the reluctance of certain politicians, and was able to send a small liaison contingent to Northcom, there is nothing to indicate that the evolution of these two institutions will follow the pattern observed since the dawn of the twentieth century — the pattern that I have labelled North America's liberal order.

The current Canadian fears would not seem to augur well for the future of that order. Might it prove to be another victim of 11 September, to be supplanted by a big-R "Republican" order, one resting on a vision of US global primacy? The question needs to be raised, even if it is obviously far too early for it to be answered. At the very least, we can say that the institutional fabric of North American security has not attained its final shape or size. The attacks on New York and Washington have certainly been an impetus for accelerating the process of integrating the security of North America, but it is difficult at the moment to know whether this acceleration signals continuity or rupture. It is much easier to note that many Canadians simply do not accept the thesis that their country *is* becoming "Americanized," and if we are to believe Michael Adams, rather the reverse is occurring: social, political, and economic divergence is on the rise, and might even be said to cast a dark shadow over the prospects of a North American "community" held together by the glue of common liberal-democratic values![8]

In some ways, current attitudes of Canadians resemble those held in the nineteenth century, to the extent suspicions of American policy are based on assumptions of a degenerating American democracy. Today, many who express a distrust of the US tend also to deprecate the democratic credentials of the Bush administration, as a result of the messy outcome of the 2000 election, its Florida denouement supplying the icing on this cake. But the distrust is also fed by other issues, including a perceived oil-industry stranglehold on policymaking in Washington, as well as disquiet engendered by passage of the Patriot Act, and the legal questions attending the detention of prisoners held at Guantánamo Bay. Some fear that the war on terror can only result in the diminishing of democracy itself. In this light, it is interesting to recall what Eric Harrison wrote more than half a century ago, and if we replace "USSR" with "terrorism," the parallel is striking:

> [T]he military dispositions fencing us in on both east and west are acceptable
> on two assumptions: the continuing political sanity of the United States, a

postulate to which Canada is inescapably committed, and the uncertain strategic behaviour of the USSR. Our existence depends on the first even more intimately perhaps than it does on the second. A viable, adaptive and humane democracy in the United States, whose expansive internationalism is kept compatible with the prejudices as well as the needs of others will not forfeit the confidence of her allies.[9]

Harrison's text serves as a useful reminder that it is premature in the extreme for anyone to sound the knell for the North American liberal order. Too many signs reveal it to be alive and functioning. Consider that in spite of the fears expressed by so many since 9/11, Canada remains today no more dependent than it had been before; indeed, as the Iraq war demonstrates, Ottawa showed a surprising capacity to withstand pressure from the Americans to follow it into combat. As Reg Whitaker has noted in a recent review article, Canada's refusal to join the coalition against Iraq hardly resulted in the catastrophes that were being routinely predicted by observers on both the right and the left.[10]

In this respect, the "crisis" that Canadian-American relations are currently weathering is no more serious or obscure than that of 1942. If History tells us anything, it surely is that the problems and tensions of the past couple of years are neither new nor insoluble. We simply have not had the chance to realize this, yet. Indeed, not only has the liberal North American order *not* expired, but it has been an order remarkably congenial to *Canadian* interests. And the bilateral institutions that frame this order have, accordingly, served Canada extremely well.

If this is so, then what the government of Canada should be doing at this juncture is confidently to commit itself to institutionalizing the North American security perimeter. Rather than limiting the objective to forging sectoral agreements negotiated piecemeal and in the heat of the moment, it would be far better, as was done in 1940 and again in 1947, to try to set forth, in collaboration with Washington, the principles that must continue to guide cooperation between the two countries, so as to determine not only the legitimate sphere of operation, but also (and especially) the limits, of the security perimeter. Doing so will not just promote Canada's security and defence interests; it will also preserve its sovereignty and identity.

Notes

[1]Kalevi J. Holsti, *Peace and War: Armed Conflicts and International Order, 1648-1989* (Cambridge: Cambridge University Press, 1991).

[2]See Alexander Wendt, "Anarchy Is What States Make of It: The Social Construction of Power Politics," *International Organization* 46 (Spring 1992): 391-425.

[3]See, for an elaboration, my two articles, "Canada-U.S. Relations: Time for Cassandra?" *American Review of Canadian Studies* 30 (Fall 2000): 135-57; and "'Honey, Are You Still Mad at Me? I've Changed You Know': Canada-US Relations in a Post-Saddam/Post Chrétien Era," *International Journal* 63 (Fall 2003): 571-90.

[4]For this evolution, see Christopher Sands, "Fading Power or Rising Power? 11 September and Lessons from the Section 110 Experience," in *Canada Among Nations 2002: A Fading Power*, ed. Norman Hillmer and Maureen Appel Molot (Don Mills: Oxford University Press, 2002), pp. 49-74; and Stéphane Roussel, "Pearl Harbor et le World Trade Center: Le Canada face aux États-Unis en période de crise," *Études internationales* 33 (December 2002): 667-95.

[5]Gordon D. Giffin, "Rethinking the Line: The US/Canada Border," a presentation to the Canadian Policy Research Conference, Vancouver, British Columbia, 23 October 2000.

[6]See, for these worries, Ronald J. Daniels, Patrick Macklem, and Kent Roach, eds., *The Security of Freedom: Essays on Canada's Anti-Terrorism Bill* (Toronto: University of Toronto Press, 2001); Stephen Clarkson, *Locked in the Continental Ranks: Redrawing the American Perimeter after September 11th* (Ottawa: Canadian Centre for Policy Alternatives, February 2002); and Michael Byers, "Canadian Armed Forces Under United States Command," *International Journal* 58 (Winter 2002-3): 89-114.

[7]Mel Hurtig, *The Vanishing Country: Is It Too Late to Save Canada?* (Toronto: McClelland and Stewart, 2002).

[8]Michael Adams, *Fire and Ice: The United States, Canada and the Myth of Converging Values* (Toronto: Penguin, 2003).

[9]W. Eric C. Harrison, "Canadian-American Defence," *International Journal* 5 (Summer 1950): 190-91.

[10]Reg Whitaker, "George Grant Got It Wrong: Coping with Uncle Sam in the 21st Century," *Inroads* 14 (Winter/Spring 2004): 118-29.

List of Acronyms

CCF:	Cooperative Commonwealth Federation
CEE:	Central and Eastern Europe
CSCE:	Conference on Security and Cooperation in Europe
CINCADCANUS:	Commander-in-Chief, Air Defense, Canada-United States
CIIA:	Canadian Institute of International Affairs
CUSRPG:	Canada-US Regional Planning Group
DCER:	Documents on Canadian External Relations
DEW Line:	Distant Early Warning Line
DPT:	Democratic Peace Theory
IR:	International Relations
IJC:	International Joint Commission
JIMPC:	Joint Industrial Mobilization Planning Committee
MCC:	Canada-US Military Cooperation Committee
MDAA:	Mutual Defence Assistance Act
MSG:	Joint Military Study Group
NAFTA:	North American Free Trade Agreement
NATO:	North Atlantic Treaty Organization
NORAD:	North American Air (later Aerospace) Defence Command
OAS:	Organization of American States
PJBD:	Permanent Joint Board on Defence

RCAF:	Royal Canadian Air Force
SAC:	Strategic Air Command
SACEUR:	Supreme Allied Commander Europe
UK:	United Kingdom
UN:	United Nations
US:	United States
USAF:	United States Air Force
USSR:	Union of Soviet Socialist Republics

Index

Queen's Policy Studies
Recent Publications

The Queen's Policy Studies Series is dedicated to the exploration of major policy issues that confront governments in Canada and other western nations. McGill-Queen's University Press is the exclusive world representative and distributor of books in the series.

School of Policy Studies

Implementing Primary Care Reform: Barriers and Facilitators, Ruth Wilson, S.E.D. Shortt and John Dorland (eds.), 2004   Paper ISBN 1-55339-040-7   Cloth 1-55339-041-5

Social and Cultural Change, David Last, Franklin Pinch, Douglas L. Bland and Alan Okros (eds.), 2004   Paper ISBN 1-55339-032-6   Cloth 1-55339-033-4

Clusters in a Cold Climate: Innovation Dynamics in a Diverse Economy, David A. Wolfe and Matthew Lucas (eds.), 2004   Paper ISBN 1-55339-038-5   Cloth 1-55339-039-3

Canada Without Armed Forces? Douglas L. Bland (ed.), 2004
Paper ISBN 1-55339-036-9   Cloth 1-55339-037-7

Campaigns for International Security: Canada's Defence Policy at the Turn of the Century, Douglas L. Bland and Sean M. Maloney, 2004
Paper ISBN 0-88911-962-7 Cloth 0-88911-964-3

Understanding Innovation in Canadian Industry, Fred Gault (ed.), 2003
Paper ISBN 1-55339-030-X Cloth ISBN 1-55339-031-8

Delicate Dances: Public Policy and the Nonprofit Sector, Kathy L. Brock (ed.), 2003
Paper ISBN 0-88911-953-8 Cloth ISBN 0-88911-955-4

Beyond the National Divide: Regional Dimensions of Industrial Relations, Mark Thompson, Joseph B. Rose and Anthony E. Smith (eds.), 2003
Paper ISBN 0-88911-963-5 Cloth ISBN 0-88911-965-1

The Nonprofit Sector in Interesting Times: Case Studies in a Changing Sector,
Kathy L. Brock and Keith G. Banting (eds.), 2003
Paper ISBN 0-88911-941-4 Cloth ISBN 0-88911-943-0

Clusters Old and New: The Transition to a Knowledge Economy in Canada's Regions,
David A. Wolfe (ed.), 2003   Paper ISBN 0-88911-959-7 Cloth ISBN 0-88911-961-9

The e-Connected World: Risks and Opportunities, Stephen Coleman (ed.), 2003
Paper ISBN 0-88911-945-7 Cloth ISBN 0-88911-947-3

Knowledge, Clusters and Regional Innovation: Economic Development in Canada, J. Adam Holbrook and David A. Wolfe (eds.), 2002
Paper ISBN 0-88911-919-8 Cloth ISBN 0-88911-917-1

Lessons of Everyday Law/Le droit du quotidien, Roderick Alexander Macdonald, 2002
Paper ISBN 0-88911-915-5 Cloth ISBN 0-88911-913-9

Improving Connections Between Governments and Nonprofit and Voluntary Organizations: Public Policy and the Third Sector, Kathy L. Brock (ed.), 2002
Paper ISBN 0-88911-899-X Cloth ISBN 0-88911-907-4